Go
Láw

Gold's Law

or

How to beat the system

Fourmat Publishing

ISBN 1 85190 061 6

First published March 1989

Apart from cases which have been heard and decided in the courts, the events and characters in this book are entirely fictitious and are not intended to bear any resemblance to any person living or dead.

Published by Fourmat Publishing
27 & 28 St Albans Place Islington Green London N1 0NX
Printed in Great Britain

Contents

To my parents David and Ada Gold

First a few paragraphs from our author

The law is out there waiting to be used. You've got to know how to use it to your advantage. I have aimed to show you how and to introduce you to some (perfectly proper and all that!) legal tricks, and to help you with legal situations which you may wish to handle yourself, without a solicitor, or on which you want some ideas before taking legal advice. The World's Longest Will, for example, may assist you to sort out in your mind what you would like to happen to your property on death, but I would hate to see you draw up anything in the least complicated without legal advice.

Here comes the bit which prevents you from suing us because I can't afford the damages and the publishers are really nice people. The law changes daily and the general principles to which I have often referred in the book may give way to some particular feature which occurs in your case. So there's no substitute for a chat with a solicitor—you may be entitled to a free chat or get a £5 fixed fee half an hour's worth and some solicitors don't even bite—to check on your particular case even though you may prefer to go it alone afterwards.

This is *Gold's Law*: my understanding of selected parts of the law of England and Wales as at August 1 1988 and reflecting my likes, dislikes and prejudices. Estate agents, insurers and others may think they have been given a hard time and ask why there's no lawyer-bashing in the book. It's about time the other lot had their fair share of bashing and if I can't shield my own profession in my own book, that's pretty rum.

There are lots of he's and she's. Usually, he can

equally be she and she can equally be he. Gettit?!

One thank you. To Cicely Rogers, a long suffering secretary who slaved over a hot typewriter with typical good humour (well I think I saw her smile—once) to produce the transcript.

I hope you have a good read—and a chuckle.

Stephen Gold
August 1988

Car chat on the dog and bone

Duff second hand motors

'This is the "Clocked Odometer" speaking. Thank you for calling. How can we take your money?'

'You've taken it. Reg Sucker I am. Sucker by name, Sucker by nature. You sold me a Triumph sports yesterday for two grand. Well, it ain't too grand. The clutch has just gone and the brakes have failed.'

'Come on, Reggie baby. It *seems* the clutch has gone and the brakes have failed. You musn't drive the beast so hard. Tell you what, we'll get it into the workshop . . .'

'. . . I'll tell *you* what. I'll have my money back.'

'You've got to be joking, my friend. Tell you what, even though you've driven the beast too hard, we'll stick by our warranty. Free parts up to a pony and you pay for the rest and for labour, naturally. Can't be fairer than that.'

'Don't waste your breath. The Sale of Goods Act covers this. Your warranty, your guarantee—whatever you want to call it, mate—may add to my rights but can't take them away. You ought to have a look at that bloke Gold's book.'

'Do me a favour, Reg. If he knew any law, he

wouldn't be wasting his time writing a book, now would he?!'

'And it's plain that not only does the Sale of Goods Act apply but you've broken it. This car wasn't of merchantable quality, it wasn't reasonably fit . . .'

'Give us a break, mate. You must have lost your brain. It wasn't twenty grand you paid. Two grand. And this was a used car.'

'My brains are with me and so is Gold's book. And he wrote that book because he cares about Suckers like me. His mother says so. And Gold says there was this big case in November 1986. Father and son had got this new Range Rover. The engine, the gear box, the bodywork and the oil seals were all defective. The vehicle was still driveable and roadworthy but each defect required repairs. The Court of Appeal held that the vehicle was not up to Sale of Goods Act standard. The buyer was entitled not just to be able to drive his vehicle from one place to another but to do so with an appropriate degree of comfort, ease of handling, reliability and pride in its outward and inward appearance. And whether the Sale of Goods Act standard had been met was to be judged at the moment the vehicle was delivered to the buyer. The fact that a defect was repairable did not prevent the vehicle from being sub-Sale of Goods Act standard if the defect was of sufficient degree.'

'How much more of this is there, Reggie boy. I've got a qucue of punters. I reckon you're suffering from verbal diarrhoea like Bold or Gold, is it? Anyway, none of that stuff has anything to do with a used car, has it now!'

'Funny you should say that. Gold says there's been another big case since, in April 1988. This case was about a used car, a second hand Mercedes.'

'A nice car the Merc.'

'Well, this one had some problems. And the Court of Appeal again ruled that the same test which was applied to determine whether a new vehicle was up to standard was to be applied to a used car. Obviously, the price paid has to be taken into account and Gold says that a buyer has to realise that when he buys a used car, defects may appear sooner or later. But the fact the used car can be driven won't be legally sufficient and Gold maintains the court must ask itself what the buyer was entitled to think he was getting. Apparently, the Court of Appeal decided this in a case in July 1987. There the customer paid £4,400 for a used Fiat X19 with about 18,000 on the clock. He thought he was buying an enthusiast's car at the going rate for that mileage. He believed that the car had a tendency to rust but expected a manufacturer's guarantee. It turned out that, having been submerged in water earlier in the year for between twenty-four to forty-eight hours, the car had been written off by insurers and the rust guarantee wouldn't apply because of its history. There was very little wrong with the car when it was bought but it was a potential "rogue". Irrespective of its condition no member of the public, learning the facts, would touch it with a barge pole unless they could get it at a substantially reduced price to reflect the risk they were taking. The customer won.'

'OK, OK, OK, Reg. What do you want from me? You want to take my business? You want to see me close down? Business isn't so good. Your car was my first to move for a fortnight. I haven't got a farthing in cash. If I wrote you a kite, it would bounce.'

'Have you heard of section 60 of the Road Traffic Act 1972?'

'What are you talking about—section 60? The Act stops at section 50.'

You must have been reading some cut price Japanese version of the Act. Haven't you ever been disqualified?'

'Maybe once or twice.'

'That's under section 93.'

'Oh.'

'Back to section 60. It makes it an offence for anyone to sell a vehicle which is in an unroadworthy condition. You would get off if you could show you had reasonable cause to believe that the vehicle wouldn't be used on a road till it had been put into a roadworthy condition. That's not on here. The police don't even need to prove that you knew it was unroadworthy when you made the sale. So I'd better get down to the cop shop on your patch—as you might say. If I can get them interested, the car will be inspected by a qualified police vehicle examiner and when I sue for my losses which aren't included in the magistrates' court compensation order, I can rely on the police evidence. And if by any chance you are a member of the Motor Agents Association and I still have a claim, then, as an alternative to going to the county court, I could opt for arbitration under their low cost, documents-only scheme (contact the Association at 75 Park Street, Bristol BS1 5PS—telephone 0272 293232). The trouble is, says Gold, it generally isn't possible to appeal against the arbitrator's award.'

'Don't be hasty, Reg. The "Clocked Odometer" would never allow a customer to be dissatisfied. We've got our reputation to think of. I'm sure we can sort out a quick refund. And, Reg, you wouldn't be interested in a job as a salesman here, would you?'

'A salesman?'

'Alright. Equal partners. And what did you say that Bold's book was called?'

Car chat on the dog and bone

Note for clever dicks

The road traffic laws are being consolidated in a new statute and section numbers are changing. This conversation took place before the coming into force of the consolidating legislation.

The name game

Name-changing is exciting and cheap

Use of a name for any fraudulent purpose cannot be permitted, although those cursed with an unspent criminal conviction or bad debt black mark do not break the law in changing their names so long as they refrain from providing false information about the past, if asked. We commend a carefully and honestly chosen new forename or surname—perhaps both—and heads may turn in appreciation or disbelief as the subject is paged in hotel lobbies: restaurants once overbooked may beg of him to accept the table over by the window. It has been suggested that a baptismal name can only be changed by Act of Parliament or bishop on confirmation or adoption. Nevertheless, it is customary to see a deed poll changing a baptismal name as well as a surname and nobody gets worked up about it. A deed poll? Yes, that's the best way of dealing with the change. Legally, no document at all is required. A snap of the fingers and a word in the ears of the subject's mates and that is legally sufficient. Yet then the banks, building societies, the Director of Savings, the Passport Office and the subject's family will allege he is an imposter and so a document is desirable. The deed poll or copies of it can be shown to whoever the subject wishes to register the change.

Have a deed poll on us. It should be witnessed by one person: it no longer has to be stamped by the Inland Revenue. There is a place on it for a legal seal to go. That would have been a wax impression in 1897: now a red wafer will do and you can get them at the stationers or artists can draw one in.

THIS DEED POLL made the 14th day of July 1988 by me MARMADUKE ADRIAN CLAPTRAP of 58 Rugby Road Haslemere in the County of Surrey formerly called MARMADUKE ADRIAN WINDSOR WITNESSES AND IT IS HEREBY DECLARED as follows:-

1. I absolutely and entirely renounce relinquish and abandon the use of my said former surname of WINDSOR and assume adopt and determine to take and use from the date of this deed the surname of CLAPTRAP in substitution for my former surname of WINDSOR.

2. I shall at all times hereafter in all records deeds and other writings and in all actions proceedings dealings and transactions and on all occasions whatsoever use and sign the said surname of CLAPTRAP as my surname in substitution for my former surname of WINDSOR hereby relinquished to the intent that I may hereafter be called known or distinguished not by the former surname of WINDSOR but by the surname of CLAPTRAP only.

3. I authorise and request all persons at all times to designate describe and address me by the adopted surname of CLAPTRAP.

IN WITNESS whereof I have hereunto subscribed my Christian name MARMADUKE my forename ADRIAN and my adopted and substituted surname of CLAPTRAP and also my said former surname of WINDSOR and have affixed my seal the day and year first before written.

SIGNED SEALED AND) Marmaduke Adrian Claptrap
DELIVERED by the above) formerly
named MARMADUKE ADRIAN) known as
CLAPTRAP in the) Marmaduke
presence of:) Adrian Windsor

A. N. Other
1A Nominal Street
Abingdon Oxon

The fast buck

and how to make one

Health warning: None of the methods explained in this chapter for using the civil law to make money should actually be tried. They could seriously damage health. Litigation is to be embarked upon only by those with genuine grievances, and courts and tribunals are adept at sussing out the "agent provocateur". Still, it's nice to dream . . .

The discrimination method

Application for a job is made to an employer and an interview refusal is secured or, better still, a refusal of employment following interview. The refusal must be on the ground of sex or race. Then, complaint is made to an industrial tribunal under the Sex Discrimination Acts 1975 and 1986 or the Race Relations Act 1976 or both. It is unlawful for an employer to refuse or deliberately omit to offer employment to an applicant on the ground of sex or race.

Just the job

Compensation may be awarded by the tribunal for injury to feelings, humiliation and insult and so it is important that the applicant does suffer that injury. If the tribunal thought the whole thing was one big joke, the applicant could be rebuffed—on the ground of farce. A woman refused a job because she had children has been awarded £100; a doctor racially discriminated against in her employment has been awarded £1,000; and a Parkhurst prisoner racially discriminated against behind bars in that he was refused the transfer he badly wanted from the prison press room to the kitchen has been awarded £500. The compensation in these cases was for the injury to feelings, humiliation and insult. The tribunal may also award compensation for earnings "lost" by being refused the job.

Discrimination will usually be inferred from the facts. The wording of the job advertisement could be a strong pointer to the employer's intentions.

> Attractive bar staff
> required. Must be
> prepared to show legs.
> Job open to men and
> women. Phone Mr. Mann
> Worthing 46791

This advertisement suggests sex discrimination against men and racial discrimination against Muslim women, amongst others who must keep their legs covered. But it is the questions at interview and statements in the rejection letter which may be the big giveaway!

White solicitor to black applicant:	"I can't understand why an English employer would want to take on a coloured girl when English girls are available."
Rejection letter:	"I was unaware that you had three children and I do feel that, with the job involvement necessary for this particular type of work, it could prove difficult for you to run your home and do full justice to the job."

In both these cases it was held that unlawful discrimination had occurred.

Bonanza for black women

Discrimination against women and blacks are the most prevalent. The job advertisement will usually give off a whiff of discrimination and there may be a discriminatory reason for a particular business not advertising a job in the conventional ways. The practice of recruiting only pesons recommended by the existing work force or from unsolicited letters of application could well be calculated to avoid discrimination detection. The hush-hush recruiters may be the very recruiters to catch out.

"Forward Mr. Rumbold— back Miss Perkins"

Sex discrimination is allowed where it is a "genuine occupational qualification". A theatre producer could get away with insisting that Marilyn Munroe is played by a woman. The lady of the house may advertise for women-only applicants for the position of her dresser. A home for the elderly where all the residents are women can demand that the required nurse who would have intimate physical contact with the residents must be a woman. Though a man's clothing shop which rejected a female applicant on the ground that the job involved measuring the inside leg of the (male) customers failed in their tribunal defence to a sex discrimination complaint: it was fact that most male customers knew their inside leg measurements and, anyway, there were seven male assistants in the shop who could have dealt with the leg bit. Discrimination had occurred. And in April 1988 a man who was turned down for the job of a part-time sales assistant in a Glasgow store retailing lingerie, girls' clothes and swimwear won his sex discrimination complaint. The manageress had said that much of the work was assisting customers in the fitting room where they sometimes stripped off to try on lingerie. But the tribunal held that the man could have carried out most of the duties, which included working at the cash desk, receiving deliveries and serving on the sales floor, while the duties he could not carry out could have been done by others.

Help!

To the industrial tribunal the aggrieved has to go within three months of the act of discrimination complained about. Some legal help from a solicitor may be available under the "green form" scheme (subject to financial eligibility, and it will be £50's worth of help initially although the legal aid people might well be prepared to raise the limit). For what they perceive as genuine cases, good advice or financial backing may come from the Equal Opportunities Commission, Overseas House, Quay Street, Manchester M3 3HN (061–833 9244) in sex discrimination cases; and the Commission for

Racial Equality, Elliot House, 10 Allington Street, London SW1E 5EH (01–828 7022) in racial discrimination cases.

The wrongful arrest by a store detective method

The shopper excites suspicion by his behaviour in a supermarket. He omits to carry a wire basket, persistently glances around, picks up and puts down goods displayed for sale and twitches nervously. He pays for whatever goods he has removed when he reaches the checkout and hurries from the store. Outside he is challenged by a store detective, invited to return voluntarily to the store and be taken to the manager's office. He refuses, is arrested and later claims damages for wrongful arrest and false imprisonment. The going rate of damages for genuine cases is £500 plus, but the actual amount awarded will very much depend on the period of the detention and the degree of humiliation and distress suffered by the aggrieved.

"I don't like the look of the short bloke with glasses. I think he's got a melon under his armpit."

All citizens have a legal power to arrest: store detectives have no greater power than Joe and Jane Bloggs and it is less extensive than any of the powers available to police constables. Section 24 of the Police and Criminal Evidence Act 1984 gives the citizen power to arrest anyone who is in the act of committing an offence of theft (and loads more serious offences) or anyone whom he has reasonable grounds for suspecting to be committing the offence. Where does that put the store detective? In difficulty. Our mischievous shopper is certainly not in the act; he is only pretending. Maybe the store detective reckons, reasonably enough, that he is in the act of theft as she watches him, but if she pounces before he has gone through the checkout she knows she will be met with the protest that it was his intention to pay as soon as he could and that there was no dishonesty on his part.

"Excuse me sir, could I have a word . . ."

So the store detective watches and waits and, almost invariably pounces outside and so *after* what she believes to be the commission of the offence. The trouble is that *after* the event, it is not what she believes has happened that matters, but what in fact *did* happen. The citizen's *after* power is to arrest anyone who is guilty of the offence or she has reasonable grounds for suspecting to be guilty of it, but the power does not arise at all if there has not been an offence. Therefore, the store detective who *arrests* our mischievous shopper outside would, along with her employers, be in danger of having to pay civil damages. To overcome the problem, the wise store detective does not herself effect the arrest; she either invites the customer to go back into the store (there's no arrest unless it's clear to the customer that he is under compulsion to go and that, in short, he can't get away) or she whistles for a police constable, who has greater powers.

Some store detectives do, some store detectives don't

But some store detectives *do* themselves arrest and, of course, it may not always be possible to get hold of a police constable before the suspect has scarpered. The probability is that he who sets out to wind up a store detective will find himself arrested by a police constable and may even be charged with attempted theft. The innocent who does not court an allegation of dishonesty by a store detective, but gets one, is under no obligation to go back to the store or the manager's office and, indeed, it would almost certainly be fatal to a civil claim to volunteer to do so. Be arrested by the store detective and sue later.

The it ain't necessary method

A minor (a person under the age of eighteen, formerly known as an infant and otherwise known as a nipper, kid, junior, lad, lass or shorthouse) obtains certain goods and services on credit and elects not to pay for them. It is essential that he refrains from acting fraudulently by, for example, pretending to be eighteen or over. If he does act fraudulently, he can look forward to being charged with obtaining by deception and, in certain circumstances, a civil court may compel him to return goods still in his possession.

Fancy waistcoats and funerals

Generally, a minor can enforce a contract but the contract cannot be enforced against him: he can have a go in the courts (through an adult) but they can't have a go at him! One of the few exceptions to the rule is in relation to contracts for what the law calls "necessaries". The minor may be compelled to pay the price—and a reasonable price, which could be less than the price he originally agreed to pay—for goods and services he has received and which are necessary to him.

The goods or services must be suitable to his station in life and his actual requirements when he receives them. In 1908 a Savile Row tailor failed in his attempt to recover through the court the price of eleven fancy waistcoats and other clothing from a Cambridge undergraduate because his under-age customer was already amply supplied with clothing suitable to his position, thank you very much. The garments were not necessaries. And in an 1868 case a court found that a pair of jewelled solitaires worth £25 and an antique goblet worth fifteen guineas were not necessaries as they had been supplied to an under-age customer with an income of just £500 a year.

If the minor has succeeded in marrying and acquiring children whilst still under age he should bear in mind that goods and services for his family as opposed to himself may rank as necessaries. Last century, a court held that a minor was liable to honour his commitment to pay for the funeral of his wife or children.

The wrong credit method

Customer of bank, building society or other savings institution receives statement or passbook showing money which has been mistakenly credited to his account. Customer relies on the statement and, as a result, he spends the money mistakenly credited or commits himself to do so. Punnets of strawberries and cream at Wimbledon (the tennis bit, not the football) for himself and his party, a holiday abroad, an order for double glazing throughout—any or all would do. The mistake is then discovered, the clerk responsible is whipped and a claim is launched against the customer for the return of the money. Provided the customer did not know there had been a mistake, he can refuse to repay the money.

The same principle would apply to a mistakenly high credit balance notified to a customer by telephone or otherwise than by a statement or passbook. And if the customer fails to check the statement or passbook or whatever else he is given to ensure it is correct, he will not be legally blamed and can still refuse to repay the money. But if the mistaken credit was primarily caused by the customer's fault in the first place, the court would order repayment.

In an 1825 case a bank had over-credited a customer's account for some five years and notified him of the credit, as a result of which he spent more than he would otherwise have done. The court dismissed the bank's repayment claim. And in a 1950 case Lloyds Bank over-credited a customer and sent her statements with the mistaken sums shown. She relied on them and spent more. The bank failed in its claim.

The principle can be extended beyond the financial institution—customer relationship. In a 1983 case Avon County Council overpaid a sick employee £1007 during an absence from work which spanned nearly two years. Of the £1007, he spent £546.61. The Court of Appeal decided he was under no obligation to repay the council any of the money—not even the unspent part! So the chances are that if the innocent recipient can show he has acted to his detriment in relation to just part of the money, his benefactor will lose the lot.

The recipient who spends money which he *knows* has been mistakenly credited to an account or paid over to him, might find himself charged with theft. But even then funny things can happen. Take the case of a Bristol gardener who earns £100 per week. Bristol & West

Building Society wrongly credited his deposit account with a cool £20,000. He protested it was not his. Staff insisted that it was. So he used about half the money to refurnish his council flat, buy a new car, a dog and tropical fish, pay for a family holiday and settle some outstanding bills. When the Society discovered that another investor with the same name should have had the money, the police were notified and our gardening friend was charged with twenty alleged offences of theft. In June 1988 at Bristol Crown Court the jury acquitted him on all the charges. And also in June 1988 a sales representative was acquitted of stealing £18,700 from her employers on the basis she had not acted dishonestly. A computer error had given her a tenfold increase in her wages so she spent it on meals, clothes and holidays after the money had been paid into her bank account. She testified to believing the money was compensation for an injury at work.

TAKE-AWAY BANK PLC
Money Buildings High Street
Orpington Kent GU6 1LL

Our ref: G/PG
Mrs Winnie Fall
2 Smiley Lane
Orpington
Kent   14 July 1988

Dear Mrs Fall,

It has come to our attention that on June 20 1988 the sum of £1,500 was wrongly credited to your account numbered 1416872 as was shown in the statement recently sent to you.

Accordingly, I write to inform you that we have debited your account in the sum of £1,500 and, as at close of business today, the debit balance was £1,750. This is totally unacceptable to the bank and you should make arrangements to put the account back into credit forthwith. In the meantime, you should return your cheque card and not draw any further cheques without my prior approval.

Yours sincerely

A. Squeeze-Dry

Arthur Squeeze-Dry
Manager

Registered in England No 4624389502217
Registered Office: Yup Towers, Fenchurch Street, London EC4 QYP

2 Smiley Lane
Orpington
Kent
15th July 1988

Dear Mr Squeeze-Dry

I was devastated by your letter. As you will know from my file, I am not the world's best organised person when it comes to matters financial. On receiving last month's statement I was very surprised but pleased. I have not had a holiday since Norman left me last year and so I immediately booked a week in Morecambe with a girl friend. My dining room suite was a disgrace and I replaced that with a bargain from X and Z. It would have been too good to miss even if I hadn't got the money, though, come to think of it, you are telling me I did not have it. Also I bought Gold's Law. It is an excellent little book on the law. Perhaps you have heard about it? He has quite a go at banks, you know! At the end of the day the £1,500 has gone on things I would never have spent out for had that statement not shown me to be better off than I had thought.

Anyway, I've read up on how I stand over precisely what has happened here so I can tell you that your statement last month was prima facie evidence of the accuracy of the entries in it (sounds good even though I haven't got a clue what it means!) and you are estopped from claiming the return of the £1,500. You are to confirm to me that you will immediately credit the £1,500 back to my account and will not debit any interest or other charges relating to the £1,500. In the circumstances, I will retain my bank card.

Yours sincerely

Winnie Fall

Winnie Fall

Sorry, service was off tonight

Aggro at the bistro

A large helping of guts is a prerequisite for a customer who wishes to challenge the management in a restaurant, for he can never be sure who will come off the better. Given the guts, any food or drink below standard under the Sale of Goods Act 1979 (it must be of merchantable quality and reasonably fit to be consumed, and in your Savoy Grills and Ritzes the higher expectations of the customer must be met) should be rejected before any more than a taster has been consumed, or the menu price will be payable. It is advisable for the customer to complain loudly so as to encourage management to promptly remove and replace the offending offering in advance of co-diners being distracted from their coq-au-vin.

The 10% joke

The service charge may turn out to be contentious. If the customer has not been notified of the intention to levy the charge before giving his order, he can refuse to pay it. It may have been brought to his attention on a sandwich board or, more likely, on the menu. In fact, it's effectively an offence for a priced menu to omit reference to a service charge if one is intended to be levied, and the law requires the menu to be displayed outside the restaurant.

Even a customer who was aware of the charge in advance can decline to pay it where the service has been below what he could reasonably expect.

Non-payment of the service charge will generate one of a varied selection of responses by management. Pursuit out into the street by the head waiter wielding a meat cleaver in the left hand is quite popular. One way to avoid the embarrassment of a confrontation with management is to scarper. Whilst it is a crime under the Theft Act 1968 to dishonestly make off without having paid as required and with intent to avoid payment—a "bilking"—a customer who scarpers refusing to settle the service charge because he geniunely believes it is legally unwarranted, cannot be guilty. Still, we are unable to rule out an arrest on suspicion of bilking by an unsympathetic police constable who is suffering from station canteen food poisoning or is very hungry.

The customer should demonstrate his genuineness and honesty by leaving a note on the table and taking a copy for evidential purposes before withdrawal. It should contain particulars sufficient to enable management to locate the customer if intent on pressing a service charge claim.

It is conceivable that management will summon the police and do so before the customer makes good his escape. In that event it would look bad to go in the knowledge that the police were on their way. If the original note has by then disappeared into the rear of

MESSAGE ON A PLATE
The service was
pathetic and I will
give full details if called
on to do so. We will not pay the
service charge. The bill total
less the charge is on the plate.
We wish your waiters
instant recovery from
their paralysis
WATA KNIGHT
Top Flat
15b Arcadia Avenue
Catisfield
Tel: Catisfield 1234

the kitchen cat the copy should be handed to the constable immediately he arrives.

Cowards

Customers who have stayed on for a service charge confrontation which has gone against them, and are paying with a credit card will find it strategically difficult to tender the bill total less service charge. They should endorse the credit card voucher with the words "service charge paid under protest" before signing, and this will ease a subsequent claim for its return. Access and Barclaycard holders are in a particularly strong position by virtue of the equal-responsibility laws (see page 299).

And "Sorry, I'm off tonight"

A London restaurateur recently recovered around £80 damages against a customer who never was, somebody who had reserved a table but failed to appear. It is breach of contract to reserve and, for whatever reason short of outbreak of war or destruction of the restaurant, then stay away. A cancellation call should be made wherever possible and as soon as possible. Cancellation call or no cancellation call, if a particular restaurateur is into litigation it would be wise to check on whether he has been able to serve others in place of the cancellor and his party. This can be done by telephoning and asking for a table or snatching a quick look from the pavement through the gap between the net curtains. If the restaurateur does serve others who would have gone unserved had the cancellor turned up and they spent no less than the cancellor would have spent, he has suffered no loss and can have no provable claim despite the contract breach. Otherwise, his provable claim will be for the profit he has lost, which will be slightly less than the menu price of the meal. Did food really go into the refuse bin, or was it served up the next evening, a little greener than it should have been? Might the cancellor have eaten only one bread roll and one truffle if he had appeared, thereby keeping the bill total to a minimum?

Some restaurateurs are maintaining records of persistent cancellors. Giving a false name when reserving with a view to frustrating this practice presents problems for those paying otherwise than in cash, and could lead to a charge of attempted obtaining by deception.

Alternative conveyancing

Including the mini land contract

Contract breakers can normally be sued even though everything was agreed by word of mouth only. It is different with contracts for the sale, purchase and leasing of houses, flats and land. Generally, unless all the terms agreed were written down and signed by the contract breaker, he cannot be sued however diabolical his behaviour. But it would be madness for most homeowners to commit themselves to an enforceable written contract without legal advice. In advance of binding himself to a contract, the buyer will want to sort out finance and have his conveyancer make searches and investigate what legal nasties ownership of the property may have in store. And both sides will probably need to synchronise any dependent sale or purchase and hope to provide for all manner of things going wrong in a detailed contract which conveyancers are skilled at producing.

P × 3

Every now and then, the entrepreneur with a wad of bank notes but without a lawyer in his back pocket will be inflicted with an insatiable urge to sign up the man he has just met in the pub to sell him his nice bit of freehold. And the dejected homeowner who has spent an eternity vainly waiting for the six local estate agents to find him a buyer and by chance encounters outside the village papershop a stockbroker down for the weekend and desperate for a terraced two bedroomed property for his ageing mother, dare not risk the sun setting without an enforceable contract. For situations quirky and urgent, we have devised the barest contract of all time. It is legal. It is dangerous. It is enforceable. It may be written out on the back of two beer mats—prudent for it to be in duplicate—or on parchment. If any other terms have been agreed they can go in. It contains the minimum terms to ensure enforceability: the 3 P's—parties, property and price. Each side should keep one copy.

Talking contract

If our contract is signed up as it stands it implies, amongst other things, that the vendor will be able to prove within a reasonable period that he owns the place; that completion will occur as soon as the vendor has proved ownership; and that vacant possession will be given on completion (although possibly not if someone other than the vendor was occupying the property when the purchaser inspected it). Where it is intended that any of these points should not be implied, the contract must say so. The purchaser signing up a naive elderly homeowner who does not have the opportunity of prior legal advice may find that the court effectively rips up the contract should the vendor change his mind about selling out at what turns out to be an undervalue.

The mini land contract

```
Date:       July 14 1988
Parties:    Ena Rush, 62 Birdcage Walk, Albatross
            Way, Eagleton (Vendor)
            Ivor Cash, Top Flat, 15b Arcadia
            Avenue, Catisfield (Purchaser)
Property:   62 Birdcage Walk, Albatross Way,
            Eagleton
Price:      £60,000 (Sixty thousand pounds)
It is agreed that the vendor will sell and the
purchaser will buy the property at the price
subject to such covenants and other matters to
which the vendor purchased.
(Signed)    ..Ena Rush..........
(Signed)    ..Ivor Cash..........
```

Won't pay today, may not pay tomorrow

H M Prison closed to debtors

"Cheque book is at home. I'll be in tomorrow to settle up with you, George. Honest—on me nipper's life." By tricking a trader into giving him credit the debtor stands a reasonable chance of making it into the criminal court dock. But simply refusing to pay after the debt has been run up is not a crime. And these days the debtor cannot be sent to prison for non-payment unless he owes money for a fine and certain other payments due to a criminal court, money under a maintenance order, rates or tax or national insurance arrears.

Dealing with a mug

Some believe that a trader mug enough to give credit deserves to be knocked or subjected to a heavy sweat. Provided they will not be requiring credit from that trader again, their response to his demand for payment will depend on the manner of the demand. If accompanied by a threat of violence to the head or any part of the body below the waist, the police will be notified immediately with the possible result that activity by them will overshadow the debt's existence. More likely, there will be a demand by letter from the trader, or a solicitor or debt collector on his behalf. It will contain a threat of civil court action if the debt is not settled within one week. How earnest is the trader about suing? The size of the debt and his organisation, and whether a solicitor is in the picture, will be relevant factors in deciding. An early calculation will be made. Unless convinced of the trader's commitment to court, the debtor may ignore the letter and any followers-up in the hope that the trader will lose heart; or will attempt to discourage him with a counter-attack. Generally, the trader has six years to sue: after that, it is too late.

Reluctant credit

The debtor should beware. A miscalculation of the trader's intentions could prove costly. Once the trader sues, the debtor will be liable for the court fee to start the case, and, if the trader has sued through a solicitor, his charges as well. The bill for the court fee and the trader's solicitor's charges goes up with the claim but it will seldom exceed £123.75, so long as the debtor settles before judgment can be obtained. More worryingly, the trader now has a right to claim interest on the debt at the rate of £15 per cent per annum and this can relate back to when the debt should have been paid. But assuming there was no agreement by the debtor to pay interest if late in payment, the trader cannot usually seek interest without suing; so the debtor who pays up late, though before the trader has issued a writ or summons, may refuse to volunteer any interest. On a large debt it will probably make financial sense for the debtor with cash flow problems to decline to settle and so gain what could be a few months' extra credit whilst the trader gets his court act together. In return, the debtor will have to pay the trader's court fee, solicitor's charges and interest.

Perfect timing

Very cunning debtors never allow a court judgment to be obtained against them as this could affect their creditworthiness with other traders in the future. They know they have a fortnight's grace from receiving the trader's writ or summons and, if it has arrived through the post, there could be an extra week: so there are often three weeks available before the trader is able to pounce. And where the debt has been outstanding for a long time and the interest claim is potentially massive once the trader sues, they will string out settlement for as long as possible, but come up with the loot seconds before the trader reaches the court office with his paperwork.

Play nice

Section 40 of the Administration of Justice Act 1970 is capable of performing a crucial role in the debtor's counter-attack. It makes it a crime for anyone—and so this covers the trader and a debt collector—to harass a debtor. Conviction carries a fine of up to £200. The crime is committed by making demands which are likely to cause the debtor or his family alarm, distress or humiliation because of their frequency or the way they are made or any threat or publicity which goes with them. Announcements of default by means of a flashing sign erected on the roof of a motor vehicle progressing slowly along the debtor's street, threats of prominent advertisement of default on the trader's premises, 2 am telephone calls and even one-off letters which pack too many punches. These are the sort of actions which the legislation has in mind—actions which many traders believe are *morally* justified.

COUNTER-ATTACK

Dear Mr Trader,
You claim I owe you £500 under invoice 4628 about which I make no admissions at all. I shall state my case fully to the court should you be misguided enough to sue me. My purpose in writing to you now is to protest at the number and content of the communications rained on me by yourself and, subsequently, the debt collection agents you have instructed. I reserve my right to draw the communications to the attention of the police so that they can consider whether an offence of unlawful harassment has been committed under section 40 of the Administration of Justice Act 1970 and/or an offence of sending a letter with intent to cause distress or anxiety under section 1 of the Malicious Communications Act 1988, and to report your agents to the Director-General of Fair Trading with a request that he review their suitability to continue to hold a licence under the Consumer Credit Act 1974. I suggest you call off your agents immediately and stop pestering me.
Yours faithfully
I. O. Yew
I.O.Yew

Since September 29 1988 it has also been a crime under the Malicious Communications Act 1988—a maximum fine of £1,000 this time—for a person to send a threatening letter to another if his purpose is to cause distress or anxiety to the recipient or to anyone else he intended should see the letter. It is a defence for the threatener to show he believed the threat was a proper means of reinforcing his demand.

Lousy seats

A pillar at the opera—a stanchion at the football

Anyone who has bought a ticket for a theatre or cinema performance or a sporting event is entitled to a reasonable view of what is going on. If the view is not going to be reasonable, he should be told before the ticket is sold, and then he cannot complain. But if he has not been told, he should be able to claim damages. It is no answer to the claim that the restrictiveness of the view was unavoidable; that, for example, the theatre pillar had to be there to prevent the dress circle from falling down or that the football ground uprights and netting were only put in to comply with the Safety of Sports Grounds Act 1975. They were not forced to sell the ticket, and they could have warned you before they did sell it.

Michael Walker from Portchester, Hants supports Portsmouth Football Club. On January 22 1986 (before they went up and then down again) Portsmouth were playing Oxford United (before they went down) away in the Milk Cup quarter final. Walker had bought stand tickets at £10 a time for himself and his three children. The tickets stated that they were sold subject to conditions displayed in the ticket office, but it transpired that at the time there were no conditions displayed there. It was a disastrous evening. Walker and his children had a poor view of the match due to barriers and pitch perimeter fencing in front of the stand, and Portsmouth lost. Walker sued Oxford United for damages. He lost, but on the facts not on the law. The judge was satisfied that he and his children were able to watch the flow of the game and see how it evolved and how the goals were scored. As poor as the view was, it was not so poor that Oxford were in breach of contract in selling the seats. Had the seats not been reasonably fit for their purpose, Walker would have scored!

1 Esplanade Walk
Bognor
July 14 1988

The Manager
Bognor Empire
Bognor
West Sussex

Dear Sir or Madam

Yesterday evening I escorted my wife to your theatre for the performance of the "Rocky Horror Show". To be more precise, I believe it was the "Rocky Horror Show" from the notices outside. Nothing on the stage permitted me to test my belief, as the stage was hidden from view by a tall, well-built pillar in front of me, and my wife, who was in the next seat, underwent the same experience. I expect you know the pillar. It is at the end of Row F. I did not know it as I had not previously patronised your establishment and the young man or woman in your box office failed to draw my attention to the deficiencies of the seats. Had he or she done so, I would never have purchased the tickets. The evening was ruined for us on what should have been a happy and joyous occasion, our thirtieth wedding anniversary.

I paid £15 for each ticket. I consider that the true value of each ticket was £1. I claim a refund of £14 per ticket and £10 for each of us to compensate for the distress, disappointment and inconvenience. The total claim, therefore, is £48 and I await your cheque within the next seven days. If it is not forthcoming, I will sue the theatre in the county court.

Yours faithfully

A. Noyed

Mr A Noyed.

I hate my insurers

A chapter which speaks for itself

Another way

There's a cheap alternative to slashing the claims manager's tyres when a policyholder has a dispute with his *own* insurance company. It's a complaint to the Insurance Ombudsman or an application for arbitration under PIAS (Personal Insurance Arbitration Service). They both deal with *personal* insurance including life cover. They both offer a *free* service to the policyholder. They can both make a financial award: up to £100,000 from the Ombudsman, up to £25,000 from PIAS. They both usually come to a decision on documents only. The threat of either may persuade the insurers to change their mind: certainly, it will force the file out of the hands of the manager or clerk dealing with it and into the hands of the top man for internal complaints purposes, because neither the Ombudsman nor PIAS will touch till the insurers' internal complaints procedure has been exhausted. A policyholder has six months from the time the insurers notify their final decision to refer to the Ombudsman.

Dear Mr Claims Manager
Your claims reference X247151149-MOV-ABC-XYZ4ZL
I shall be grateful if you could take a short break from causing misery to other of your policyholders and pass my papers to your chief executive for the purpose of your internal complaints procedure. The offer to pay me £35 for my beloved £5,500 MG Midget contained in your second class stamped recycled letter received today is rejected and unless my claim is settled in full I intend to refer the matter to the Insurance Ombudsman/PIAS.
Yours faithfully,
Anne Gree
Anne Gree

Alas, the policyholder can only go to the Ombudsman or PIAS if his insurers belong to one of the schemes. If his insurers do belong, they will abide by the decision of the Ombudsman or, in the case of PIAS, the decision of the independent arbitrator who will have been appointed by the Chartered Institute of Arbitrators. If the policyholder reckons that the Ombudsman's decision stinks, he can go on and sue the insurers in court. But with PIAS, the arbitrator's award is virtually final, which means the dissatisfied policyholder cannot then go to court unless he can show the arbitrator had a mental wobbly and got his law wrong. The Ombudsman can be contacted direct: an approach for PIAS arbitration should be initiated with a request to the policyholder's insurers. The schemes are useful in the same sort of circumstances as we have commended a complaint to the Banking Ombudsman (see page 107). What we must emphasise is that neither scheme can be used for a complaint against the insurers for somebody else: for example, they won't apply where a claimant cannot get the insurers of a bloke who drove into the back of his car to answer correspondence.

The Insurance Ombudsman's Bureau is at 31 Southampton Row, London WC1B 5HJ (telephone 01–242 8613) and The Chartered Institute of Arbitrators which runs PIAS can be found at International Arbitration Centre, 75 Cannon Street, London EC4N 5BH.

Who plays?

We give some of the main players. There are others. An enquiry to the policyholder's own insurers will confirm whether they play if they are not shown. Should the enquiry result in a banged down receiver, the Bureau or The Chartered Institute of Arbitrators can be contacted.

Insurer	*Insurance Ombudsman*	*PIAS*
Ansvar Insurance Co Ltd		√
Avon Insurance PLC		√
Bishopsgate Insurance PLC	√	
Commercial Union Group	√	
Co-operative Insurance Society Ltd		√
Cornhill Insurance Co Ltd		√
Dominion Insurance Co Ltd		√
Europa Insurance Co Ltd		√
Excess Group	√	
General Accident Group	√	
Guardian Royal Exchange Group	√	
Halifax Insurance Co Ltd		√
Hibernian Insurance Co Ltd	√	
Ideal Insurance		√
Legal & General Group	√	
London & Manchester Assurance Co Ltd	√	√
Minster Insurance Co Ltd	√	√
Municipal Mutual		√
National Insurance and Guarantee Corporation Ltd		√
N.E.M.	√	
Northern Star Insurance Co Ltd		√

Norwich Union Group	√	
Pearl Assurance Group	√	
Provincial Insurance Co Ltd		√
Prudential Assurance Group	√	
Royal Insurance Group	√	
Royal London Group	√	
Sun Alliance Insurance Group	√	√
Sun Life Group	√	
Trafalgar Insurance Co Ltd		√
Westgate Insurance Co Ltd	√	
Zurich Insurance Group	√	

Taste the Ombudsman

The Insurance Ombudsman publishes annual reports. These give a valuable guide to how he thinks and what he may do on a particular complaint, although different policy wording in another case might well lead to an opposite decision:

- *No claims bonus*: A policyholder's no-claims bonus must not be affected by a claim against the policyholder which was invalid and has been turned down.

- *Economic vehicle repairs*: Where a car repair bill would be less than market value of the car, insurers must not try and force the policyholder to settle on an economic write-off basis. Take this situation. Cost of repairs—£1,000: pre-accident market value of car—£1,100: salvage value—£350: insurers say "You can have cost of repairs less the value of the salvage which you keep. Here's £750." Wrong. The policyholder may prefer a cash settlement and go out and replace the car without having to wait for repairs. But if an enthusiast wants to repair, and the cost is less than the value, the only option for insurers under normal current policy wording are to have the repairs done, or pay their estimated cost and let the owner have them done.

- *Premium refund after total loss*: Where insurers pay a total loss claim on a car, there is no refund of the premium due in respect of the unexpired portion of the policy year. The insurers will often allow an *ex gratia* credit but the policyholder does not have a *right* to it.

- *Policy changes*: Failure by insurers to properly communicate to the policyholder changes in policy terms may result in a claim being dealt with on the basis of old terms which are more favourable to the policyholder.

- *No receipt*: It is outrageous and contrary to principle for insurers to accept that property has been lost or destroyed and then knock off a percentage of the amount claimed for no better reason than the policyholder has estimated the value himself and he has no independent evidence of value such as a receipt.

- *Under-insurance*: If a building is only insured for half its reinstatement value, the policyholder cannot expect to be paid the full value when it is destroyed. But if the insurers' agent, rather than the policyholder, fixed the sum insured, there might be grounds for allowing a proper value to be backdated to the taking out of the policy so as to secure payment of the full claim less the premium difference.

- *Secret excess*: If in the space in the policy schedule for recording the amount of an excess the word "None" appears, the policyholder should not be expected to have to look to his policy booklet to find out that there is a compulsory excess where the vehicle insured is a motorcycle.

- *Investigating third party claims*: Insurers should go to reasonable lengths to investigate a claim against the policyholder, but it is not obliged to go to extraordinary lengths simply to preserve or re-instate the policyholder's no-claims bonus.

Baby blues

Affiliation proceedings, bye-bye

The illegitimacy rate might have more than doubled in the last ten years but only a tiny proportion of mothers go to court for their rights in the form of an affiliation order. So there won't be too many tears shed for the passing of affiliation proceedings. They will be killed off when, as is likely in the near future, an important part of the Family Law Reform Act 1987 is brought into force. Of course, the mother must still have the ability to get the court to order the father to pay maintenance if necessary. She'll have that ability when, with the 1987 Act coming in, the Guardianship of Minors Act 1971 is extended to cover applications by the mother of an illegitimate child for financial help from the father. In fact, more extensive financial help than she can get at the moment: in addition to regular weekly or monthly payments she'll be able to ask for a lump sum payment to cover expenses she has already incurred (no limit on it except in magistrates' courts where the limit will be £1,000) and an order that the father passes over property for the child's benefit (but not from magistrates' courts).

The court won't be able to punish the father, or to reduce maintenance to reflect the mother's eagerness for intercourse. The aim will be to provide for the child's reasonable needs. Existing affiliation orders will remain in force notwithstanding the abolition of affiliation proceedings. Mothers who have left it too late to apply for affiliation orders under the present law (there are strict time limits) will be able to take advantage of the new law and, indeed, even mothers with an affiliation order who fancy their chances of obtaining a hefty lump sum or some property order for the child will be able to have a go when the new law comes in: the court will have power to cancel the affiliation order because of fresh provision it makes.

"Blood, hair and that sort of thing"

"It isn't mine, it was Roger the lodger."

"She's been with the whole darts team."

"He's the spitting image of the bloke down at the Kebab takeaway. Hasn't got my conk."

"I was speaking in a debate on the pollution of our waterways when she conceived. Take a look at *Hansard*."

It will continue to be open to a man to deny he is the father. Magistrates' courts can already order blood tests. The Family Law Reform Act 1987, when the relevant section is in force, will give power to order other "scientific" tests and that should lead to the widespread use of DNA fingerprinting which, for the moment, can only be used in paternity cases if the parties agree.

DNA fingerprinting (forget the finger bit—it's a colloquialism to indicate the uniqueness to each individual of the chemical signals which show up as a series of bands on an autoradiography film) has been used to convict murderers and rapists. Soon it will habitually be nailing the careless fornicators of the country. Conventional blood testing techniques can only conclusively *exclude* a man as father. *Cellmark Diagnostics*, which holds the monopoly on the new process, claim that the statistical chance of a second individual selected at random possessing all the same DNA bands as the true father is 30,000 millions-to-1 against, which ought to satisfy most judges and beaks. In short, DNA will *exclude or establish* fatherhood. And DNA can cope with any human tissues, not just blood. The total bill for sampling and testing under DNA fingerprinting currently comes out at £315 plus VAT: legal aid may be available. DNA enquiries should be made to Cellmark Diagnostics, Blacklands Way, Abingdon Business Park, Abingdon, Oxfordshire.

The refusal of either party to submit to a blood test can be held against them when the court comes to consider a paternity issue. In due course, it will be the same with a refusal to submit to DNA.

£25 per week for eighteen years—it's a pleasure

But should mother be able to persuade father to sign an acceptable agreement to maintain the child she will avoid court attendance so long as he complies with it. If father defaulted with payments, the mother could sue him in the county court for arrears in much the same way she might sue the greengrocer for short changing her upon the purchase of a sack of potatoes, and a personal attendance for a court hearing would probably be unnecessary. But if father is a bad payer, mother might prefer a court order because of the enforcement back-up machinery available. Though it could prove necessary to kick the backsides of the enforcing staff more than once, she will find that there are ways of extracting money from men who have the capacity to pay it (but see "Working it off" at page 144).

Maintenance from heaven

Mother who has been seduced by a man of social standing or wealth is in a strong bargaining position provided she has her evidence (a portable tape recorder strategically placed at bedtime could prove invaluable). He should be glad to avoid the risk of publicity which may be attracted by court proceedings or the coincidence of a vindictive mum and a hungry Sunday newspaper hack. And because, except under old commitments, the day of tax relief for father on the regular maintenance he pays are over, there is no tax disadvantage to father in weighing more heavily with a lump sum. Father can be invited to agree to the regular maintenance continuing beyond him pegging out so long as the child remains dependent. Mother may have peculiar knowledge of bedroom factors relevant to his life expectation, and what's the good of an agreement which is going to die off before the child is out of short trousers? But a maintenance rate which seems generous in 1988 may be only enough to buy a bag of gobstoppers come 1998. The agreement itself might provide for progressive increases, but a prudent father would want to fight against that.

When the Family Law Reform Act 1987 is in full swing, mother with a maintenance agreement *in writing* will be able to apply to the court for more if that is reasonable because of some change in circumstances since the agreement was made (for example, mother has lost job, child has become ill or father has won "Spot the Ball"), or if the agreement was a lousy deal for the child in the first place. And where father agreed that his estate should go on paying for a dependent child after his death, mother will be able to go to the court to alter the agreement after his death.

THIS DEED is made on the 14th July 1988 BETWEEN JACK LAD of 38 Elephant Walk Gosport Hampshire ("Mr. Lad") and LAVINIA FISGUARD of 31 Dalrymple Grove Portsmouth Hampshire ("Ms. Fisguard")

BACKGROUND -

1. On the 1st June 1988 at St. Mary's General Hospital Portsmouth Ms. Fisguard gave birth to an illegitimate child Stephen Fisguard ("the child")

2. Mr Lad is the father of the child OR Mr Lad denies he is the father of the child

3. Ms Fisguard is to retain the custody and care and control of the child

4. Mr Lad has agreed to make financial provision for the child as set out below and in consideration thereof Ms Fisguard has agreed not to bring any court proceedings as mentioned below so long as Mr Lad complies with his obligations under this agreement

NOW THIS DEED WITNESSES as follows:

1. (1) Mr Lad hereby covenants with Ms Fisguard to pay to Ms. Fisguard or to such other person as she may from time to time direct in writing for the maintenance and support of the child the sum of £25 per week ("the maintenance") payable weekly

(2) The first payment of the maintenance shall be made on the date of this agreement and all subsequent payments shall be made on Thursday in each week

(3) Subject to clause 1(4) the maintenance shall be paid so long as the child shall be alive and until the occurrence of the later of the following events -

(a) the child attaining the age of eighteen

(b) the child ceasing full-time education

(4) the maintenance shall cease to be payable upon the death of Mr Lad OR The maintenance shall continue to be payable notwithstanding the death of Mr Lad and the obligations of Mr Lad under this agreement shall be enforceable against his estate

2. (1) In addition to the maintenance Mr Lad hereby covenants with Ms Fisguard to pay to Ms Fisguard a lump sum of £1,500 towards Ms Fisguard's confinement expenses and otherwise for the maintenance and support of the child

(2) The said lump sum shall be paid as to £500 on the date of this agreement as to £500 on or before the 14th July 1989 and as to £500 on or before the 14th July 1990

3. Ms Fisguard hereby covenants with Mr Lad to retain the custody and care and control of the child and to provide the child with prompt and sufficient food clothing accommodation education and medical attendance

4. Ms Fisguard hereby further covenants with Mr Lad that so long as Mr Lad shall comply with the covenants contained in clause 1 she will:-

(a) keep Mr Fisguard indemnified from and against all actions proceedings costs claims and liabilities of any kind in respect of the maintenance education or otherwise of the child

(b) not take or cause or permit to be taken any proceedings to affiliate the child to Mr Lad or to obtain financial relief under section 11B of the Guardianship of Minors Act 1971 (whether or not the said section shall yet be in force at the date of this agreement) or otherwise to compel him to make payments in respect of the maintenance and support of the child beyond those specified in clause 1

(c) not apply for any alteration of this agreement under section 15 or section 16 of the Family Law Reform Act 1987 (whether or not such section shall yet be in force at the date of this agreement)

(d) keep confidential the terms of this agreement

(e) not molest or otherwise interfere with Mr Lad

IN WITNESS whereof the parties have hereunto placed their hands and seals the day and year first before written

SIGNED SEALED AND DELIVERED)
by the said JACK LAD in the) Jack Lad
presence of:)
Millie Combes
147 Abbeywood Drive
Catisfield Hants

SIGNED SEALED AND DELIVERED) Lavinia
by the said LAVINIA FISGUARD) Fisguard
in the presence of:)
Millie Combes
147 Abbeywood Drive
Catisfield Hants

Health warnings: No stamp duty is payable on this agreement. The "I won't go to court to get an alteration" (see clause 4(c) of the agreement) provision may well be unenforceable, but its inclusion would not invalidate the remainder of the agreement.

How to eliminate your neighbours

. . . nuisance!

Love thy neighbour

It is a pity that having to live next door to next door neighbours is apparently unavoidable. They will be overflowing with pleasantness and incessant analyses of the weather and the National Health Service. Or, almost as bad, they will make excessive noise, fail to cultivate their gardens and devaluate all other properties in close proximity. If the noise, in a legal sense, amounts to a nuisance—it causes substantial inconvenience and no reasonable person would put up with it—an action could be brought in the county court or High Court for an injunction to stop it, and for damages. The same course could be taken in respect of smells and any anti-social behaviour emanating from next door.

In January 1988 Ronald and Patricia McSorley from Maidenhead Road, Windsor were awarded £23,632 damages plus interest and costs in their High Court nuisance action against two members of a Hell's

Angel chapter which had taken up residence next door and ultimately driven the McSorleys out by their behaviour.

Most neighbouring nuisances are in a different league. For the less serious noisy nuisance, the local authority has power under section 58 of the Control of Pollution Act 1974 to serve on the neighbours an abatement notice—belt up or else—and prosecute in the magistrates' court any failure to comply. And if the local authority won't pull its finger out or refuses to help, the aggrieved occupier may extract the cotton wool from his ears and bring an action himself in the magistrates' court under section 59 of the 1974 Act. If successful, the occupier will obtain an abatement order—belt up or else—against his neighbour. If the order is contravened, an offence is committed attracting a fine of up to £2,000 and up to £50 for each day after conviction that the noise continues. This is a sort of low-key injunction. In the magistrates' court, a group of affected occupiers may get together, pool resources and back an action by one of their number: some legal aid help from a solicitor in preparing the case will be available for any occupier financially eligible. What an action by the council or by the aggrieved occupiers under the 1974 Act will not bring is damages; for those an outing to the county court or High Court must be embarked upon, but it may be costly. For flat occupiers there will be the additional course available of complaining to the landlord or the managing agents that the neighbour is in breach of the terms of his tenancy by carrying on as he is.

And so to bed

Before the local authority or the court is asked to come in, it is desirable for the aggrieved to communicate with his nuisance neighbour and beg him to desist. All being well, a pattern of reasonableness on the part of the aggrieved, and unreasonableness on the part of the neighbour, will then be established and the exchange of correspondence and abuse can be relied on thereafter:

42 Hunch Road
14th July 1988

Dear Mr and Mrs Royds,

I am typing this letter as my hand would be too shaky to write. I have been kept up through the night by the noise from your home: the dog barking in the kitchen, your son broadcasting in the basement and yourselves bonking in the bedroom. This happens almost every night and for the last three months Bert and me have been here you have made our lives a misery. The party wall is thin and we hear everything. You are so inconsiderate and everything you do seems to be done at maximum volume. When I have tried to speak to you, I have been met with abuse. Bert is not a wimp.

Unless you show more consideration in the future and keep down the noise to a moderate level, we will take what action we are advised is suitable.

Yours truly

A. Dalrymple

Agnes Dalrymple

The neighbours respond

WE'VE BEEN HERE FOR YEARS
NOBODY ASKED YOU TO MOVE IN.
GO AWAY. DROP DEAD.
EMMA ROYDS

The fact that the aggrieved came to the nuisance will not give the neighbour a defence. But if the neighbour can show that his behaviour has been the same during the previous ten years and that the previous occupiers never complained, the court might wonder whether the aggrieved is over-sensitive.

Love thy neighbour's garden

Since we do not have the legal right to a pleasant view, the only comfort available for he who looks out on to an eyesore next door may be opthalmic drops. And, if he were still alive, Mr. Giles would tell you that a neighbour who neglects to cut back his thistles resulting in seeds being blown in large quantities on to the adjoining land is not civilly liable to its aggravated owner. Mr. Giles unsuccessfully sued a Mr. Walker in such circumstances and had his appeal thrown out in the High Court in 1890. Chief Justice Lord Coleridge disposed of the matter in four and a half lines beginning "I have never heard of such an action as this."

But for 'orribly overgrown gardens, it may be possible to persuade the local authority to take action against the neighbour under section 92 of the Public Health Act 1936—land in such state as to be injurious or likely to cause injury to health or a nuisance—or perhaps more appropriately, under section 4 of the Prevention of Damage by Pests Act 1949 on the ground that there are rats or mice on the land or that something should be done to keep the land free of rats or mice. And under section 83 of the Public Health Act 1936 the local authority can give a clean-up notice to the owner or occupier of land or premises which are verminous or in such a filthy or unwholesome condition as to be prejudicial to health. The authority can clean up itself if the stink-out continues, and can also prosecute. In October 1974 a couple living in a Rhos-on-Sea council house which was filthy and full of rubble and bags of rubbish were prosecuted under the 1936 Act and convicted. Magistrates fined each of them £25 and £2 a day so long as the offence continued.

Love thy neighbour's business

The neighbour may be carrying on a business from home which is a source of irritation to other occupiers in the road, whether immediately next door or not. Men in dirty raincoats straining their necks for Number 96: nightly discussions in the road about "this nice little motor which I bought for my wife but which I've got to get rid of quickly for half its value because I've just been told she is suffering from a serious illness and I am desperate for cash to pay the medical fees." But it would take more than proof of a business and resulting irritation to show that a legal nuisance was being perpetrated. What other laws can be invoked against the business-conducting neighbour? Quite a lot. Planning permission may be needed to change the use of a property from a private dwelling to a mixture of private dwelling and business. The change must be *material*. Using a desk in the corner of the living room, not employing any staff at the property and receiving one business caller a month would probably not be material. But putting aside one room for the business, having a part-time secretary work there, using the address in all business advertisements and for all business communications and attracting a dozen or more callers a day could well demand permission. It is a question of degree. And though planning permission may be avoided it is possible that the neighbour is breaching a covenant in his deeds not to use the property for any business and that the covenant could be enforced by the complaining neighbour or by the estate developers.

Anonymous note

Dear Mr Businessperson

Would you care to reconsider the wisdom of running a dating agency from your home? You may find that:-

(a) the local authority serves you with an abatement notice under section 58 of the Control of Pollution Act 1974 on the ground that the conduct of your property amounts to a legal nuisance;

(b) one or more of your neighbours brings private proceedings in the magistrates' court under section 59 of the Control of Pollution Act 1974 on the same ground;

(c) the local authority serves you with an enforcement notice requiring you to stop using your property for the purpose of a business because I understand you have never obtained or even applied for planning permission to change its use;

(d) the rateable value of your property is increased;

(e) if you rent your property you will lose the security of tenure to which you would otherwise be entitled under the Rent Act because that is not designed for business tenants and if the business use actually constitutes a breach of the terms of your tenancy, your landlord may decide to ask the court to evict you;

(f) if you own your property and are subject to a covenant not to use it for the purpose of a business or for any purpose which may cause a nuisance to adjoining owners then those adjoining owners or the developers may take action against you to stop the use and the adjoining owners for damages; and

(g) if you have set aside any part of the property exclusively for the use of your business you may jeopardise escaping capital gains tax on the whole of the profit you make when you sell your property.

Yours sincerely

A. W. Wisher

A Well Wisher

Out shopping

Some conversation pieces

- "I'll have to send it back to the manufacturer."
- "My dear man, you can send it to Timbuktoo if that be your wish. However, I bought it from you and not the manufacturer. My contract was with you and not the manufacturer. My claim is and must be against you and not the manufacturer. Give me my money back."

- "We can't do anything about it unless you can produce the receipt."
- "I threw the receipt away because I did not realise I would need it. I had not expected you would sell me rubbish. I bought the thing. I bought the thing from you. I will swear on oath in court if I have to that I bought it from you. There is no law which requires me to produce the receipt before I can obtain legal redress. By being awkward you will increase your obligations because I will have to sue and that will involve costs which I will claim against you. Give me my money back."

- "It was in the sale. That's the sort of thing you must expect."
- "What I expect from something I buy in a sale is

that it should be cheaper than it was when not in a sale. The fact my purchase was in a sale does not alter your legal obligations. It should have been of merchantable quality and reasonably fit for its purpose. It was neither. Give me my money back."

- "Is there something wrong with your eyesight, madam? This was in a display marked "SECONDS" and "SLIGHTLY IMPERFECT". What do you want—blood?"
- "What I want is something which will work. I recognise I cannot expect perfection. But the law says I can expect something which is of use. This isn't. Give me my money back."

- "The manager is busy/out/engaged stocktaking/interviewing/gone to head office."
- "I'll wait until the manager is available. If I get fed up waiting, I'll pop along to Trading Standards who I expect to have more time for dissatisfied customers than your manager. If he is prepared to grant *you* an audience during the next hour, perhaps you could pass on my feelings."

- "There's no question of a refund but we are prepared to give you a credit note."
- "There's no question of a credit note. This was not of merchantable quality. This was not reasonably fit for its purpose. I've come back quickly. I reject the article and you can't force a credit note on me (unless you want to make it redeemable for substantially more than the price I paid). Give me my money back."

- "Maybe it doesn't fit her but we sold you what you asked for."

- "I bought this on the strict understanding that you would replace it with a garment of the correct size if it didn't fit. You are bound by what you promised. It doesn't fit. Give me a garment which will fit. If you are not prepared to do this, give me my money back."

- "Our salesman had no right to tell you that. It's against company rules. We can't be held responsible for him."
- "Oh yes you can. What he said was in the course of his employment by you. It may have been against company rules, alien to the way his mother brought him up and justifying forfeiture of his "Salesman of the Year" sash and trophy. But you're stuck with it. His sins are your sins. Give me my money back."

- "The pears were quite edible when you bought them. The fact they were black when you got them home is your bad luck, madam."
- "Perishable goods must be up to Sale of Goods Act standard when they are handed over and they must remain so for a reasonable time afterwards, sir. These pears failed to. Give me my money back."

- "The price label on the article and the price ticket on the display counter were both wrong. They should have said £4.99, not £1.99. You will have to pay £4.99 even if you stand in the queue for the rest of the day. Actually, we are closing in half an hour."
- "I accept I cannot compel you to sell the article to me at any price. As a matter of courtesy however, I would like to direct your attention to section 11(2)

of the Trade Descriptions Act 1968 which makes it an offence to offer to supply goods at a price less than that at which they are in fact being offered. Perhaps you made a mistake but I suggest you could not show you took all reasonable precautions and exercised all due diligence to avoid an offence and so you have no defence. Trading Standards or £1.99?"

- "A carrier bag will be 4p madam."
- "Before you ring up the prices and so accept my offers to buy each of the items I have just emptied out of my wire basket and conclude binding contracts, I have one important condition to impose. I am not prepared to buy unless you supply me with a carrier bag FREE OF CHARGE. So do you put this lot back on the shelves or risk liquidation by providing the plastic for me to take away what you are going to sell me?"

- "Madam, those paper bags are there to be used by customers for items they have just bought. I believe you have three dozen bags and one packet of Polos."
- "I thought they were free to customers who made a purchase. There's no sign up restricting the number to be taken or circumstances of their removal. I was acting within what I thought were my rights. Therefore, I was not acting dishonestly. Therefore, I am not guilty of theft."

- "The goods were perfect. You can't blame us because the box fell to pieces and the goods fell on to the pavement and smashed."
- "It's not just the goods which have to be of

merchantable quality and reasonably fit for their purpose, mate. It's the packaging too. You are as legally responsible for that as for the goods."

- "This is Efficiency Stores, Catisfield, speaking, sir. It's about the microwave you bought on Access this morning. I'm afraid we have lost the voucher you signed. Could you be so kind (unctuous grovel, creep etc) to pop back in and sign another voucher if it is not too much trouble and do have a cup of coffee and biscuits with the manager. Bring the wife? The children? Your dog? Mother-in-law . . .?"
- "Actually, sorry. Legally, my signature on the voucher this morning discharged my obligation to pay. Must fly. I've got a potato baking . . . in my new microwave."

Shopping special

In three rounds

Fast rejection

A customer may have the strongest case this century under the Sale of Goods Act, but if, aware of their deficiencies, he carries on using the goods or just waits too long before making it clear to the seller that he rejects them, he will lose his legal right to reject. He will still be entitled to damages to reflect the defects and losses he has suffered as a result of them. It's the valuable right to reject which will be gone. As Lord Justice Stephen Gold once said: "A purchaser stands no chance of the return of the price for the goods if he has sat on his bum."

In a 1986 High Court case which has come in for a good deal of criticism, the judge held that the buyer of a new car had legally accepted it though he had had it for only three weeks and had been ignorant of any defect until it conked out. Leslie Bernstein bought a new Nissan Laurel from Pamsons Motors (Golders Green) Limited for £7,995. During the following three weeks he made two or three short trips for the very purpose of trying it out and then, with just 142 miles on the clock, the engine seized up. The cause was a drop of sealant which had gone into the lubrication system when the car was assembled. This was responsible for a blockage, depriving the camshaft of lubrication. The judge said that Mr. Bernstein had "accepted" the car by having it for three weeks without sending it back. A buyer was to have a reasonable time to inspect his purchase and try it out: once that time was up, no money back. What was a reasonable time? It depended on the nature of the goods: what was reasonable for a bicycle would scarcely be adequate for a nuclear submarine. Mr. Bernstein still got some damages but the story had a happy ending for him. He put in notice of appeal to the Court of Appeal and shortly before the hearing the sellers (with some assistance from the manufacturers) did a deal with him. He was paid all the damages he had been after (by then the car had been sold) based on a right to reject and he withdrew his appeal, which means that the High Court judgment stands.

Round 1

Dear Mr Trader

On the 14th July 1988 you agreed to sell me a Whitesmalls Superlative Extra De Luxe washing machine for £486 which I paid by cheque. The machine was delivered two months ago. It was badly dented. It is not of merchantable quality and I reject it. I claim the immediate return of the price. Please make arrangements to collect the machine.

Yours faithfully

Ena Spin

Ena Spin

Round 2

Dear Ena Spin

If your Whitesmalls washing machine was dented when it was delivered, I find it hard to understand why you did not draw this to the attention of our delivery person and, indeed, why you signed a copy of the delivery note to confirm receipt and satisfaction. Further, our solicitors advise us that you have accepted the washing machine by retaining it for two months without rejection and that you are too late to claim the return of the price.

Assuring you of our best attention at all times,

Yours faithfully

M. Trader

Mr Trader

Round 3

Dear Mr Trader

Your delivery person said he had another seven calls to make and it was already 5.05 p.m. when he came to my home. The washing machine was in a large cardboard box which was secured with staples, tape, glue and string. It was still in the box and secured in this way when your delivery person left. Maybe I did sign the delivery note. This did not remove the dents which I later discovered were present.

I do not consider that any county court would say I had held on to the machine for too long before rejecting it. Anyway, I am advised that I am still entitled to damages for the diminution in value of the machine by virtue of the dents. I have expert advice to the effect that it is worth £150 less. Strictly without prejudice, I am prepared to accept a replacement machine without dents in satisfaction of all claims against you. Otherwise you will have to pay the £150.

Yours faithfully

Ena Spin

Ena Spin

Ena in a bit of difficulty there. The greater the damages to reflect defects, the greater the incentive to the trader to come to a compromise agreement which involves him taking back the goods. In practice, it will often be the case that neither side is absolutely confident about which way a judge will decide on whether the buyer was too late to reject. If a buyer cannot reach an agreement and has to sue, he should sue on the alternative bases that he has effectively rejected or is entitled to damages for diminution in value: in either event, other losses can be claimed.

Bear a repair?

The present state of the law presents a potential trap for the customer who is invited by the trader to have the defective goods repaired. He'll be in a more favourable position if the goods were taken on HP. Then he isn't the legal owner of them until he completes all the payments and this will have some bearing on his legal capacity to "accept" soon after he has got them when they're on the duff side. In one case a customer had a duff motor bike on HP but allowed an opportunity for repairs; after some time there were still defects and with four HP instalments already paid he said he had had enough and the finance company repossessed the machine. Did consent to the repair and the four payments mean he was too late to reject? The court said "No". And Lord Denning pointed out that the customer had complained from the beginning of the defects. "He did not elect to accept it unless they were remedied. But the defects here were never satisfactorily remedied."

With a cash purchase, the customer who wants to say "Yes" to repairs should do it this way—

> Dear Mr Trader
>
> I reject the white two piece silk suit I bought from you yesterday for £499.99 because it is stained on the lapel. You have said you can remove the stain. If you do remove the stain, I will then consider whether I would be prepared to take the suit back. For the moment, you must treat rejection as unconditional.
>
> Yours faithfully
>
> C. Customer
>
> Cutie Customer

And if the trader does not at first succeed with his repair attempts, the customer should be very, very careful about giving him a second chance.

Till divorce us do part

Passport to freedom

For the spouse after quick liberation from marriage, an allegation of adultery or unreasonable behaviour may be the very thing. That's because the other divorce grounds depend on husband and wife having lived apart for specified periods—two years when the other spouse consents to the divorce, five years without consent and two years when one has deserted the other. Sadly, a spouse cannot bring divorce proceedings on the ground of his own misconduct (in contrast, a spouse can bring nullity proceedings on the ground of his own impotence), and has to wait as long as one year from the celebration of the marriage before starting the proceedings.

Anonymous adultery

As the law currently stands (there has been a high powered recommendation for change, but there is no sign of it yet) when adultery is alleged, the *other* man or woman must be made co-respondent and so a party to the proceedings. This entails that other man or woman being named in the papers and being sent copies. It is all very well if the co-respondent has been alerted to the prospect of the papers hurtling through his letter box, for then he is prepared—"Just another confounded questionnaire from Censuses and Population, darling. I'll see to it."—but collapse and the outbreak of gibbering have been registered in some cases. The court only has power to make an exception about involving the other man or woman if some "special ground" can be shown—and it rarely can.

What if the spouse bringing the proceedings hasn't a clue who the other person is? Then, he cannot do the impossible. The divorce petition should contain a statement that the person's identity is unknown and the case can go ahead without the person being named, made a party or served with any papers. It is imprudent to tell a lie about this. It may lead to a criminal charge of perjury and to the divorce decree being rescinded if and when the truth emerges.

Almost adultery

The prospective co-respondent may himself be married and feel obligated to defend the allegation of adultery against him because his wife will come to hear of it. That could turn what should be a straightforward undefended divorce case into a protracted defended one. Or the spouse who has committed adultery may be unprepared to make a generous financial arrangement with his wife unless she refrains from naming his girl friend. In situations like these, the spouse wanting to bring divorce proceedings would dearly love to leave out the other person. Is there a legitimate way round this when the other person's identity is known? Yes.

Instead of relying on adultery, the spouse can allege unreasonable behaviour and pray in aid the improper association of the other spouse "with a person who can be named by the Petitioner if called on to do so". This will usually work. An allegation of unreasonable behaviour on the strength of an improper association can also be made in addition to, or as an alternative to, an allegation of adultery where there is some doubt whether adultery can be proved (but some hanky panky can) and the other spouse might refuse to admit adultery or even defend a lone adultery allegation. The petitioning spouse has to prove it is more probable than not that adultery was committed. An admission by the other spouse will do fine. And in the absence of an admission? Bedroom evidence is best but not essential. Circumstantial evidence may do: evidence of strong inclination, mixed with opportunity!

Unreasonable behaviour as a divorce ground can take in more than a bare allegation of an improper association. It can extend, for example, to allegations of physical violence, mental "cruelty", extreme meanness, and abstinence from sex: all are capable of amounting to unreasonable behaviour. The other spouse must have behaved in such a way that the one seeking divorce could not reasonably be expected to live with him. Would a right-thinking person, knowing the couple and all the circumstances, consider it reasonable to expect her to live with him? That is the test.

"Him divorce me!—*I'll* divorce *him*!

It often happens that one spouse, in bringing divorce proceedings against the wishes of the other, actually triggers the other into going after a divorce herself. In fact she can do this in the same proceedings by always drop out, allowing the cross-petition to go ahead undefended. Effectively the original petition has been used as a device to stir or even provoke the other into doing something about bringing the marriage to an end.

"Which way to the Grimsby County Court?"

The divorce proceedings may be brought in London's Divorce Registry or most local county courts. It is not necessary for the spouse who brings the case to actually live in the area in which the court is located, although a defended case will be fixed for hearing at the most convenient venue. Where that is will depend on where the couple and the witnesses are living. It is the practice of some local newspapers to publish particulars of divorce decrees pronounced in the county court on their doorstep. A spouse whose local newspaper gets its kicks this way and wishes to avoid publicity will be keen to patronise a divorce county court a few hundred miles away.

A free booklet can be obtained from the Divorce Registry and county courts explaining the procedures and how to start the case. Most firms of solicitors will take on divorce and other matrimonial cases. If money is rationed, there may well be an entitlement to help from a solicitor under the "green form" legal aid scheme. Any person bringing divorce proceedings who is being helped this way is exempt from paying court fees and gets the paperwork drawn up by the solicitor. There's also an exemption for people on income support or family credit (supplementary benefit or family income supplement to you and me). Otherwise, the court fee for starting the case is £40, for applying for maintenance £15 and for applying for the decree absolute £10. The fees can be claimed back from the other spouse through an order for costs which has to be asked for in the divorce petition. In an adultery case, the order for costs could be sought against both spouse and co-respondent, thereby doubling the chance of getting the money. But the court might well decline to make an order against the co-respondent when the adultery was not directly responsible for the marriage breakdown.

Here is an example of a divorce petition:

* Delete as appropriate

IN THE HAPPINESS COUNTY COURT*

~~IN THE DIVORCE REGISTRY*~~

No. of matter: 88 D 674

Between

MELANIE GARFIELD Petitioner

and

IVOR ADENUF McGREGOR GARFIELD Respondent

and

MANDY CLORE Co-respondent

1 This is the petition of Melanie Garfield ('the petitioner') who was lawfully married to Ivor Adenuf McGregor Garfield ('the respondent') on the 1st day of June 19 70 , at the Church of St. Mary's Union Street Happiness in the County of Great Joy

2 The last address at which the petitioner and the respondent lived together as husband and wife was "Chez Garfield" 41 Albert Road Happiness aforesaid

(1) If this is not so, delete and insert the details required by MCR 1977, Appendix 2, paragraphs 1(c) and (d)

3 The petitioner is domiciled in England and Wales.(1)

4 The petitioner resides at "Chez Garfield" 41 Albert Road Happiness aforesaid

and ~~[his]~~ [her] occupation is housewife

The respondent resides at Flat 15a Sin Row Happiness aforesaid

and [his] ~~[her]~~ occupation is schoolmaster

(2) Here set out the details required by MCR 1977, Appendix 2, paragraphs 1(f) and (g)

(3) Delete these words in a wife's petition

(4) If this is not so, delete and insert the details required by MCR 1977, Appendix 2, paragraphs (i) and (j)

5 ~~[There are no living children of the family.]~~
[There ~~[is]~~ [are] now living two child[ren] of the family(2):
Simon McGregor Garfield born on the 1st day of March 1971 and
Sarah McGregor Garfield born on the 14th day of February 1983.
]

[~~As far as the petitioner knows~~(3)] no other child now living has been born to the [petitioner] ~~[respondent]~~ during the marriage.(2)

Petition for divorce (adultery) *s.1(2)(a), MCA 1973*

Form F901

27/28 St. Alban's Place
London N1 0NX
January 1981 E

6 There are and have been no other proceedings in any court in England and Wales and elsewhere relating to the marriage or to any child[ren] of the family or between the petitioner and the respondent with regard to any property belonging to either or both of them.(4)

7 There are no proceedings continuing in any country outside England and Wales relating to the marriage or which are capable of affecting its validity or subsistence.[4]

8 ~~There has been [no] [an] agreement or arrangement made or proposed to be made between the parties for the support of [the petitioner] [the respondent] [or any child of the family] [namely][5]~~

(5) Where five years' separation is *also* alleged, this paragraph must be completed (with appropriate deletions) and details of any agreement or arrangement set out. Otherwise this paragraph should be deleted.

9 The marriage has broken down irretrievably.[6]

(6) Delete if judicial separation sought

10 The respondent has committed adultery with MANDY CLORE ('the co-respondent') and the petitioner finds it intolerable to live with the respondent.

<u>Particulars</u>

Between on or about the 1st day of January 1988 and the date of the presentation of this petition at Flat 15a, Sin Row, Happiness aforesaid and at other places unknown to the petitioner the respondent has habitually committed adultery with the co-respondent.

OR

Between on or about the 1st day of January 1988 and the date of the presentation of this petition at places unknown to the petitioner the respondent has committed adultery with the co-respondent when opportunity and inclination have coincided.

OR

10. The respondent has committed adultery with a woman whose identity is unknown to the petitioner and the petitioner finds it intolerable to live with the respondent.

<u>Particulars</u>

On or about the 1st day of January 1988 and on other dates unknown to the petitioner at a place or places unknown to the petitioner the respondent has committed adultery with the said woman.

11. Further and in the alternative, the respondent has behaved in such a way that the petitioner cannot reasonably be expected to live with the respondent.

<u>Particulars</u>

(a) Between on or about the 1st day of January 1988 and the date of the presentation of this petition the respondent has conducted an improper association with the co-respondent.
(b) Between on or about the 1st day of January 1988 and the 30th day of April 1988 when the petitioner and the respondent ceased living together, the respondent habitually spent more of his social hours with the co-respondent than with the petitioner well knowing that such practice caused distress to the petitioner.
(c) Between on or about the 1st day of January 1988 and the 30th day of April 1988 the respondent frequently lavished gifts on the co-respondent including lingerie, leather accessories and perfumes.

(d) Between on or about the 1st day of January 1988 and the 30th day of April 1988 the respondent frequently telephoned the co-respondent from the matrimonial home at "Chez Garfield" aforesaid and spoke in hushed tones so that the petitioner would not hear him.

(e) On or about the 5th day of January 1988 at the Railway Hotel, Happiness aforesaid the respondent took afternoon tea with the co-respondent having previously told the petitioner that he was committed throughout the day on foreign business discussions.

(f) On or about the 1st day of April 1988 in Archibald Street, Happiness aforesaid the respondent publicly kissed the co-respondent on the back of her neck.

(7) Amend the prayer as appropriate

(7) The petitioner's prayer is for:

1 dissolution of the marriage

2 an order for the custody of the said children Simon McGregor Garfield and Sarah McGregor Garfield

3 an order that the [respondent] [co-respondent] do pay the costs of these proceedings.

4 an order that ancillary relief be granted to the petitioner as follows:

(a) an order for maintenance pending suit
a periodical payments order
a secured provision order
a lump sum order

(b) a periodical payments order
a secured provision order
a lump sum order
} for the children of the family

(c) a property adjustment order

(8) Insert name(s) and address(es); if any person to be served is under disability, see MCR 1977, r.113

The following person[s] ~~[is]~~ [are] to be served with this petition(8):

Respondent: Ivor Adenuf McGregor Garfield, Flat15a, Sin Row, Happiness, Great Joy

Co-Respondent: Mandy Clore, Flat 15a, Sin Row, Happiness, Great Joy.

(9) See MCR 1977, Appendix 2, paragraph 5(c), as amended

The petitioner's address for service is(9):
"Chez Garfield" 41 Albert Road Happiness Great Joy.

Dated this 14th day of July 1988

Signed... Melanie Garfield ....

If the petition is filed in The Divorce Registry, all communications for the court should be addressed to The Divorce Registry, Somerset House, Strand, London WC2R 1LP. If the proceedings are commenced in a County Court, all communications for the court should be addressed to The Registrar, Happiness County Court, The Law Courts, Misery Lane, Great Joy

The court offices are open from 10.00am to 4.00pm (to 4.30pm in the Divorce Registry) on weekdays.

Till divorce us do part

In the HAPPINESS County Court

~~In the Divorce Registry~~

No. of matter: 88 D 674

Between

MELANIE GARFIELD

Petitioner

and

IVOR ADENUF McGREGOR GARFIELD

Respondent

and

MANDY CLORE

Co-respondent

Petition for Divorce
under section 1(2)(a)
of the Matrimonial Causes
Act 1973

The dreaded drink-drive

Any chance of saving my licence?

HEALTH WARNING: Drinking and driving is bad for motorist, his licence, his pocket and his insurance premium. It is also bad for other people who happen to be on the road at the same time. The drink-drive law was revolutionised by the Transport Act 1981 which came into force on May 6 1983.

It is an offence to drive, attempt to drive or be in charge of a motor vehicle on a road or other public place with excess alcohol or under the influence. It is also an offence to fail to supply a specimen for the breath machine (two specimens are actually called for) or a blood or urine specimen instead. Before arrest, the motorist will often have given a roadside breath test—the legendary blow in the bag test—although there is more sophisticated roadside breath testing equipment available these days. This is the "screening" test. It is not mandatory for the police to carry it out, and the result is not a substitute for the analysis of breath by the machine at the police station or of the blood or urine of which specimens may have been taken following arrest.

It was intended, among other things, that the new legislation would plug loopholes in the law which had allowed drivers to escape conviction on technicalities and so reduce the level of contested cases. Loopholes it did plug, but new ones have opened up and although the prospects of casting doubt on the reliability of the Intoximeter and Camic breath machine analyses are extremely slim, the magistrates' and appeal courts of the land have been besieged by technical arguments of great ingenuity on behalf of motorists desperate to secure an acquittal or the quashing of a conviction. Some of the arguments have succeeded.

The motorist cannot elect to be tried by a jury at the Crown Court on a drink drive charge. Only a magistrates' court can try him. He can appeal against a conviction by magistrates to the Crown Court (if the appeal is on a question of fact or a mixed question of fact and law), or to the High Court (on a question of law only).

The archbishop defence

Motorist dines with archbishop before taking to driving seat. His liquid intake during the meal is restricted to two glasses of Perrier water and a bowl of non-alcoholic consommé. He appears quite sober to the archbishop and to other persons with whom he is in contact before he has the misfortune to be arrested; he calls those people in his defence. Oddly, the breath machine shows him to be over the limit.

In the course of the driver's attempt to impugn the breath machine's accuracy, the court may hear evidence of the amount of alcohol which the motorist had consumed. So evidence from persons of high moral standing, like the archbishop, will make the court sit up. But the evidence will need to be very powerful indeed and, ideally, linked with some evidence suggesting strange breath machine behaviour (a few aborts, moaning by the operating police constable that the "confounded thing hasn't been feeling well lately" would do) before the court can be expected to contemplate that the machine has had an aberration. After all, the breath machine calibrates itself both before and after each subject provides his breath specimens, and the results must be within an acceptable tolerance band. If they had been outside the band—and the calibration results are recorded on the printout—the police would not be relying on the machine's analyses.

Relevant case—Cracknell v Willis, decided by the House of Lords on November 5 1987.

The dirty play defence

If the police play it dirty, the court has a discretion to exclude evidence which they need in order to prove the motorist's guilt. The dirty play could relate to the initial stopping of the motorist. Random roadside breath *testing* is outlawed (and despite shouts for its introduction, we suggest it is really not needed and our bet is that it will not be introduced), but random *stopping* is quite permissible. So a police officer can stop a motorist for no apparent reason and, then, sniffing alcohol on his breath, require him to give a roadside test. But if, in connection with the stopping, there is "malpractice", "oppression", "caprice" or "opprobrious conduct" by the police, there may be grounds for excluding evidence of what follows, including provision and analyses of the main breath or blood or urine specimens. Random *stopping* in order to administer roadside breath tests might be "malpractice" where carried out by the police under the pretence that the drivers are committing traffic offences when the police knew perfectly well they are not.

In one case the police trespassed to get to the motorist and behaved oppressively and the screening breath test was not voluntarily undertaken. Although the motorist was over the limit, the court acquitted him.

Relevant cases—Fox v Chief Constable of Gwent decided by the House of Lords on October 17 1985; Matto v Wolverhampton Crown Court decided by the High Court on May 20 1987; Gwent v Dash decided by the High Court on June 13 1985.

The absent brief defence

As a general rule, the police can carry on with the drink drive procedures at the station, including putting the motorist on the breath machine, despite the motorist wanting legal advice and even if he is actually waiting for a solicitor to telephone or visit him. So a refusal to provide a specimen until advice has been received would not be justified. But if the police have told the motorist quite clearly that he need not provide a specimen until he has consulted with a solicitor and, still solicitorless, the police change tack and require a specimen, the motorist may have a good defence to the charge of failing to supply a specimen if he refuses. Also, if the police act "oppressively"—much more than just refusing solicitor access—over a request for legal advice, and the motorist refuses to provide a specimen and is charged, he might be able to persuade the court to exclude sufficient of the evidence against him as to ensure his acquittal.

And if the motorist says "I will, I will provide a

specimen but can I see my solicitor first?" the police must not treat this as an outright refusal to provide and go on and charge the motorist with failing to provide a specimen. If they did, he would have a good defence. Instead, the police should decide whether or not to grant the favour asked for. They could not be faulted for rejecting it.

Relevant cases—DPP v Billington; Chappell v DPP; DPP v Rumble and Corywright v East, all decided by the High Court on July 20 1987.

The no warning defence

The police must warn the motorist that failure to provide a specimen for the breath machine or a specimen of blood or urine (whichever it is to be) may render him liable to prosecution. They usually do because the warning is written down on their aide-memoire. Nevertheless, they have been known to forget. Where the warning has not been given and the motorist refuses to supply a specimen and is charged with failure, the absence of warning will be fatal to the prosecution and the motorist will be entitled to an acquittal. We submit that even where the motorist has given a specimen and is charged with driving over the limit, the absence of a warning should lead to the same result.

Relevant cases—Howard v Hallett, decided by the High Court on May 4 1984; Simpson v Spalding, decided by the High Court on November 7 1987.

The me no understand warning defence

This is a variation of the no warning defence. It works like this. "O.K. a warning was given but I did not understand it." Valid reasons for not understanding might be the motorist's inability to understand English or his anxiety or mental state. The defence has succeeded where the motorist was charged with failing to provide a specimen. We submit that, in principle, the defence should succeed on a charge of actually driving over the limit. In the decided case, the motorist was of Indian origin. He could understand English to a certain degree but he could not understand long or technical words. So that when, at the police station, a sergeant said to him: "It is alleged you have committed an offence contrary to section 5 or 6 of the Road Traffic Act 1972 as amended by the Transport Act 1981 and I require you to provide two specimens of breath for analysis by means of an approved device. The specimen with the lower proportion of alcohol in your breath may be used as evidence and the other disregarded. I must warn you that failure to provide any of these specimens may render you liable to prosecution. Do you agree to provide two specimens of breath for analysis?", he was somewhat overwhelmed. He replied "Yes" but did not understand the warning. He then went on to attempt to provide two specimens on the machine but blew insufficiently and so no analysis occurred. The sergeant had not considered there was a language barrier, did not "explain" the situation to the motorist and did not think it was necessary to get in an interpreter. The motorist won.

Relevant case—DPP v Singh, decided by the High Court on March 12 1987.

The statutory option opt-out defence

The legal limit on the breath machine is 35 (microgrammes of alcohol per 100 millilitres of breath) but, in practice, the police will not charge a motorist with driving over the limit unless the lower of the two breath specimens he should provide analyses out at 40 or more. Where the lower specimen analyses out at 50 or less, the motorist is given an option by statute. The option is to ask to be allowed to give a specimen of blood or urine. (The police will decide which it is to be, and almost always will call for blood rather than urine; but if a doctor decides that there are medical reasons for blood not being taken, the specimen is to be urine, whether the police like it or not.) So long as he then provides that specimen of blood or urine, it will replace the breath specimens. In the event of the blood or urine analysis putting him under the limit applicable to that specimen, he will not be charged despite the lower breath specimen having put him above the breath limit. The statutory option, therefore, is a valuable option. The police must inform the motorist of the option's existence. Their failure to do so will be a good defence.

Relevant case—Anderton v Lythgoe decided by the High Court on October 29 1984.

Option alternative defence

This is a variation of the statutory option opt-out defence. Although the choice as to whether the specimen to replace the breath is to be blood or urine is generally to rest with the police, the motorist must, nevertheless, still be told that the alternative to breath is blood *or* urine. If he is not told, the motorist will have a good defence. This is what one of the appeal judges had to say in the case which decided the point: "Once the constable has told the motorist of both types of specimen and has listened to anything that that person has to say as to which type of specimen he would wish to provide, the constable may decide whether the specimen . . . should be a sample of blood or urine. However, the constable's decision . . . must be an informed decision. It cannot be an informed decision unless the person who has provided the samples of breath knows that there are two possible samples which can be substituted for them and has been given an opportunity of making representations as to which of the two types of specimen it should be."

Relevant case—Hobbs v DPP, decided by the High Court on May 7 1987.

Option offput defence

This is a further variation of the statutory option opt-out defence. The motorist's statutory option must not be interfered with: his freedom of choice must not be undermined. "I've got to tell you about the option but it's a complete waste of time and could make things worse for you." That would do to give the motorist a good defence if it persuaded him against asking for a blood or urine specimen to be taken. And in one decided case, the motorist was acquitted after he had been misled by the police, albeit innocently, into believing he would have to pay there and then for the police doctor's fee in taking the blood specimen.

Relevant case—Hammond v Hunter decided by the High Court on March 6 1985.

The no reliable machine method

Generally, the police must go for breath specimens at the outset and so, generally, they cannot at the outset require the motorist to provide blood or urine specimens. There are three exceptions: where the police believe there may be medical reasons for not requiring breath; where a doctor reckons that the motorist's condition may be attributable to drugs; and, most commonly, where there isn't a breath machine at the police station which is working reliably or it isn't practicable to use the machine. So if the police go for blood or urine at the outset when there *was* a reliable machine at the station, the blood or urine requirement will be unlawful and the motorist will have a good defence notwithstanding that he gave blood or urine and the specimen showed him to be over the limit.

And, in a decided case, the police swopped from breath to blood because the breath machine failed to produce a printout but had analysed the specimens and the results had showed up on the machine's visual display unit. Both the machine and the blood specimens put the motorist over the limit but at the hearing the police relied only on the breath. They could not do so as they had treated the machine as unreliable as evidenced by their blood requirement. The motorist's conviction for driving over the limit was quashed by the appeal court.

Relevant case—Badkin v Chief Constable of South Yorkshire Police, decided by the High Court on July 10 1987.

The handy printout defence

If, as they almost always do, the police wish to prove the results of the breath machine analysis by using the printout produced by the machine (instead of giving evidence about how the machine twice calibrated itself and what recording came up on the machine's visual display unit), they must hand a copy of the printout to the motorist when it comes off the machine, or serve a copy on him at least one week before the hearing. In a decided case, the printout copies were placed on a counter at the police station for the motorist to sign, but without any indication to him that one of the copies was for him to take away. He was acquitted because a printout copy has not been "handed" to him at the station, and no copy had been served on him before the hearing.

Relevant case—Walton v Rimmer, decided by the High Court on February 4 1985.

The bloody certificate defence

This is a variation of the handy printout defence. If, as they almost always do, the police wish to prove the result of a blood (or urine) specimen analysis by producing a certificate by the Home Office scientist who actually carried out the analysis, they must serve a copy of the certificate on the motorist at least one week before the hearing. Failure to do so will be fatal to them. The fact that the motorist initially keeps quiet at the hearing about not having received a copy at least one week beforehand, or not having received a copy at all, and allows the original certificate to be seen by the magistrates will not matter. He has a good defence.

Relevant case—Tobi v Nicholas, decided by the High Court on July 1 1987.

The same bloody arm defence

Where the motorist provided blood (or urine) and he wants part of it—probably because he would like to have it privately analysed—the specimen must be divided into two parts and he must be given one part. But it is the product of a specimen taken *on one single occasion* that has to be divided. And so a motorist was entitled to be acquitted on a charge of driving with excess alcohol on the strength of a blood analysis where the police doctor took a tiny insufficient amount of blood from the motorist's *right* arm and placed it in a container and then tried again. The second time the needle went into the motorist's *left* arm and an acceptable specimen was obtained. This was divided into two parts: one part went into one container and the other part went into a separate container which already had the right arm blood and which was handed over to the motorist. Not good enough, because the blood he took away with him had not been taken on a single occasion but was a mixture of blood taken on two consecutive occasions.

Relevant case—Dear v DPP, decided by the High Court on November 20 1987.

The one blow defence

If the motorist supplies only one instead of the required two specimens for the breath machine and is charged purely and simply with driving over the limit on the strength of the analysis of the single specimen, he has a good defence. In the circumstances, he can only be convicted of failing to supply breath and so should only be charged with that offence.

Relevant case—Cracknell v Willis, decided by the House of Lords on November 5 1987.

The metei-sho defence

They call it metei-sho in Japan. Here, it has been christened intra-gastro intestinal alcohol fermentation syndrome. Either way, it is a rare disease resulting in a victim generating body alcohol upon consuming carbohydrates. He could exceed the drink-drive limit on one meal! The alcohol would show up on the analysis of a specimen, but should not count for the drink-drive law. A motorist who could show he suffered from the disease would almost certainly be acquitted on a drink-drive charge. But so far the only known human victims of the disease are in Japan.

The magic of "without prejudice"

Negotiating without fears

Apart from the occasional crank, the judiciary, lawyers, the media and court ushers, nobody relishes litigation. There will be a special anxiety to fend off litigation by those who consider themselves vulnerable to a judgment because they were to blame and those who, though convinced of their blamelessness, would prefer to spend their time and money out of court. Especially for them is a legal way to make the opposition a compromise proposal which will not count against them if it is rejected. After all, it could be prejudicial and awkward, having denied in the witness box that you are liable to pay the plaintiff a penny, to be shown in cross-examination the letter you wrote three years earlier offering £½m to get rid of the claim. So the way to do it is to make the proposal in a letter endorsed at the top with the magic words "without prejudice". Then the letter cannot be used in court against the writer before the judge has made up his mind.

The recipient of a "without prejudice" communication may send a reply which is not similarly endorsed and which sets out the proposal and goes on to reject it.

This ploy will fail. The reply is no more usable in court than the original letter.

Letters which may induce tears

It is a common misconception that simply endorsing a letter "without prejudice" will save it from being produced in court, regardless of its contents. To be immune from production, the letter must have been written for the purpose of settling the dispute. So he who writes the "Dear Sir I think you are a perverted little creep who molests young children and beats your wife" type letter will be unable to rely on the fact it was endorsed "without prejudice" when sued for libel damages. And a "without prejudice" letter which contains damaging admissions but was written to aggravate, or for some other non-settlement purpose, will backfire. It can be used in court and the writer should be informed of the intention to use it at an early stage so that he can reflect on his boob.

Trying to settle

62 Magnolia Gardens
Fareham
14th July 1988
WITHOUT PREJUDICE

Dear Miss Cyclist

I refer to the unfortunate accident which occurred today when I understand there was some connection between Lady Poofoo, my pet chihuahua, and your pedal cycle as you rode by my home. Whilst I regret that you appear to have fractured your clavicle, I am bound to join issue with you over the suggestion that Lady Poofoo did not look before going to cross. However, I am prepared to make an ex gratia offer to you with a denial of liability of £150 in full and final settlement of all claims you may have against me and the members of my household. If not accepted within the next 7 days, this offer is to be treated as withdrawn. Please let me know whether or not you do accept.

Yours sympathetically

Ian Ajam

Ian Ajam

PS Hope you are out of hospital soon.

PPS Lady Poofoo sends her regards.

Goodbye

Including the longest Will in the world

Anyone who believes that he extricates himself from the rule of law by dropping dead is mistaken. The law dictates who gets the dead person's property if he scarpers without a Will, or makes a Will which is duff because, for example, he only had one instead of two witnesses when he signed it. The law of intestacy they call it. And the law can give a share of the kitty to certain "relatives" who passed out because they were passed over. Or it can give them a bigger share than the dead person wanted.

Who can make a claim?—the dead person's husband or wife; a former husband or wife who has not remarried; a legitimate or illegitimate child of the dead person, and that would include a great big ugly boy of forty-three; a child treated by the dead person as being of his marriage—like a step-child—and, again, the great big ugly ones are included; and mistresses or, to be precise, "any person . . . who immediately before the death of the deceased was being maintained, either wholly or partly, by the deceased." The court will decide whether it is *reasonable* for the claimant to score, or to score more. Attention will be paid to a host of factors such as the present and future financial circumstances of the claimant, how much is available and how the claimant has behaved. The Will-maker may favour the idea of watching from Heaven's front stalls on his nearest and dearest as they scrap over the loot and waste most of it in legal costs.

A gift of back editions of *Motoring News* to the wife and children in equal shares and the rest of the dead person's property to "our window cleaner Bert who always had a smile" ought to ensure some lively litigation. The Will-maker with no greater love for litigation in death than in life should sign a statement to go with the Will explaining the reasons for what he has done. A wisely composed statement may deter the disappointed from launching a claim, or persuade the judge not to interfere if a claim is made. The statement can be taken into account by the judge. It will not be available after death for public consumption like the Will itself, but those involved in the dispute and, later, the court, will get to see it. What man wants the world to know that he nightly donned the attire of a girl guide and slept in the back garden, which is why his Will-making wife walked out on him and willed him just a few pairs of panties and nothing more?

Here is an example:

I BENNY FACTOR of 31 Deep Water Bristol Avon hereby state as follows:-
1. I have this day executed my last will.
2. In my will I have not made any provision for MELANIE SLAGG of The Very Top Flat, The Terraces, off Railway Cuttings, Bristol. I have known Miss Slagg for some years and made contributions towards her flat rental and other outgoings. My wife must not be distresed by this revelation. It is only for my wife that I have had true love. I have attempted on many occasions to terminate my relationship with Miss Slagg but on each she has threatened to send a message to my wife tied to a brick and delivered through my front living room window. Miss Slagg has other male friends from whom she has received money and I am confident nothing will change in the future. I believe she has

accumulated substantial savings in a foreign bank account and would be well able to support herself without any help from me or my estate. In the last twelve months, I have acceded to her requests to purchase her a mink stole for some £4,000 and to acquire a freehold residence in Stockport for her mother and in her mother's name at a cost to me of £23,500 and legal expenses.

3. Further, in my will I have not made any provision for my former wife Estelle Factor. On our divorce I made a capital payment to her of £5,000 and transferred to her my interest in the matrimonial home. I have also continued to pay her maintenance under court order. Although I realise that the court order will die with me, I feel that she is well able to become financially independent and that I would have been justified in asking the court years ago to revoke the order. I also understand that I could have made application to the court on divorce or subsequently for an order precluding my former wife from claiming against my estate under the Inheritance (Provision for Family and Dependants) Act 1975. It has only been my invincible hatred of ignorant, bullying and power crazy court ushers which has prevented me from adopting such courses.

4. Finally, I have not made any financial provision for my son by my former marriage, SMALL FACTOR. He has had little to do with me since my remarriage and has caused me much hurt. He is profligate and I believe that any money he might otherwise have received from my estate would have been squandered. He could work and if he worked he could lead a comfortable life style. He prefers to lead a comfortable life style but not to work.

Signed Benny Factor
Dated the 14th July 1988

On your marks

A claimant has six months in which to start court proceedings. The six months start from the date on which whoever is winding up the dead person's affairs has been given authority to do so in the form of probate (where there is a Will) or letters of administration (where there is no Will). It can be tiresome and hypocritical to make regular phone calls to the home of the prospective stiff to enquire of his decline, and worse still to visit in person, although there are recorded instances of death being accelerated by an attempt to muster the energy to raise two fingers in the air upon the sudden appearance of a disfavoured relative. Still, the would-be claimant needs to keep an eye on what is going on, and once death occurs he can make a standing search at the Probate Registry for £1 which will entitle him to be sent a copy of any grant of probate or letters of administration in relation to the person in whom he has an interest during the following six months; if need be, he can keep renewing the search period. Should the six months from the grant of probate or letters of administration elapse without him starting proceedings, he may be able to get an extension from the court, but it will not be lightly granted.

Wisdom of a Will

"Nobody will argue about what I have got and the intestacy laws will do quite nicely, thank you very much." In the absence of a Will, the surviving husband or wife takes the first £75,000 of money and property plus personal chattels (clothes, car, instant shave, etc.) and the rest is divided up: the husband or wife gets a *life* interest (that means the income during lifetime) in one half, with that one half going to the children on the death of the husband or wife; the other half goes to the children outright. And where there are no children but there are parents or brothers and sisters, the husband or wife takes the first £125,000 plus personal chattels and one half of the remainder outright.

But, say the house was in the dead person's name and is worth more than the surviving spouse gets under the intestacy laws? Unsympathetic family members might demand that it is sold up immediately so that they can grab what is due to them. A Will could have avoided that. And say a married couple and their children perished together? A much hated relative instead of the Battersea Dogs' Home may stand to cop the lot. A Will could have avoided that. A Will enables personal choice of executors and trustees. And a Will may reduce the Inheritance Tax which has to be paid on death or avoid it entirely. Generally, no Inheritance Tax is payable where the value of what is left does not exceed £110,000. Even when the value exceeds that sum, Inheritance Tax is avoided on what goes to the surviving husband or wife. The survivor has to watch the likely tax bill on his or her death and might do well to make lifetime gifts. Survival for seven years after the gifts means they will be ignored on the death of the person who made them. Survival for between three and seven years means they will be partially ignored, and survival for less than three years means they will all be taken into account and added to the value of what is left to see whether Inheritance Tax is payable.

So, because there was no Will, or because the Will-maker was unable to tell the difference between Inheritance Tax and margarine, does he have to be called back from the dead or is there some other way? There is another way: the section 142 of the Inheritance Tax Act 1984 way, which is the topic of discussion in far too few funeral parlours. It enables the Will or distribution of property under the intestacy laws to be "re-written"—just once—with the agreement of everyone concerned. This must be done within two years of death, and great care must be taken to avoid procedural and other traps which are queuing up to outwit the family.

Look—no Will!

One way for a disappointed relative to overcome the terms of a Will is to destroy it. This should lead to criminal charges and a lynching by other members of the family. Because we have no system of *compulsory* registration of Wills, the disposal of an unhelpful Will could easily occur. Can this be protected against? Yes. The original Will may be deposited with a solicitor or bank and copies kept with personal papers and handed to the executor. Or the Will can be lodged with the Probate Registry who would not allow letters of administration to be granted to anyone on the basis that the deceased had left no Will and would not grant probate in respect of any earlier Will. The fee is £1 and details can be obtained from the Principal Registry, Family Division, Somerset House, Strand, London WC2 (01–405 7641) or from any District Probate Registry.

Responsible form

A Will should be signed in the presence of two witnesses—a sort of death trio. Adult witnesses are preferred although a minor who knows what he is doing will be acceptable if all the big kids are out. No beneficiary or spouse of the beneficiary should act as a witness or the gift to him will be lost. Generally, marriage automatically revokes a Will and a gift to the spouse is cancelled if it is followed by divorce or annulment of the marriage. It's a responsible document, a Will, but who says responsibility cannot be tempered with a bit of fun? Here goes—

THIS WILL dated the 14th July 1988 is made by me BENNY FACTOR of 31 Deep Water Bristol Avon

1. I revoke all former wills made by me.
2. I wish to be cremated/I do not wish to be cremated.
3. I wish that certainty of my death shall be confirmed by a medical practitioner cutting my wrists and that I shall be buried with a hammer in a coffin into the top of which twelve airholes shall be made.
4. If my wife FREDA FACTOR survives me by thirty days:-
   - (a) I appoint her as my sole executrix;
   - (b) I give her the sum of Five hundred pounds for her to spend on a party for my relatives and personal friends to be held in the public bar of The Black Death Bristol Avon at which I wish there to be two minutes of silence in memory of me and during the "Coronation Street"commercial break; and
   - (c) Subject to (b), I give the whole of my estate to my wife.
5. If my wife does not survive me by thirty days the following provisions of my will shall take effect.
6. I appoint my solicitor MEL PRACTICE of 38 Coke Road Bristol Avon and my friend ROBIN GOODFELLOW of 2 Chorley Grove Bournemouth Dorset to be the executors and trustees of this my will and I declare that the expression "my trustees" shall mean the trustees of this my will and of any trusts arising under it.
7. I appoint the said ROBIN GOODFELLOW and TRACY-ANNE GOODFELLOW his wife to be the guardians of any of my children who are under the age of eighteen years.
8. I give to my trustees the sum of Two thousand seven hundred and fifty pounds for them to spend on a party for my relatives and personal friends to be held at The Fishnet Stocking Greek Lane Bristol Avon at which I wish there to be in memory of me a rendering of "All the Nice Girls Love a Sailor" by the artiste Miss April May.
9. I give to NELLIE SCRUBBIT of 122 Reinforcement Road Bristol Avon the sum of Five hundred pounds provided she is in my employment at my

death and not under notice of termination of such employment given by me.

10. I give to the Society for Distressed Former Old Bailey Hacks care of Temple Underground Station London EC4 the sum of Two thousand pounds and declare that the receipt of the person who appears to be a proper officer of the said charity shall be a complete discharge to my trustees.

11. I give the sum of Five hundred pounds to each of the following persons:-

(a) the said Robin Goodfellow;
(b) the said Tracy-Anne Goodfellow;
(c) my friend Gerard Combes of 12 Jellicoe Road Gosport Hampshire on condition that he is not at the date of my death a member of the Church of Scientology or any religious sect society or body to which he is under an obligation to give his property or the income thereof and if such condition shall not be satisfied this gift shall fall into residue;
(d) my friend Mirabel Myerson of 40 Gregson Arcade Fareham Hampshire on condition that at the date of my death she has not married Greaser Gattree and if such condition shall not be satisfied this gift shall fall into residue; and
(e) Gloria Hunniford care of BBC Broadcasting House London W1A 1AA for the many hours of enjoyment she has given to me and without seeking to impose any obligation on her I express the wish that she shall play a record in my memory on the air and preferably any rendering of "All the Nice Girls Love a Sailor".

12. I give any motor vehicle in my ownership or possession at my death to my neighbour Jose Parker "Chez Costa" 29 Deep Water Bristol Avon and if such vehicle is in my possession under the terms of a hire purchase or other consumer credit agreement my trustees shall take steps to vest ownership of the same in the said Jose Parker at the expense of my residuary estate.

13. I give to my trustees such sum as at my death equals the maximum amount which could be given to them by this will without inheritance tax becoming payable in respect of the gift to hold on trust in equal shares for such of my children of my former marriage Estelle Factor

junior and Frank Factor as survive me and attain the age of twenty one years.

14. I release Arthur Con of 13 Cottagefield Close Guildford Surrey from his indebtedness to me in respect of a loan made by me to him in or about 1984 together with any interest thereon which he is liable to pay.

15. I give to my son of my said former marriage Small Factor of YMCA Church Street Bristol Avon my collection of stamps.

16(a) Subject as aforesaid I give such of my furniture plate and articles of household domestic or personal use or ornament to my trustees to transfer to my relatives and personal friends who are not otherwise beneficiaries under this my will such items as each of them shall select provided that no one person shall select items worth in the opinion of my trustees more than £100 and my trustees shall decide who shall be entitled to so select; and

(b) any articles not so selected under sub-clause (a) of this clause shall form part of my residuary estate.

17. My trustees shall hold the remainder of my estate on trust to sell call in and convert into money such parts as do not already consist of the same at such time or times and in such manner as they shall think fit with power to postpone such sale calling in and conversion for so long as they shall in their absolute discretion decide without being liable for loss and

(a) to pay my funeral and testamentary expenses and debts;

(b) to pay any inheritance tax which shall be payable in respect of property passing under this will;

(c) to divide the residue (hereinafter called "my residuary estate") equally among such of my children of my marriage to the said Freda Factor who shall survive me by thirty days and attain twenty one years or marry under that age but if none of such children so survive me or attain a vested interest in my residuary estate my trustees shall divide my residuary estate equally between the said Robin Goodfellow and Tracy-Anne Goodfellow;

(d) to pay any money to which a beneficiary who is still a minor is entitled to his parent or guardian for his benefit;

(e) to pay or apply capital for advancement or benefit of any beneficiary under section 32 of the Trustee Act 1925 as if the said section applied to the whole of the presumptive or vested interest of such beneficiary and not to one half thereof and

(f) to invest as freely as if they themselves were beneficially entitled.

18. Any of my trustees being a person engaged in any profession shall be entitled to charge and be paid for work done by him or his firm or company including work which an executor or trustee not being in any profession could have done personally on the same basis as if he were not one of my trustees but employed to carry out such work on their behalf.

19. I wish that my trustees shall read this my will as soon as practicable after my death to a gathering of such of my relatives and personal friends as it is practicable for my trustees to invite and whether or not I have made provision for them in this my will and that immediately preceding such reading there shall be recited to the said gathering by my trustees in unison the lyrics to "All the Nice Girls love a Sailor".

20. I wish that my trustees shall consider the appropriateness and advisability of a deed of family arrangement and/or variation and/or disclaimer under section 142 of the Inheritance Tax Act 1984.

21. I have this day made a statement explaining the reasons I have not made provision for certain persons and for a token gift only for the said Small Factor.

SIGNED by the Testator)
in our joint presence and) Benny Factor
by us in his presence)

Millie Combes
747 Abbeywood Drive
Catisfield Hants
Housewife

Nosie Parker
29 Woodbine Park
Catisfield Hants
Civil Servant

Health warnings

These questions should be answered and the Will should cater for the answers—

Q If my child fails to inherit but has a child of his own, do I want my grandchild to collect what my child would have collected?

Q Do I prefer some charity to collect the bulk of my property because all my family and friends have money pouring out of their ears as it is?

Q If my wife survives me, do I want to ensure that my children will collect after her death by giving her only a life interest in what I own? If I did that, would she have sufficient to live on? If I give her only a life interest, do I want it to come to a sudden end should she remarry or cohabit with someone?

Q Do I want to give my interest in my jointly held home to someone other than my spouse? If so, do I have to change the basis of ownership because if my spouse and I hold the property as joint tenants, my interest will automatically pass to her on my death even though my Will says it is to go elsewhere?

Q So far as our home is concerned, shall I prevent my wife from living there with another man after I am dead and gone, by gifting the property to someone other than my wife, but directing my trustees to allow my wife to live there so long as she remains my widow and does not cohabit with another man?

Q Although Inheritance Tax will not be payable on so much of what I own as is collected by my wife under my Will, what sort of Inheritance Tax bill am I mounting up to be paid when she dies? Would it not be wise for me to give away in my Will the maximum possible, currently £110,000, without incurring any Inheritance Tax charge, with the rest going to my wife but also make some gifts during my lifetime? The gifts will not be taken fully into account in valuing my worth on my death so long as I outlive the gifts by three years, and I can also give away £3,000 a year (my wife can give away the same amount in her own right) as well as make a number of small gifts each year, all of which will be disregarded on my death even if I die very soon.

It is possible to attach a condition to any gift in a Will. But a condition, if it is challenged in court, may be held void because, for example, it is contrary to public policy or it is too uncertain and then, if void, it will be disregarded:

> "I give to each of my executors fifteen thousand pounds provided they do not disclose to the Inland Revenue details of the investments to which relating documents are to be found in deposit box number 132 at the Hush Bank of the August Moon, Kensington, London . . ."

That would be void.

> "My trustees shall pay the income from my residuary estate to my son Alfred for life so long as he shall not marry Angela Scrubbit."

Valid. And this one as well—

> "My trustees shall pay the sum of Seven thousand five hundred pounds to my son Alfred upon marrying Mary Angelwise and in default of . . ."

Last century, courts held to be valid conditions against marriage to a Scotsman, to a domestic servant and to anyone "beneath her". More recently, a gift "provided he shall be a Roman Catholic" was given the Blessing of the House of Lords, and a condition to conform to and be a member of the Church of England was also judicially approved. And so was a direction to trustees under a Will to pay income "to the Baronet for the time being if and when and so long as he shall be of the Jewish faith and shall be married to an approved wife." An approved wife was defined as "a wife of Jewish blood by one or both of her parents and who has been brought up in and has never separated from and at the date of her marriage continues to worship according to the Jewish faith as to such facts in case of dispute or doubt the decision of the Chief Rabbi in London of either the Portuguese or Anglo-German community shall be conclusive." The direction could be adapted for other religions.

Conditions which would effectively require the beneficiary to behave himself in future are also quite safe:

> "I give to my friend Harry "The Lad" Scratcher the sum of ten thousand pounds provided he has given up low company and is following the path of virtue and the decision of my trustees as to whether these conditions have been satisfied shall be conclusive and . . ."

is fine.

If a husband and wife make Wills saying substantially the same things and agree between themselves not to change them, can they trust each other to keep to the agreement once the first to go is watching *Neighbours* on a television set in the sky? As a general rule a Will can be changed. So, although a couple may have agreed not to change, one can go ahead and change during the lifetime of the other, and there is nothing the other can do about it except to protest, moan and nag for the rest of his days. It's changing contrary to an agreement after the death of the one who has kept to the agreement which the law does not like. Then, provided it is proved that the couple made an agreement not to change and that they intended to be bound by it, the beneficiaries under the original Will would be able to get the court to enforce its terms and, effectively, to rip up the later Will insofar as it broke the agreement. The Will should spell out a no-change agreement:

> "This will is made pursuant to an agreement between myself and my wife. Under the agreement my wife is also making a Will in substantially the same terms as this Will and neither of us will revoke our respective Wills without the consent in writing of the other."

A Will is a tricky document. It's easy to go wrong. It makes sense to get it drawn up by a solicitor; his charge for a Will will not be prohibitive.

Cab chat

Taxi! Taxi! Taxi! Taxi! . . . I'll walk

Dedication: To those who have been drenched, mugged and convinced life was not worth living as they stood on the kerb, waving pathetically, waiting for a London taxi driver to agree to take them to the destination of their fading dream.

A London cabbie (that's one of your pukka, hackney carriage lot) who is waiting for business at a rank or at the roadside must accept a passenger, provided his destination is within the metropolitan and/or city police district, and the journey is not more than six miles (or twenty miles from Heathrow Airport)—unless he has a reasonable excuse. For example, he believes on reasonable grounds that the passenger has insufficient money to pay for the fare, is drunk or is on the way from the scene of a crime in which he has participated. Any of these should do and if the cabbie can rely on the lot, he's likely to win an acquittal, costs and a handsome tip from the stipendiary. A cabbie is not under a duty to stop when hailed.

In practice, erring cabbies are not prosecuted, but complaints are logged and persistent offenders now stand in jeopardy of losing their licence. London cabbie complaints should be made to the Public Carriage Office, 14 Panton Street, London SW1. Taxi drivers outside London can refuse to accept a passenger who wants to go outside their operating area. Complaints about them should be made to the local authority which handles their licensing.

Tender Taxi

Dedication: To the cab driver who collected the writer from Waterloo on June 20 1988 at 10.40 a.m. approx., conveyed him to St. Pancras and could still be heard raving and ranting as the writer made his way to the 11.35 a.m. to Market Harborough:

- £3.20

(Searches pocket for change and then produces £10 note.)

- I'm afraid this is all I've got.
- I can't change that.
- Then I'll have to give you a cheque with a bank card.

(Reaches for pad, snatches £10 note from writer.)

- No good. The law is I give you my name and address, take your details and I will send on the change. I've been done twice with cheques.
- I've got a bank card.
- I've told you the law.
- That isn't the law. You'll have to get some change.
- I can't leave this taxi, cab law says so.
- This is your problem. It's a substantial fare. You

should be equipped to change a £10 note. I've offered you a cheque with a card. A £10 note is legal tender. Don't be so obstinate.

(Raises volume of voice to high angry screaming; attempts by screaming louder and gesticulating to solicit support of railway porter who looks on with glazed expression.)

- Look, I'll take you to the police station. Can't you get it into your thick head that I don't have to change that note? Can you understand English? Have you got saw-dust between your ears?
- There's no need for you to be offensive. I thought you were trouble from the start. I'll have to report you to the Public Carriage Office.
- I'll give you the address.

(Makes way to rear of cab—writes down licence and registration numbers.)

- It's not necessary, I know it.

(Driver gets out of taxi—writer gingerly steps back with terrorised expression on face—driver goes to another taxi and changes £10 note for two £5 notes and returns to his own taxi—driver gives writer change but no gratuity is offered.)

- You shouldn't pick up lawyers.

- You might be a lawyer but you don't know anything about cab law. It's cab law that counts. I don't have to give you change. Cab law says that I take . . . did you hear that . . . made me leave my taxi . . .

(Writer walks away irritated that because of confrontation he has missed the 11.35 a.m. to Market Harborough and searches recesses of his mind for law on legal tender.)

There is no obligation on he who has to be paid to give change. The customer should tender the exact amount due. Insofar as coins are concerned, there are legal rules about the maximum value of coins which the customer can insist be accepted as part of the exact amount due. These are the rules—

Coin	*maximum*
50p and 20p pieces	£10
10p and 5p pieces	£5
2p and 1p pieces	20p

So the driver was right when he said he did not have to give change. But a passenger can reasonably expect a driver to be in a position to deal with the sort of change which was required here.

And the driver was not under any legal obligation to accept a cheque even though it would have been backed by a bank card, so he was right about that too. But a passenger who is clearly worth £10 in cash and does not justify suspicion about his honesty can reasonably expect a driver to accept a cheque backed by a card where the driver is unable to come up with an unexceptional amount of change.

The driver was wrong to have snatched the £10 note and detain it. If he had not fetched change himself, his legal choice would have been to have allowed the writer to fetch it or to have allowed the writer to send on cash when it was available. So long as he had an intention to pay when he could, the writer would not have been committing any criminal offence by walking off having recovered his £10 note. Then, as an indicator of good faith, the writer would have been wise to thrust a note of his name and address at the taxi driver before leaving. It is an offence for a taxi passenger to refuse to pay his fare on demand (and a magistrate may order him to pay it), but the writer would not have been refusing.

I hate my bank

Another chapter that speaks for itself

Dear Mr Bank Manager

I refer to my complaint about -

- ☐ You debiting my account for £100 in respect of a cash withdrawal when, in fact, the cash dispenser produced only £50.
- ☐ The bouncing of my cheque for £5 when you knew or should have known my account would be credited with my £1268 monthly salary the next day.
- ☐ You charging me £3 for notifying me that I had exceeded my overdraft facility by £2 and then charging me £5 for dismissing my letter of protest.
- ☐ Waiting in Miss Smithie's queue for twenty five minutes the other lunch time and then on reaching the front having her put a "closed" sign up so that she could go and eat her sandwiches.
- ☐ The insolence over the telephone of your jumped-up pip-squeak of a deputy-assistant under sub-temporary manager when I urgently required to know the balance in my current account.
- ☐ You charging me for holding the title deeds to my property when no mention of a charge had been made when you agreed to take them.
- ☐ You refusing to cancel my standing order in the absence of at least ten days' prior notice.
- ☐ You failing to act on my instructions to

countermand my cheque for £20,000 in favour of Miss Brenda Streetwalker.

- ☐ My being thrown to the ground by an attempt robber on account of your inadequate security while waiting at your counter.

I am dissatisfied with your rejection of the complaint and refusal to make me an offer of compensation. I require you to arrange for my complaint to be considered under your internal complaints procedure until that procedure has been fully exhausted (unless, before exhaustion, you uphold the complaint and make me a compensation offer which I find acceptable). Should I remain dissatisfied, I will follow up my complaint with the Banking Ombudsman.

Yours faithfully

C. Acious

Claude Acious

Have a go

The Banking Ombudsman will look at most complaints against a member bank. His service is *free* and he can award compensation—up to £100,000 for complaints about something which has happened since 24 January 1988. The bank complained about will pay out under his awards. But the customer can reject the Ombudsman's decision and take the case to court. So the Ombudsman is good news for the customer too nervous to invest in court proceedings; whose complaint does not have sufficient monetary value to make court proceedings viable; who is after an apology rather than money; whose complaint has dicey merits; or who wishes to flush out the full arguments of the bank to give him an advantage in court proceedings should the Ombudsman decide against him.

Provided the complainant isn't after too many favours from his bank manager in the foreseeable future, there really is nothing to lose from going to the Ombudsman. What, however, he won't touch is any complaint by a company about a bank's commercial judgment (was it wrong to refuse an unsecured loan to a customer wishing to start a training school for Gorillagram deliverers?); or about the way a bank has exercised its discretion under a Will or trust. Subject to this, complaints are in if they're about accounts, cheques, standing orders, direct debits, cash dispenser machines, loans, mortgages and overdrafts. The complaint must be sent to the Ombudsman within six months after the customer last heard from the bank's head office in respect of the internal complaints procedure.

Who plays?

The member banks—and the Ombudsman cannot deal with complaints against others—are:

Bank of Scotland
Barclays—and that includes Barclaycard
Clydesdale
Co-op
Coutts
Girobank
Lloyds
Midland
National Westminster, Royal Bank of Scotland, Standard Chartered, Yorkshire,
TSB, Bank of Ireland, Allied Irish Banks, Northern, Ulster
Joint Credit Card Company—Access to you and me—
National Westminster Home Loans and other associates of the lot we have mentioned

House of Ombudsman

For a complaints form and bumph apply to the Office of the Banking Ombudsman, Citadel House, 5/11 Fetter Lane, London EC4A 1BR (telephone 01–583 1395).

Joint account blues

One day in 1986 a respectable Hampshire man in decent, well-remunerated employment went into his branch of the National Westminster to withdraw the credit balance in the account he held there jointly with his wife. Either could sign. He had known the manager for years. He confided in him that he was separated from his wife and wanted to put the money into a building society: it was a tax reserve. He learned from the manager that his wife had herself recently withdrawn £800 from the same account. "Account frozen," declared the manager: the bank would only operate the account from that time onwards on the signature of both respectable man *and* his wife. The wife had not asked the bank to alter the mandate. Telephone protests to the bank by the man's solicitor were of no avail. The man subsequently complained through the bank's internal procedures, again to no avail. The man, said the bank, had not suffered any loss. If he was entitled to the money in the account, it would be paid to him either with his wife's agreement (which was not forthcoming) or under court order. The bank had to act impartially and protect the interests of both husband and wife. The man then took advantage of the Ombudsman's free service. No luck.

Different banks act in different ways when learning that all is not well between joint account holders.

Midland say that when they hear of a dispute which apparently extends to the joint account balance or might reasonably be thought to do so, they may decide that the account should be operated against both signatures. TSB say it would take an extreme case to lead them to go to the customers for "clarification" of whether the one signature only mandate still applies. "The general rule is that the mandate is to be honoured." And a shy High Street bank thinks that there is little merit in the argument that a bank has a right to freeze and believes freezing can create more problems than it solves. "However, it must be said that in some unusual cases this may be the most equitable way of handling the situation."

The moral is clear. Nobody in their right mind should open a joint account if she is thinking of one day falling out with the co-account holder. Or if she does, she should withdraw most of the credit balance before she gets too chatty with the manager.

Bank charges

If a bank has said its services will be provided *free* (pigs do occasionally fly!), no charge can be made. Otherwise, the bank can make a charge. Should the amount of the charge not be agreed in advance, it can only be a *reasonable* one. The customer usually discovers it when he looks at his bank statement. He is not precluded from challenging it simply because the bank has debited the charge to his account.

Chase the debt

Interesting for traders

The trader must refuse to tolerate nonsense from any customer to whom he has extended credit because it is likely he will have only hassle to look forward to if compelled to bring court proceedings to get his money. True, he will be able to claim interest on the debt from the date it should have been paid but, as a general rule (to which bounced cheques are a notable exception), there will not be an interest entitlement without actually suing. So the trader is denied interest if the customer settles very late but before the trader has stirred himself to going to court. By requiring the customer to *agree* to pay interest before extending credit, the trader overcomes the problem and can then sue for the interest despite the fact that the original debt is cleared before court proceedings.

It is inappropriate to hide the interest obligation in a plethora of small print. Let it be written boldly on the order form which the customer signs. Then there is no doubt (well, not much) that the customer appreciates the consequences of late payment, and the trader can hope that the interest obligation will act as an incentive for prompt payment. The interest rate? Going over the top could turn interest into a penalty instead of a genuine pre-estimate of the loss to the trader resulting from default, and civil courts do not like penalties. Fifteen per cent simple interest (less for philanthropic traders) should be in order; possibly more if the trader is borrowing heavily at high rates.

"I agree to pay £1,000 within 28 days but £1,500 if I am late." Leave it out!—a penalty. Something like this will do (draw the customer's attention to it before the order is finalised)—

> If the amount due is not paid within 28 days of the date of this order the customer shall be liable to simple interest thereon as from the expiration of 28 days from the date of this order until payment of the amount due at the rate of 15% per annum.

In the majority of cases, there is no *agreement* to pay interest. Here, the trader has a big question to answer. Does he ask for payment of the debt without interest if this is going to avoid the trouble of suing, or does he sue so that he can get interest ordered by the court? Interest will not complicate the claim; it is almost invariably added on automatically. The age of the debt may determine how the big question is answered. The older the debt, the more the interest which can be recovered. If the trader decides on a quest for interest, he should sue without giving the debtor a chance to pay up in response to a seven days' threatening letter or similar demand (see below). Otherwise, the trader can use the interest factor to encourage the customer to pay up fast.

MEAH'S GENERAL STORES
15 High Street, Anywhear, Hants
Proprietor - Meah Succour
1st December 1988

Dear Sir

Despite persistent demands, you have failed to pay me £575 due under my invoice dated July 14 1988 for goods sold and delivered. I hereby give you notice that unless, within the next 7 days, I receive £575, I shall institute court proceedings against you without further notice for the recovery of that sum together with interest on it from July 14 1988 until judgment or earlier payment at the rate of 15% per annum and costs.

Yours faithfully

Meah Succour

Meah Succour

Bankruptcy taster

There is a special treat for all creditors be they traders, former friends of the debtor or others who are owed at least £750 and who are unbothered about interest or have an agreement for interest. Not tea and blancmange with a county court bailiff—but a statutory demand. This is the first step towards the debtor being made bankrupt. The demand is a form requiring the debtor to pay up within three weeks of getting it and if he fails to do so, the creditor can issue a bankruptcy petition against him. Fees of £245 have to be paid to the court when a petition is issued so the creditor will not be jumping over his cheque book at the prospect of that. With luck, the service of the demand alone will scare the designer pants off the debtor and send him to the pawnbrokers without the creditor having to issue a bankruptcy petition. What makes the demand such a treat is that it can be served on a debtor without any prior court judgment (but if the debtor disputes he owes the money or maintains the creditor owes him money which cancels out the debt, he can ask the court to set the demand aside; to do this he must act within eighteen days of getting the demand). And what adds to the treat is that it can be served without reference to the court. It is vital that the demand is accurately completed for otherwise the debtor might succeed in having it set aside, or any bankruptcy proceedings brought on the strength of it might collapse. Either way, the trader could end up paying the debtor's legal costs. The creditor should check with his local county court or take legal advice in the county court on whose name and address is to be inserted in Part A on the third page of the demand. We are showing you the demand to be used when the creditor has not previously obtained a court judgment. If he has, a different form is required:

Rule 6.1

Form 6.1

Statutory Demand under section 268(1)(a) of the Insolvency Act 1986. Debt for Liquidated Sum Payable Immediately

Notes for Creditor

- If the creditor is entitled to the debt by way of assignment, details of the original creditor and any intermediary assignees should be given in part C on page 3.
- If the amount of debt includes interest not previously notified to the debtor as included in the debtor's liability, details should be given, including the grounds upon which interest is charged. The amount of interest must be shown separately.
- Any other charge accruing due from time to time may be claimed. The amount or rate of the charge must be identified and the grounds on which it is claimed must be stated.
- In either case the amount claimed must be limited to that which has accrued due at the date of the demand.
- If the creditor holds any security the amount of debt should be the sum the creditor is prepared to regard as unsecured for the purposes of this demand. Brief details of the total debt should be included and the nature of the security and the value put upon it by the creditor, as at the date of the demand, must be specified.
- If signatory of the demand is a solicitor or other agent of the creditor the name of his/her firm should be given.

Warning

- This is an **important** document. You should refer to the notes entitled "How to comply with a statutory demand or have it set aside".
- If you wish to have this demand set aside you must make application to do so **within 18 days** from its service on you.,
- If you do not apply to set aside **within 18 days** or otherwise deal with this demand as set out in the notes **within 21 days** after its service on you, you could be made bankrupt and your property and goods taken away from you.
- Please read the demand and notes carefully. If you are in any doubt about your position you should seek advice **immediately** from a solicitor or your nearest Citizens Advice Bureau.

Demand

To ARTHUR CON

Address 13 Cottagefield Close,
Guildford, Surrey

This demand is served on you by the creditor:

Name MEAH SUCCOUR

Address "Meah's General Stores", 15 High Street
Anywhear, Hants

The creditor claims that you owe the sum of £ 1,500, full particulars of which are set out on page 2, and that it is payable immediately and, to the extent of the sum demanded, is unsecured.

The creditor demands that you pay the above debt or secure or compound for it to the creditor's satisfaction.

~~[The creditor making this demand is a Minister of the Crown or a Government Department, and it is intended to present a bankruptcy petition in the High Court in London.]~~ [Delete if inappropriate]

Signature of individual Meah Succour

Name MEAH SUCCOUR

(BLOCK LETTERS)

Date July 14 1988

~~* Position with or relationship to creditor~~ ________

~~* I am authorised to make this demand on the creditor's behalf~~

~~Address~~ ________

~~Tel. No.~~ ________ ~~Ref.~~ ________

* Delete if signed by the creditor himself

N.B. The person making this demand must complete the whole of pages 1. 2 and parts A, B and C (as applicable) on page 3.

Form 6.1 contd.
page 2

Particulars of debt
(These particulars must include (a) when the debt was incurred, (b) the consideration for the debt (or if there is no consideration the way in which it arose) and (c) the amount due as at the date of this demand.)

The said Arthur Con is indebted to the creditor in the sum of £1,500 for one box of tools, one umbrella and two sideboards sold and delivered by the creditor to the said Arthur Con on July 31 1987 under the creditor's invoice numbered 467214 and bearing the said date.

Notes for Creditor
Please make sure that you have read the notes on page 1 before completing this page.

Note:
If space is insufficient continue on page 4 and clearly indicate on this page that you are doing so.

Form 6.1 contd.
page 3

PART A
Appropriate Court for Setting Aside Demand

Rule 6.4(2) of the Insolvency Rules 1986 states that the appropriate court is the court to which you would have to present your own bankruptcy petition in accordance with Rule 6.40(1) and 6.40(2). In accordance with those rules on present information the appropriate court is [the High Court of Justice] [
County Court]
(Address)

Any application by you to set aside this demand should be made to that court.

Part B
The individual or individuals to whom any communication regarding this demand may be addressed is/are:

Name MEAH SUCCOUR (BLOCK LETTERS)	
Address "Meah's General Stores"	
15 High Street, Anywhear, Hants	
Telephone Number Anywhear 12121212	
Reference 467215	

PART C

For completion if the creditor is entitled to the debt by way of assignment

	Name	Date(s) of Assignment
Original creditor		
Assignees		

How to comply with a statutory demand or have it set aside (ACT WITHIN 18 DAYS)

If you wish to avoid a bankruptcy petition being presented against you, you must pay the debt shown on page 1, particulars of which are set out on page 2 of this notice, within the period of **21 days** after its service upon you. Alternatively, you can attempt to come to a settlement with the creditor. To do this, you should:

- inform the individual (or one of the individuals) named in part B above immediately that you are willing and able to offer security for the debt to the creditor's satisfaction; or
- inform the individual (or one of the individuals) named in part B immediately that you are willing and able to compound for the debt to the creditor's satisfaction.

If you dispute the demand in whole or in part you should:

- contact the individual (or one of the individuals) named in part B immediately.

THERE ARE MORE IMPORTANT NOTES ON THE NEXT PAGE

Form 6.1 contd.
page 4

If you consider that you have grounds to have this demand set aside or if you do not quickly receive a satisfactory written reply from the individual named in part B whom you have contacted you should **apply within 18 days** from the date of service of this demand on you to the appropriate court shown in part A above to have the demand set aside.

Any application to set aside the demand (Form 6.4 in Schedule 4 to the Insolvency Rules 1986) should be made within 18 days from the date of service upon you and be supported by an affidavit (Form 6.5 in Schedule 4 to those Rules) stating the grounds on which the demand should be set aside. The forms may be obtained from the appropriate court when you attend to make the application.

Remember! -	From the date of service on you of this document: (a) you have only 18 days to apply to the court to have the demand set aside, and (b) you have only 21 days before the creditor may present a bankruptcy petition.

Light blocking without tears

Only twenty years . . .

He with a bit of land at the back of his house might like to add on an extension. He who suspects that she next door is nosing over the garden wall when he is at work might like to heighten the wall. The law on right to light should be watched, because if the extension or the heightened wall would block out or substantially reduce the quality of light entering any window of a next door building (or just a next door greenhouse) an injunction and damages might be sought—but only if them next door had acquired a legal right to have light entering that window. One way such a right might have been acquired (unless the title deeds say otherwise) is by light having entered the window for an uninterrupted period of twenty years. Uninterrupted, we said.

Light interruptus

It is possible to interrupt the twenty years by registering what is called a light obstruction certificate with the local authority under the Right of Light Act 1959.

Registration has the same legal effect as if a giant screen had been placed in front of the window enjoying the light, but it is less inconvenient and cumbersome. It is a notional obstruction and the registration has to be made before the twenty years have been scored. Then, once twelve months following registration have elapsed, next door need to restart counting the twenty years. Nineteen years later a fresh registration can be effected. A light obstruction certificate can be re-registered and re-registered until either the building burns down or the owners of the adjoining plots become bosom pals, obtain planning permission to stick up a giant block of flats on the land and swim out to Benidorm with £1½m each in their trunks.

A land owner, anxious to ensure he is not frustrated or restricted in his development ambitions and who could be caught out by the twenty years rule in relation to a building on adjoining land would be stark staring bonkers not to take advantage of the light obstruction certificate procedure. Statistics suggest there are plenty of stark staring bonkers land owners in England and Wales.

Registration recipe

And this is what has to be done. An application is made to the Lands Tribunal, 48/9 Chancery Lane, London WC2A 1JR for a "temporary certificate" or a "definitive certificate". A temporary certificate will be issued where there is some exceptional urgency and it may not have been possible for anyone or everyone likely to be affected by the registration (like the building owner with *that* window) to have been told about it. Fee? £80 for a definitive certificate only, otherwise £90. The building owner with *that* window who unleashes his anger on the Lands Tribunal will be wasting his time as there is no discretion to refuse a certificate and the certificate application will be "rubber stamped". Armed with the certificate, application is then made to the local authority to register the certificate with them. Fee? £32.25 and, when a definitive certificate is registered after a temporary one, a further £1.30. Registration application forms are available from local authorities. Well, that, at least, is the theory, although it may be necessary to kidnap the mayor's chauffeur before one is produced.

Dear Neighbour
You know what today is, don't you? It's 19 years 364 days after you started counting from the date your side window went in. Sorry, but you'll have to go back to zero. I've registered a light obstruction certificate at the council office.
Yours
M.N.D.
Me Next Door

Fishin' for commission

Or some of our best friends are estate agents

We are told that estate agents have been observed helping infirm persons across the road and that they are delightful employers. Now, let's get down to business!

All fall down

A large number of deals set up by estate agents fall through. Whether or not the agent is, nevertheless, entitled to commission or to damages will depend on the agreement which the property owner has reached with him. Because he has no automatic legal right to be paid by the owner for abortive work, the agent will have to show that the agreement catches the situation which has arisen. The basis on which the agent was engaged might well have been agreed at his office desk on a Sunday afternoon (like the Windmill, estate agents these days never seem to close) by the wretch of a property owner harassed by his wife (who has picked up particulars relating to fourteen possibilities for an alternative property all of which she insists on viewing before teatime) and tugged at by little Eric who has a finger up his nose and sweet Victoria who is making eloquent, high pitched representations for a vanilla cornet to be served up with a chocolate flake.

"We write to confirm the agreement we did not reach."

There may follow in the post a day or two after the agent has been engaged a letter of confirmation from him. It could well spell out terms of engagement which are different from those agreed. So, in truth, it is not a letter of confirmation, but a letter of trickery. There is a risk that the owner could be deemed to have accepted the different terms set out in the letter of confirmation by continuing to deal with the agent without challenging them. The letter of confirmation, therefore, must be closely scrutinised and any departure from the agreed terms taken up with the agent immediately.

Getting in on the Act

The Estate Agents Act 1959 requires the agent to tell the owner *in advance* what he will charge and in what circumstances he will have to be paid. If he fails to do so, the Director-General of Fair Trading can do horrible things to him and, more interestingly, the agent cannot enforce his commission claim without a court order. Should he apply for an order, the court could refuse him one where it is reckoned this would be justified because of "prejudice caused to the client by the agent's failure to comply with his obligation and the degree of culpability for the failure", or the court could knock down the agent's commission to compensate the property owner for any prejudice he has suffered.

2 Yuppee Walk
Wapping
London E1
14 VII 88

The Manager
Haggle, Deception & Complete
1068 Fleet Street
London EC4

Dear Sir

14 Egham Rise EC4

I refer to your commission account of yesterday's date in the sum of £6020 inclusive of value added tax relating to the sale of the above property. It appears you have sought to charge me commission at the rate of 4.15 per cent on the property and 4 per cent on the price of the musical (classical) toilet roll holder and light bulbs which I sold to my purchaser separately.

You have not previously notified me of your commission rate or the circumstances in which commission would be payable. I am advised that this constitutes a breach of section 18 of the Estate Agents Act 1979. Accordingly, I am referring the matter to the Director-General of Fair Trading so that he can investigate and consider whether to prohibit you from doing estate agency work or warn you. Furthermore, I decline to pay your account. Had you taken me into your confidence and actually told me how much you intended to charge I would have told you what you could do with your display board.

If you wish to pursue the matter you will have to make an application to the court for permission to enforce the contract under section 18(6) of the 1979 Act which I will oppose. OR Strictly without prejudice, I am willing to pay you £1150 inclusive of value added tax in full and final settlement of your claim and with a denial of liability that I am under any legal obligation to pay you anything. The offer is open for a period of seven days from the date of this letter. If it is not accepted I shall oppose any court application you make under section 18(6) of the 1979 Act.

Yours faithfully

J. Pirahana-Smyth

Jeremy Pirahana-Smyth

Sole selling rights

Never, never, ever, ever grant an estate agent SOLE SELLING RIGHTS. If they are granted and the property owner manages to sell to someone he has found himself and has personally conducted all the negotiations, the estate agent is lawfully entitled to commission—for doing nothing.

Sole agency

Granting an estate agent a SOLE AGENCY is fair enough and it should lead to a lower commission rate. Indeed, a sole agency may well spur the agent on to great things as his chances of earning on that particular property are stronger. But it could have the opposite effect with the lack of competition sending him to sleep, and so a time limitation should be placed on the sole agency—say, six weeks, and the owner should be careful not to instruct a second agent during the life of the sole agency because, if the second agent finds a purchaser, the owner could find himself legally liable to pay both agents.

Ready, willing and able

It is not uncommon for a property owner to agree to pay an estate agent commission on the introduction of a purchaser who is "ready and able to purchase" or "ready, willing and able to purchase" or "prepared to purchase"—there are a number of variations on the same theme. Such form of words should be avoided. Although virtually every purchaser will make an offer which is conditional—like "subject to contract" or "subject to survey" or both—with the result that, legally, the purchaser does not *then* fall into the "ready, willing and able" type category, there is a risk that a court might decide he did fall into that category at some point before contracts might have been exchanged. Take this situation. A purchaser who has agreed to buy "subject to contract" sorts out his mortgage, and his solicitor deals with the conveyancing work and sends his part of the contract and the deposit cheque to the owner's solicitor asking for contracts to be exchanged. But along comes Joe Gazumper through another estate agent and offers the owner an extra £5,000 with an exchange of contracts immediately. The owner wants to drop the original purchaser and do a deal with Joe. A court might hold that the owner was liable to pay commission to the first estate agent despite the fact contracts were never exchanged with the buyer he introduced, and that the owner had to pay commission to the agent who instructed Joe as well. Two lots of commission on one sale. There's nothing novel about that!

Double your money

In March 1985 a High Court judge held that an owner was legally compelled to pay commission to two agents even though only one purchaser was ever involved. He had agreed to pay Lordsgate Properties Ltd if they introduced someone who purchased the property, and he had also agreed to pay Brian Lack and Partners Ltd if they were *instrumental* in negotiating a sale, even if they had not introduced the purchaser. The actual purchaser was first introduced by Lordsgate but subsequently made a number of offers through Brian Lack: the last offer was accepted and a sale ensued.

In a 1982 case, a Saudi Arabian princess, Noura

Bint Abdulla Bin Abdulrahman Al Saud, was shown round the property by two rival agents at the same time with each agent being ignorant of the presence of the other. To be fair, the property did have fourteen bedrooms, eight bathrooms and an assortment of other rooms.

The risk of a claim by two agents, or even a liability to two agents is a real one and the owner is not given an opportunity to escape by paying one set of commission over to the court and leaving it to the two agents to fight it out between themselves. Agree to pay an agent if he introduces a purchaser who enters into a binding contract or (better still) who completes the purchase.

The link

Before an agent can become entitled to anything there must be some link between the agent and the prospective purchaser: the agent must be an effective cause of the purchaser making his offer. And he isn't legally prevented from being an effective cause because the property has been put with another agent, or the owner has himself conducted most of the negotiations with the purchaser. It is also irrelevant that the purchaser deceives the owner into thinking the purchaser just happened to hear from a friend of a friend that the house might be on the market and did not come through an agent and did not notice the 'For Sale' boards and has never received particulars of the property through the post and goes to church regularly and thinks all agents are parasites.

The secret link

It might even suit the agent himself to allow the owner to believe that the applicant has come privately and not through the agent when there are competitors for the property. The owner then exchanges contracts with the applicant, smiling at the thought of having avoided estate agent's commission and promptly receives a commission account. The owner could have a good defence to the agent's claim: that the agent was in breach of his duty to the owner in failing to warn him that he had sent along the applicant. Certainly, if the sale had been negotiated by a sub-agent when the owner had not given authority for a sub-agent to be instructed there will usually be no liability to pay commission.

For the owner who still has or has had his property on the books of an estate agent but has decided to sell to the ostensibly agent-free applicant, here's a bit of protection to go into the contract—

(1) In consideration of the vendor entering into this contract with the purchaser, the purchaser hereby warrants to the vendor that
  (i) he has not received particulars of the property from or had any contact relating to the property with any estate agent and has not otherwise been introduced to the property by any estate agent;
  (ii) that his initial contact with the vendor did not result from or arise out of an estate agents' 'For Sale' or other notice or communication advertising the property as being available for sale or otherwise or from any step taken by any estate agent

(2) The purchaser hereby agrees to indemnify the vendor against all claims demands actions or other proceedings by any estate agent or agents relating to the sale of the property to the

```
purchaser for commission expenses damages or
otherwise and arising out of this agreement,
events preceding this agreement or completion of
the said sale to the purchaser and this
indemnity shall extend to all costs expenses or
otherwise incurred by the vendor in connection
with such claims demands actions or other
proceedings.
(3) Paragraphs (1) and (2) above shall not merge
with the assurance of the property to the
purchaser.
```

Them boards, them boards, them ruddy boards

More than one agent must not mean more than one board, and one board must be within the size legally allowed without planning permission (see page 277). The owner can insist that there be no 'For Sale' board or, perhaps of greater importance to him, no 'Sold' board. After all, it's bad enough having to let on to the neighbours that you may be moving. It's verging on the intolerable to have to announce that you *will* be going and, impliedly, that if they ask enough questions they will eventually discover the price the property has fetched. In a 1979 case the owner stipulated to Benham & Reeves that they were not to put up a 'For Sale' board. The agents obeyed. But once contracts were exchanged up went a 'Sold' board. The court held that in view of the express instructions which had been given, no board should have been put up. The owner was awarded £5 nominal damages to reflect his annoyance, but had deducted ten per cent of the commission amounting to £101.92 representing his advertising charge against the agents and so, at the end of the day, he lost. £5 for annoyance then and the board can always be taken out and put in the garage: add a couple of quid for the hassle of that!

Extortion

Very *interesting* . . .

To get a civil court to help, it is not essential that the borrower should have got his loan in a public bar from an armed, eye-patched unlicensed moneylender at a 150% per annum rate of interest, had his pension book confiscated and been threatened with *Neighbours*. Both the county court and the High Court have powers under the Consumer Credit Act 1974 to re-open extortionate credit agreements—cash loans, mortgage loans, hire purchase agreements, credit sale agreements—entered into with any person or any business; even a loan made by the next door neighbour could be re-opened. The level of the loan matters not: the limit of £15,000 which so often applies to consumer situations does not apply here. But a company cannot take advantage of the Act's re-opening provisions: an individual, whether or not he is in business, can. The borrower (or his guarantor) may go to the court on his own initiative to ask for re-opening, or he can do the asking when sued by the lender because of default.

But not very funny

The interest rate was high—not enough. The borrower was unwise—not enough. The agreement must have been *extortionate* in that it required the borrower or a relative to make payments which were exorbitant, or in that it otherwise grossly contravened ordinary principles of fair dealing. The court will take into account anything which is relevant including—

- interest rates prevailing when the agreement was made;
- the borrower's age, experience, business capacity and state of health;
- the degree to which the borrower was under financial pressure and the nature of the pressure.

Particularly important will be the extent of the risk accepted by the lender having regard to any security provided. An unsecured loan is bound to call for a higher interest rate then a secured loan. A loan of £10,000 on the security of a £25,000 property in poor repair is bound to call for a higher interest rate than a £5,000 loan on the security of a new £50,000 house.

The provisions at work

In a 1982 case, a man borrowed £400 from a company which had advertised in a national paper. The interest was shown in the loan agreement as 184% per annum (the APR would have been 320%). The trial judge reopened and reduced the interest from 184% to 40% per annum taking into account that the money could have been borrowed elsewhere at 20% per annum and the man's lack of business capacity. The lenders had argued that their interest rate was high because they operated by mail and one third of their clients had a bad debt record. Our borrower had no such record.

But in a 1980 case a couple who needed £20,500 in a hurry borrowed it at a 48% per annum interest rate.

The lenders had insufficient time to deal with status enquiries, conveyancing searches and an inspection of the property. Principally because of the high risk which the lenders assumed, the court refused to interfere. And so did the court in a 1986 case involving a mortgage loan of £17,450 at an interest rate equivalent to 21.6% APR. Although the court should be astute to protect borrowers, this loan was not extortionate. The borrowers had had independent legal advice before taking up the loan and had been told the mortgage was expensive.

Case No 88/79160

IN THE CAMBRIDGE COUNTY COURT

BETWEEN:

WE HAVE WAYS OF MAKING YOU PAY LTD Plaintiffs

- and -

JOSEPH SOAP Defendant

DEFENCE AND COUNTERCLAIM

DEFENCE

1. The Defendant admits that on the 14th July 1987 the Plaintiffs lent him the sum of £25,000 secured by way of second charge on 52 Coercion Street, Cambridge with interest at an APR of £150 per centum and otherwise on the terms alleged in paragraph 1 of the Particulars of Claim.
2. The Defendant will ask the Court to re-open the said agreement with the Plaintiffs under section 139 of the Consumer Credit Act 1974 on the ground that it is an extortionate bargain.
3. The said bargain is extortionate in that it requires the Defendant to make payments which are grossly exorbitant and, further or alternatively, in that it otherwise grossly contravenes ordinary principles of fair dealing.

Particulars

(a) the said agreement requires the Defendant to pay an APR of £150 per centum whereas at the date of the said agreement an APR of £15 per centum would have been readily available to the Defendant from other commercial sources on terms no more onerous than those otherwise provided for by the said agreement;

(b) the Defendant was twenty one years of age at the date of the said agreement and had no business capacity;

(c) the Defendant was under severe financial and domestic pressure at the date of the said agreement in that due to periods of unemployment he was in arrears with payments under loan agreements into which he had previously entered and was being subjected to threats of violence by his creditors and to threats by his wife to desert him if he did not extricate himself from the particular indebtedness which then existed;

(d) there was no or, in the alternative, no material risk accepted by the Plaintiffs in that the Plaintiffs had the said property valued prior to entering into the said agreement and such valuation established an equity in the said property of £32,000, in that the Plaintiffs satisfied themselves as to the marketability of the said property and the Defendant's interest therein by the usual searches and inspection of the Defendant's charge certificate and in that the Plaintiffs knew that the Defendant was again in remunerative full-time employment; and

(e) the Plaintiffs represented to the Defendant before he entered into the said agreement that their lending terms were "the best in town" and the Defendant believed that when he entered into the said agreement the said representation was true.

4. Save as hereinbefore expressly admitted, the Defendant denies each and every allegation of fact in the Particulars of Claim.

COUNTERCLAIM

5. By way of counterclaim, the Defendant repeats paragraphs 3 and 4 of his defence and claims to have the said agreement re-opened as aforesaid. The Defendant therefore counterclaims:-

(1) an order that the said agreement be re-opened under section 139 of the Consumer Credit Act 1974;

(2) an order directing that accounts be taken between the parties;

(3) an order setting aside the obligation by the Defendant under the said agreement to pay interest;

```
(4) an order requiring the Plaintiffs to repay to
    the Defendant all interest on the said loan
    which the Defendant has paid; and
(5) costs.
Dated this 14th day of July 1988
(Signed) .J...Soap...........
Joseph Soap
52 Coercion Street
Cambridge
Defendant
To: The Registrar
And to the above-named Plaintiffs
```

Nice one

There's an alternative way which a *defaulting* borrower may be able to get his interest rate down. Often, the lender will be obliged, before he can sue or take other enforcement action, to serve the borrower with a "default notice" under section 76 of the Consumer Credit Act 1974. The borrower can then apply to the court for a "time order". This may do more than give the borrower further time to pay what is owed having regard to his means. It may actually change the interest rate if the court reckons to do so would be just. And this power could be exercised even when the interest rate was not so diabolical as to be classed as "exorbitant". A similar power can be exercised when the lender has been the first to get to court because the borrower has defaulted.

Take this case which was before Sheffield county court in 1987. Cedar Holdings Ltd. had lent £2,258 to a borrowing couple on second mortgage at a £22.80% per annum interest rate. The borrowers defaulted and a "default notice" was served on them. The borrowers countered with an application for a "time order" under section 129 of the Consumer Credit Act 1974. The court registrar decided the couple could only afford £45 per month instead of the £52.56 they had agreed to pay to Cedar and so reduced the interest rate to £17.40% per annum which brought down the mortgage instalments to . . . £45 per month. The judge upheld the registrar.

Anti-gazumping kit

Well, it's got to be worth a try . . .

"£75,000 then, and you'll think about buying the loft insulation and hot water cylinder jacket on top. I'll ring my solicitor in the morning. Here's to an early completion . . . And the next one right in here please."

It's immoral—and it makes you sick

Until contracts have been exchanged, either side can back out of a house or flat sale and neither is legally responsible for the expenses which the other has incurred. That's the general situation and it means that the seller may accept a higher offer elsewhere and ditch the hapless first person to have agreed to buy "subject to contract" who is beavering away getting his financial act together, paying out for the property to be surveyed and valued and having his solicitor get on with the legal work. And it means that, alternatively, the seller may accept a string of further "subject to contract" offers, perhaps at the same price, perhaps at different prices, and announce that whoever is first to come up with an unconditional contract and deposit cheque, will have the place.

Option to purchase

The risk of being gazumped can be eliminated by an option to purchase agreement. We have to concede that it would not work on the vast majority of home moves. But it could work on some. Have a look at how it goes—

AN AGREEMENT made on the 14th July 1988 BETWEEN GRANT CHANCE of 422 Euston Parade Portsmouth Hampshire ("Mr Chance") of the one part and AVA GRAND of "Throgmorton" Cherry Drive Brighton East Sussex ("Ms Grand") of the other part WHEREBY IT IS AGREED as follows:-

1. In consideration of £1,000 ("the fee") now paid by Ms Grand to Mr Chance (the receipt whereof Mr Chance hereby acknowledges) Mr Chance grants to Ms Grand the option to purchase the freehold property 422 Euston Parade Portsmouth Hampshire ("the property") which is registered with title absolute at H M Land Registry under title number HP 467215 at the price of £100,000.
2. The option shall be exercised by notice in writing by Ms Grand to the solicitor for Mr Chance at any time on or before the 14th September 1988 and the notice shall only be effective if accompanied by £9,000 as a part deposit and if so accompanied the fee shall be treated as the balance of the deposit and Mr Chance shall give Ms Grand credit for the deposit on completion.
3. If Ms Grand shall exercise the option in accordance with clause 2 -
   (a) the property shall be sold subject to The Law Society's General Conditions of Sale (1984 Revision) ("general conditions") so far as they are not varied by or inconsistent with the terms of this agreement;
   (b) the date for completion shall be 14 days from the expiration of notice in writing by Mr Chance to Ms Grand requiring her to complete or on the 28th October 1988 (whichever is the earlier);
   (c) for the purposes of general condition 1(b) the contract rate shall be 4 per cent above the base rate from time to time of Midland Bank Plc;

(d) Mr Chance shall sell as beneficial owner;
(e) Ms Grand shall have authority to inspect the Register and to obtain office copies thereof;
(f) the property shall be sold with vacant possession on completion;
(g) the property shall be sold subject to entry number 1 in the Charges Register of the above mentioned title; and
(h) the £9,000 part deposit shall be held as agents.

4. If Ms Grand shall not exercise the option in accordance with clause 2 the fee shall belong to Mr Chance absolutely.

SIGNED by GRANT CHANCE
in the presence of: Grant Chance
Millie Combes
147 Abbeywood Drive
Catisfield. Housewife

SIGNED by AVA GRAND
in the presence of: Ava Grand
Nosie Parker
29 Woodbine Park
Catisfield. Civil Servant.

The property buyer is paying—£1,000 here—for the right to buy a house within a specified period. If he does buy, the £1,000 is counted towards the price. If he does not buy he loses the £1,000. The £1,000 compensates the prospective seller for holding on and demonstrates the prospective buyer is not a time waster. The option agreement may suit a prospective seller who, for example, must move, has yet to find an alternative property but wants to know he has a sale close to being in the bag. And it may suit a prospective buyer who has sorted out everything except finance but is confident all will be well.

Our option agreement provides for some flexibility with the completion date (clause 3(b)) in contemplation that Mr. Chance may want Ms. Grand to buy earlier rather than later, but there is a longstop date specified. This can be adapted in any case to fit the circumstances, as can the option fee and the period available for the exercise of the option—in fact, it can all be adapted! The longer the prospective buyer is to be given to exercise the option and then to complete, the higher the price for the property or for the option which the prospective seller would wish to ask.

Health warnings

- Under no circumstances would we commend either side to enter into an option agreement without legal advice.
- The prospective seller should check that the option agreement would not trigger the payment of commission to any estate agent he has engaged (see page 122) and, if it could, seek to persuade the agent to waive commission if the option is not exercised with completion following on.
- The option agreement will need to be registered at the Land Registry or Land Charges Registry. A solicitor will advise.

The pre-contract deposit agreement

This is an agreement for an agreement! It has been devised by the Law Commission but has not taken off. We believe it has deficiences but we acknowledge it will cater for the needs of some. It works this way. Prospective seller and buyer strike a "subject to contract" bargain which is carried through into the Deposit Agreement. It's called a Deposit Agreement because each party pays ½% of the price. The agreement provides that contracts are to be exchanged within four weeks. If they are not because one of them withdraws or is unwilling to exchange otherwise than for a permitted reason, that party forfeits his ½% deposit to the other. Beyond forfeiture there is no penalty for the refusal or paralysis.

The agreement shows good faith and the forfeited deposit gives the "innocent" party some compensation for his losses. However, the deposit lost will not of itself deter a prospective seller from dropping his buyer and negotiating elsewhere if the increase in price elsewhere is to exceed the deposit. To cater for this problem, the deposit percentage could be increased if both sides agreed. And we would suggest that the four weeks period for exchange is lengthened: the prospective buyer could find it far too short, particularly in relation to fixing up a mortgage which is acceptable to him and especially if the proposed lender has to carry out status enquiries. Any part of the agreement can be modified as the parties may agree. Here's the agreement in its unmodified form—

Please read the notes overleaf before completing this form

Pre-Contract Deposit Agreement

as recommended by the Conveyancing Standing Committee

1. We have agreed "subject to contract" on the sale and purchase of

Insert address of house or flat: 422 Euston Parade Portsmouth Hampshire

Insert price: for £ 100,000.

2. Each of us has paid a pre-contract deposit of $^1/_2$% of the price to

Insert Vendor's Solicitor or Licensed Conveyancer: Eagle, Eagle & Co.

as stakeholder.

3. If contracts are exchanged within four weeks both deposits shall be repaid.
4. If contracts are **not** exchanged within four weeks because one of us withdraws or is unwilling to exchange, both deposits shall be paid to the other.

But both deposits will be repaid **if**

a) the Purchaser withdraws or is unwilling to exchange because:
- he has discovered something reducing the open market value of the property by more than his deposit;

or • he has been refused a reasonably acceptable offer of a mortgage loan of £ 75,000 by Grand National Building Society; (Insert amount; Insert name of bank or building society to which applying)

or • any condition of sale proposed in good faith is not reasonably acceptable;

†[or • contracts cannot be exchanged for the sale of his present dwelling]; (Delete † if no "chain" needed by purchaser)

or b) the Vendor withdraws or is unwilling to exchange because:
- any amendment made in good faith to the proposed conditions of sale is not reasonably acceptable;

†[or • contracts cannot be exchanged for the purchase by him of another dwelling]; (Delete † if no "chain" needed by vendor)

or c) both the Vendor and the purchaser withdraw or neither is willing to oxohange.

5. The four weeks period for exchange must be complied with strictly †[but this period may be extended at any time by the Purchaser until one week after replies to local authority searches and enquiries have been received]. (Delete † if Vendor to supply with draft contract)

6. Date of Agreement 14th July 1988 (Insert)

Signed:

Vendor[s]:	Purchaser[s]:
Grant Chance	Ava Grand

Guidance Notes

A. Before signing
Read the Agreement and these Notes carefully. Fill in all the blanks. Consult a solicitor or licensed conveyancer if the form has been altered or if anything seems unclear.

B. Purposes
Each of you guarantees his genuine interest in the sale of this dwelling by putting down a sum of money which will be lost on backing out. The amount lost should ordinarily be compensation for the other's wasted expenditure, such as valuation fees and legal costs. No additional legal liability is intended.

C. Exchange
This Agreement does **not** make the sale legally binding before your solicitor or licensed conveyancer has exchanged contracts. Then the purchaser's pre-contract deposit may be used in part payment of the full deposit.

D. Conditions
The pre-contract deposit should not be lost if there is a good enough reason for backing out. For example, if a survey or search reveals to the purchaser a defect or other matter costing more than the amount of the $^1/_2$ % deposit to put right, then normally he need not go on. Remember that the price agreed is not necessarily the same as the open market value, which may not be affected by the defect or other matter, and that the Vendor can avoid this risk by disclosing any known defect or other matter at the outset.

Similarly, if the purchaser duly applies for a mortgage loan of the amount mentioned (usually financial credit should be already ascertained, eg by obtaining a "mortgage certificate") but the loan is either refused or made subject to unreasonably onerous conditions, then he can get back his deposit.

Again the precise terms and conditions of the sale may still have to be negotiated and, if agreement as to these cannot reasonably be reached both sides will be entitled to back out without loss of their deposits. A solicitor or licensed conveyancer will be able to advise you about what is "reasonably acceptable" here. However, if the condition of sale or amendment is not put forward in good faith, this may be taken to show an unwillingness to exchange.

E. Deletions
The form caters for two situations which may not always apply. First, it recognises that the vendor may not want to sell the property until he has actually bought somewhere else to live and that the purchaser may not want to buy this property until he has sold his present house or flat. If exchanging contracts must depend on this sort of "chain" of transactions, then the relevant parts of Clause 4 should be left in. Otherwise, they should be deleted. Second, in some areas is still takes longer than 4 weeks to get replies to local searches and enquiries. This difficulty can be overcome if the vendor has got the replies ready for the purchaser, but otherwise the whole of clause 5 should be left in.

Although the 4 weeks period should be complied with strictly, (ie time is of the essence), it may be extended by agreement (or by the purchaser where clause 5 applies without any deletion).

F. Definitions
The expression "as stakeholder" means that the person concerned holds the deposit on behalf of both sides, unable to pay the money to either without the other's consent except in accordance with the provisions of the Agreement.

Generally in the Agreement, singular words include the plural (eg "Purchaser" also covers joint purchasers) and the masculine includes the feminine).

Form F500 Fourmat Publishing 27 & 28 St Albans Place Islington Green London N1 ONX February 1987

Playing detective

The buyer shoudl reduce the risk of being gazumped by—

1. Asking the seller to take the property off the market and, if he has promised to do so, checking that he has kept to his word. Does the seller's estate agent still regard the property as up for grabs? It would not be proper for us to suggest that the buyer put on his best Edna Everage voice, telephone the agent and enquire whether it is possible to view the property.
2. Asking the seller for a commitment that he will not issue a second or subsequent contract for a minimum period. Although this will not compel the seller to actually exchange contracts with the buyer at any stage, it may discourage the seller from courting other offers.
3. If the seller is doing his own conveyancing or is not represented by a solicitor or licensed conveyancer, asking the seller for an undertaking that he will notify the buyer immediately any second or subsequent contract is sent out. The professional codes of the solicitor and licensed conveyancer will require him to notify the buyer if any other contracts are issued. A particularly devious seller might deliberately steer clear of a solicitor or licensed conveyancer so as to ensure that his buyer remained ignorant of the competitors until such time as he wanted him to be in the know.
4. Checking whether any "For Sale" board becomes an "Under Offer" board.
5. Sitting outside the property and making ugly faces at anyone who seems remotely interested in it.

Working it off

A fine mess . . .

If a person who has been fined by a Crown Court or magistrates' court defaults, his goods may be seized under order to cover what is due: or he may so move the court that it decides it is just, in view of some change since the conviction, to wipe out the fine although moving fine enforcement courts is as easy as moving Judge Jeffries after an argument with his wife. Most probably, a sentence of imprisonment will be imposed and this will wipe out the fine. Orders for compensation, costs and so on which have also been imposed and gone unpaid are similarly wiped out. The period of imprisonment depends on the amount unpaid—

Debt	*Maximum imprisonment (magistrates' courts)*
up to £50	5 days
£50 – £100	7 days
£100 – £400	14 days
£400 – £1,000	30 days
£1,000 – £2,000	45 days
£2,000 – £5,000	3 months

£5,000 – £10,000	6 months
£10,000 – £20,000	12 months
£20,000 – £50,000	18 months
£50,000 – £100,000	2 years
£100,000 – £250,000	3 years
£250,000 – £1 million	5 years
£1 million or more	10 years

Imprisonment is costly to the State and denies the prisoner the company of his spouse and screaming children. Prisons are filled with defaulting offenders who have decided to work it off and there are some who time their incarceration so as to coincide with Christmas. There is a national allotment to prisons to be used for holiday extras for Christmas and when prison kitchen staff have saved on their budget over the year and put aside the occasional cow and turkey, these can be turned to the seasonal advantage of the customers. There is no statutory obligation on prison governors to display menus outside their establishments (unlike restaurants) and so discreet enquiries should be made of the available fare before submission to the magistrates' court warrant of commitment to prison for non payment.

"He was a no-good when I married him and he's a no-good now."

Rates and maintenance defaulters cannot be put inside for longer than six weeks. But for maintenance defaulters the imprisonment does not wipe out the debt. It's rare, however, for the court to do anything too drastic over arrears for which imprisonment has been served, and the practice is to direct that arrears which are more than twelve months old be wiped out whether prison or no prison has been suffered, provided, of course, that the non-payer is not flush with cash.

Generally, non-payment of a civil debt cannot lead to imprisonment—maintenance, rates and tax or national insurance arrears are the exceptions (see page 26)—and so there is no question of working off the civil debt by getting banged up.

"Closed for delivery of goods on credit. Gone bankrupt. Back in two years."

Bankruptcy is an option open to the masochist so long as he owes debts of at least £750 which he cannot pay. It is actually on discharge from bankruptcy that, generally, the debts are wiped out. Discharge now comes automatically for first time bankrupts after three years or, if the liabilities were less than £20,000, after two years, but the court does have the power to stop the clock when the bankrupt has failed to co-operate as he should. For those bankrupted by a criminal court and old hands (anyone who has been an undischarged bankrupt at any time during the fifteen years before the later bankruptcy) there is nothing automatic about discharge. An application for discharge has to be made to the court and it can be made after five years: the court can order discharge conditional on a bankrupt handing over some future loot for the benefit of his creditors. There are special rules for those bankrupted before 29 December 1986.

The principal debts not wiped out by discharge from bankruptcy are awards of damages for personal injuries, money payable under a maintenance or some other matrimonial order and debts which were *fraudulently* run up. During the bankruptcy, there are restrictions on what the bankrupt can get up to: for example, any money he receives or earns belongs to his trustee (although he'll be allowed reasonable amounts to live on), he can't manage a company or be a company director and he can't obtain credit of £250 or more.

Anyone anxious to be made bankrupt but who cannot find a creditor willing to oblige, may present his own petition to the county court for which he will have to pay a fee of £15 (which can be reduced or waived on the ground of exceptional circumstances), plus £100 towards the Official Receiver's tea fund. But the court will want to help him to avoid bankruptcy!

A woman scorned

Including the cohabitation contract

Dear Madam

My Husband

I am the wife of the gentleman who recently deserted me and my children and with whom you have taken up residence. He is called John Dictive. For your sake, I am anxious that you should be under no illusions about what the future holds for my husband. It would be unfair for you to suffer the same disappointment as me. Therefore, I am writing to tell you of my intentions.

It remains the Law of England and Wales - or so I am reliably informed - that a man may not lawfully enter into a ceremony of marriage with a woman so long as he remains married to another woman. My husband remains married to me and will do so for a good many years yet. I cannot imagine for one moment that among the promises he has made to you has been one of marriage in the foreseeable future as my husband is cognisant of my feelings but it is best I should put you straight on this point. For my part, I have not committed adultery and do not desire contact with any adult male except, possibly, in the course of spitting him in the eye. Nor have I behaved unreasonably towards my husband or deserted him. I will never consent to a divorce following any period of separation. It follows that my husband is without any grounds to divorce me until we have been separated for a minimum of five years. Whilst I gather it would be extremely difficult to succeed, I have found out that even then I might defend the divorce saying that if it went ahead I would be caused grave financial or other hardship and that it would in all the circumstances be wrong to dissolve the marriage.

Simon and Sarah are at school. I shall encourage them to go on to university. Already Sarah is showing an aptitude for the academic life whilst only 5 years. The other day I caught her browsing through an encyclopaedia when she should have been watching television. The children look like being a financial drain for many years to come. That is where my husband comes in.

I shall require substantial maintenance for the children and, of course, for myself as well. I will apply for this as part of my suit for judicial separation about which next week I have an appointment to see my solicitor (very aggressive and sharp, she is - a lady magistrate who sits on the domestic panel highly recommended her). The court can grant a decree of judicial separation on exactly the same grounds as a decree of divorce and give the wife exactly the same financial relief as it could give her with divorce. But unlike with divorce, the husband and wife remain married to each other after the judicial separation case is over.

The idea of my taking employment, even part-time is unthinkable until the children are very much older. Anyway, I cannot imagine to what I could put my hands even if a job were possible. My husband always insisted I should be at home. Before our marriage I did a little typing but in those days it was manual typewriters, pencil sharpeners, rubbers and postage stamps. You know what I mean. All this modern gadgetry is another world to me. I would expect the maintenance for me to be paid as long as my husband and myself are both alive.

By the way, I hear you have a nice little number job wise, thank you very much. Whilst you may not be under any obligation to maintain me or my children, you did, after all, take my husband subject to all known prior incumbrances (!) and I assume he is deriving some benefits from your income and capital. For a start, he is living in your flat. I am advised it will be appropriate to ask the court to compel your attendance at the maintenance hearing so that the court will have the advantage of personal evidence from you about your financial circumstances.

Now the house. It is in joint names. It may have six bedrooms and be expensive to run but to me and the children, it is home. It would break the children's hearts to even hint of moving and, frankly, there are no reasonably priced three or four bedroomed properties within walking distance of the children's schools. I do not drive. I shall be seeking the transfer of my husband's interest in the house to me and he will have to continue to make the mortgage repayments. It is an endowment mortgage we have and so I am advised to go after a large share (if not the entirety) of the maturity monies under the endowment policy.

Insofar as access to Simon and Sarah is concerned, I will not allow my personal feelings to come between them and their father whom they love. I shall encourage contact. This Xmas I have already arranged to stay at my parents which means the children will not be available down here. Otherwise, I will be suggesting that my husband sees them one day a week at the weekends (subject to Simon's football and Sarah's ballet commitments). Whilst Simon would be prepared to go out for the day with his father, Sarah flatly refuses to do so and I cannot bring myself to force this on her, especially after all the trauma she has gone through. Simon and Sarah must be kept together and their father will have to exercise his access here for the day. I shall have a room available. I expect you will welcome the chance to get on with some flat cleaning - or perhaps you have a domestic?

There it is. Continued good luck with your career because some of your success is my maintenance!

Yours sincerely
V. Dictive
Vinney Dictive

Hussy hits back

Dear Mrs Dictive

Thank you for your considerate letter. As it happens, I read law at Birmingham University and before John joined me, we obtained legal advice from a big city firm which specialises in these cases. Therefore, *I* am well qualified to put *you* straight on a couple of things.

If you intend to string out your farce of a marriage for another five years, that is a matter for you and your conscience. Just remember that you will be sentencing yourself to five years of bitterness in the wilderness. You will forever be looking over your shoulder to see whether we are watching. Should you form another relationship which becomes a full one, you will then become the adulterer and John will be able to divorce you and ask for your maintenance to be cancelled or reduced on account of your relationship: that he had committed adultery first or that you had already obtained a judicial separation decree from the court, would make no difference.

On the question of you blocking John's attempt at getting a divorce after five years (if it comes to that), you do not have a hope in hell of getting the case thrown out. John's solicitors have yet to hear of anyone who has succeeded with the defence you mention.

The whole spirit now of the maintenance laws which apply on divorce or judicial separation is that the wife should stand on her own two feet and become independent of her husband whenever this is reasonably possible. She is not automatically entitled to a meal ticket for life. I do not pretend for one moment that, with two young children on your hands, you could become independent for some while. But if you think you can sit on your backside when the children are older and you could be doing some part time work, and can continue to sit on your backside once the children are off your hands and you could be doing full time work - you are mistaken! The court can attribute you with the income you could reasonably earn.

You might ask your switched-on, aggressive and sharp solicitor to tell you about the "clean break". Even when permanent maintenance and property are first considered, the court can order a clean break and dismiss the wife's maintenance claims or direct that her maintenance order shall only last for a fixed period and preclude her from coming back after it. This may now be done against the wife's consent. A clean break is a particularly real possibility when the husband can come up with a lump sum payment which will enable the wife to cope quite nicely. A whopping great lump sum might even result in a clean break though the wife is to have the children but an order for their maintenance would also be required. Sometimes a clean break immediately will be regarded as premature. It will crop up again. When either husband or wife applies for the original maintenance order to be varied (husband worse off, wife better off, rampant inflation) the court is now under a duty to consider then whether to finish off the order or limit its life. The husband who has capital available can undertake to pay a lump sum and against that undertaking the maintenance order could be killed off; a belated clean break and even without the wife's consent.

Whatever maintenance order should be made for you and the children, it cannot be for the payment out of my income or capital: it must be for payment out of John's means. You could argue that whilst he is with me and I am working he has a greater part of his income and capital "freed" and available for you. I concede this sort of argument has found favour with the courts but it won't do you any good. John pays his way with the bills as my bank statements will bear out. Our personal relationship does not enter into the financial agreement we have reached. We want our own family and if I become pregnant I shall have to stop work. John will have moral responsibilities towards me and, later, legal responsibilities towards our child. Though his responsibilities to you and Simon and Sarah must come before those towards me, all his responsibilities must be taken into account.

Your house is much too big and expensive to run. The court could order a sale on a judicial separation as well as on a divorce. If it did this, the sale proceeds could be used to buy a more reasonably sized property with no mortgage, or with a small mortgage on which I expect John would be able to help.

It would be better all round if you were less bitter and emotional and tried to sort out everything with John in an amicable way.

Yours sincerely

V. Hussy

Virginia Hussy

Devious dictive

My dear Virginia

I have read and re-read your recent letter and you are right. My mind is unchanged about not going for divorce and about fighting for what is just for me and Simon and Sarah, but I will try and see things from John's standpoint as well.

Some of the points you raised did worry me a little and so I showed your letter to my solicitor. She said that my right to maintenance would not be forfeited if I met somebody else. If I actually cohabited with someone, my maintenance could be subject to review on John asking the court to vary my order but it is extremely unlikely it would be wiped out altogether whilst the children remain around. Interestingly, my solicitor tells me that in January 1988 the Court of Appeal refused to end a maintenance order in favour of an ex wife for 5p a year. It seems that the nominal amount was simply to keep the order alive so that the ex wife could apply for it to be increased if she needed to. The wife was 48 and earning £10,000 a year as a teacher and the ex husband was 53 but had been made redundant. By a 2-1 majority, the court held that nominal orders were useful in case unforeseen contingencies deprived an ex wife of the ability to provide for herself and made it necessary for her to look again to her former husband.

My solicitor tells me more. In June 1988 the Court of Appeal apparently over-ruled a county court judge who had ordered after divorce that a wife's maintenance should come to an end four years later. The wife had been trying to find full time employment but it was not possible to predict when, if ever, she would do so. The four year time limit was removed and the Court of Appeal accepted the wife's undertaking to inform the husband if and when she found a job. It would remain open to the husband to require the wife to account for the steps she had taken to find work and, if she failed to do so, he could always extract this information when applying to the court to have the order varied.

Anyway, so far as a clean break is concerned my solicitor says there will not be one without my consent now.

Let me turn to the house. If I have to move I shall undoubtedly insist on the new property going into my sole name so that John has no claim on it.

I have not received my allowance from John for a fortnight and his last cheque bounced twice before being cleared at the third attempt. He has told his mother that he has never had it so good. It is much cheaper for him to stay with you than living in digs and he can now afford to buy a few rounds in the pub at lunch time. It is sad that I should be rewarded this way for so many years' devotion and care. If this is how he treats me his wife, what sort of chance do you stand should the two of you fall out? I suggest you mug up on cohabitation law!

Sincerely

V. Dictive

Vinney Dictive

Cohabitation contract

Dear John

There's some nut roast in fridge. I've got a P-T meeting and, afterwards, a few of us are going out for a curry so don't wait up. I've been thinking. We ought to enter into a cohabitation contract. It's the thing to do, I'm told. The lawyers aren't 100% convinced that the courts will enforce them - apparently, there hasn't been a test case yet - but the betting at the 'Wig and Pen' is that they will be O.K. I mean, this is the enlightened 80's! I've found a precedent in pip-squeak Gold's Law. It's intended for a man who owns his own house and takes in a woman. We could adapt it. Let me know what you think.

G. x

Ginnie.

THIS AGREEMENT is made the 14th July 1988 BETWEEN JONATHAN PLAYSAFE of 31 Woodbine Park Catisfield in Hampshire ("Mr Playsafe") and TERRY BEA KEENE of 6a Navigators Walk Gosport in Hampshire ("Ms Keene")

BACKGROUND:

(1) Mr Playsafe and Ms Keene wish to live together as man and wife at 31 Woodbine Park Catisfield ("the home") or such other home as Mr Playsafe shall from time to time acquire.

(2) The home is owned solely by Mr Playsafe

(3) Mr Playsafe and Ms Keene wish to be financially independent of each other
(4) Mr Playsafe and Ms Keene have both obtained or been aware of their right to obtain legal advice on this agreement and have carefully read and understand its contents

NOW IT IS HEREBY AGREED AND DECLARED as follows:-

1. Mr Playsafe and Ms Keene shall live together at the home as from the above date until this agreement shall terminate in accordance with clause 10.
2. Mr Playsafe has neither made nor held out any promise inducement proposal or offer to Ms Keene to grant her any licence other than that granted by clause 6 and Ms Keene has terminated her right to occupy 6a Navigators Walk Gosport in the knowledge that her licence to occupy the home shall be limited to the said licence.
3. Neither party has made nor held out to the other any promise inducement proposal or offer to make any provision for the other in his or her will.
4. Ms Keene acknowledges that she has no beneficial interest in the home or its proceeds of sale by way of resulting constructive or other trust or otherwise and that she shall not acquire any such interest in the home or its contents (save and except in respect of such contents as she may purchase) and she shall not acquire any right other than that granted by clause 6 to occupy the home by virtue of any payment of money or act she shall make or do in respect of the improvement maintenance repair decoration cleaning tidying or otherwise of the home or its contents or by virtue of any payment of money she shall make under any mortgage or in respect of any other outgoing on the home or its contents and no such payment or act shall entitle Ms Keene to make any claim against Mr Playsafe or his estate.
5. Neither party shall have any claim against the other or the estate of the other by virtue of having lived with the other (however long such period of living together may be) or by virtue of any payment having been made or act having been done as referred to herein or otherwise for the benefit of the other.

6. Mr Playsafe grants to Ms Keene personally a bare licence to live at the home with Mr Playsafe and such other person or persons (if any) as Mr Playsafe shall from time to time permit to occupy the home.
7. Ms Keene covenants with Mr Playsafe for himself and his personal representatives that she will within 28 days of the termination of the licence granted by clause 6 vacate the home and remove her property (if any) therefrom and it is hereby agreed that such termination shall occur upon the death of Mr Playsafe or upon notice in writing to terminate being given by Mr Playsafe to Ms Keene.
8. This agreement shall continue in force notwithstanding the birth to Ms Keene of any child.
9. In the event of Mr Playsafe disposing of his interest in the home and taking possession of any dwelling with Ms Keene this agreement shall in all respects apply to the other dwelling as it shall apply to the home.
10. Subject to clause 7, this agreement shall terminate upon the occurrence of any of the following events (whichever shall first occur):-
    (a) the intermarriage of Mr Playsafe and Ms Keene;
    (b) the expiration of 28 days notice in writing by one of the parties to the other; and
    (c) the desertion of Mr Playsafe by Ms Keene
11. For the purposes of clauses 7 and 10 notice shall be deemed to have been given by Mr Playsafe to Ms Keene if Ms Keene having ceased to live at the home and her whereabouts being unknown to Mr Playsafe such notice shall be delivered by ordinary prepaid post or personally to her last known address

IN WITNESS whereof the parties have hereunto placed their hands and seals the day and year first before written

SIGNED SEALED AND DELIVERED) J. Playsafe
by the said JONATHAN PLAYSAFE)
in the presence of:)
Nosie Parker
29 Woodbine Park Catisfield
Civil Servant

SIGNED SEALED AND DELIVERED) T. B. Keene
by the said TERRY BEA KEENE)
in the presence of:)
Nosie Parker
29 Woodbine Park Catisfield
Civil Servant

Health warnings for liars

When a gentleman acquires a property to be lived in by himself and his prospective cohabitee, or when he takes a cohabitee to his existing property, he is well advised to tell the truth about his intentions. Ask Mr. E. He met Ms. G: each was married to another. In due course and after their respective spouses separated from them, a close relationship developed and Ms. G gave birth to a son. Mr. E. was the father. Mr. E. and Ms. G. decided to live together permanently. He purchased a house in the joint names of himself and his brother. He told Ms. G. that but for the fact there were then pending matrimonial proceedings between herself and her husband her name would have gone on to the deeds: he did not want to prejudice her position in the proceedings by giving her a share in his property. In fact that was not the real reason. Mr. E. never had any intention of replacing his brother with Ms. G. on the deeds when her proceedings were over. In 1986, after eleven years' cohabitation, the Court of Appeal, awarded Ms. G. one half of the property. She had relied on Mr. E's statement and, whatever may been locked away in his head, his statement was evidence of the intentions of the couple!

And in 1975 the Court of Appeal gave the woman a one-quarter share of the property. The man had falsely told her when he purchased that the reason for the property not going into joint names was that she was then under twenty-one. Despite her youth, she wielded a fourteen pound sledge hammer, broke up a large area of concrete, filled a skip and did other things in renovating the property after its purchase.

To score, the woman whose name is off the deeds needs to show that the couple intended she should have an interest plus some acting to her detriment in the reasonable belief that she was acquiring an interest—something over and above what might be done out of love and affection for the man. And the courts will treat the man's lies as the truth. It could pay to tell the truth from the start.

Stop the clock

Miles better off

Show us an accurate odometer reading on a used car and we will show you a happy corpse. A dealer who displays or offers to sell a vehicle with a false reading falls foul of the Trade Descriptions Act 1968 even though he was not responsible for "clocking", and may genuinely believe that the reading is accurate—unless he has disclaimed. He may well earn himself an acquittal if he was ignorant of the inaccuracy and had taken the trouble to inform prospective purchasers on a notice stuck on the odometer glass that the reading may be wrong. In December 1987 the High Court held this notice to be good enough for the quashing of a conviction under the notoriously feared section 1(1)(a) of the 1968 Act—

> Trade Descriptions Act 1968. Dealers are often unable to guarantee the mileage of a used car on sale. Please disregard the recorded mileage on this vehicle and accept this is an inaccurate reading.

Sorry— look at clause 479 sub-clause 12!

Excluding the exclusions . . .

Those who sell goods and supply services often contemplate that the goods will fall to pieces and the services will be sub-standard. They prefer not to refund money and pay out damages and so they attempt to lumber the customer with a contract condition which gives them a let-out. The condition is called an exclusion clause. It may be in a notice displayed on the premises or it may be in a document handed to the customer or shown to him when the contract was made. The clause may be long or it may be short. The words of the clause may be hidden away in very small print OR THE WORDS MAY SCREAM OUT. Wherever and however the words have appeared, the customer must try and exterminate them for they will otherwise spell doom.

ARGUMENT NO. 1: *"I didn't know about it so I can't be bound by it"*

It could be that the customer *signed* the document containing the exclusion clause. No customer reads a document before he signs it. He may look at it but with an impatient queue behind or a hungry salesman in front, he doesn't *read*. That the customer failed to read before he signed will not help him legally. He is bound by what he signed unless, without being careless, he was mistaken about the nature of the document: he thought he was signing a Will but it was an order form for an indoor swimming pool.

The customer may be able to show that he isn't bound by the exclusion clause because it didn't come to his notice until *after* the contract was made. In one celebrated case, a couple who booked into a hotel made their contract to stay there whilst at the reception desk. Up to the bedroom they then went to find an exclusion notice hanging on the door. Never mind, they weren't stuck with it. The contract had already been made.

Reasonable steps have to be taken to draw the exclusion clause to the customer's attention, even when it is present and capable of being seen at contract making time. It may be obvious that a ticket is issued subject to exclusion clauses—a railway or ferry ticket, for example. Without reciting them, the ticket will probably state that the conditions—with the exclusion clauses among them—can be inspected at the main booking office. Can the customer successfully argue that he is not bound because he didn't read the ticket, he didn't read the conditions and he reckoned the ticket clerk would have collapsed with laughter if he had asked for a copy? Rarely.

But with a really nasty exclusion clause, there could be an obligation to do something extra special about communicating it to the customer before he commits himself—an obligation to sock it to him! Take this case which recently reached the Court of Appeal. It does not concern an exclusion clause but a clause in a contract which was very onerous on the customer; still, the principle it demonstrated could be put to good use by a customer battling against an exclusion clause. Interfoto Picture Library Ltd, ran a photographic transparency library. Stiletto Visual Programmes Ltd. were in advertising. Stiletto telephoned Interfoto and asked whether they had any 1950's transparencies which were wanted for a presentation. The same day, Interfoto sent them round forty-seven transparencies. They were packed in a bag. Also in the bag was a delivery note. It specified the return date and under "conditions" prominently printed, were nine conditions set out in four columns.

Condition 2 required the return of the transparencies within fourteen days and imposed a holding fee for every transparency of £5 per day plus VAT for every day of lateness. You guessed it! Stiletto went over the return date. Interfoto sent them an invoice for . . . £3,783.50! You guessed it again! Stiletto refused to pay and were sued. In the county court, Interfoto won and Stiletto then appealed. This time, Stiletto won and the bill was knocked down to under £350. It was felt that Stiletto could not have known of the proposed "very high and exorbitant charge" if their attention was not drawn to condition 2. Nothing whatever had been done to draw their attention *particularly* to that condition. Consequently, condition 2 had never become part of the contract.

This decision reflected the words of Lord Denning in a case over twenty years ago. "I agree," he said "that the more unreasonable a clause is, the greater the notice which must be given of it. Some clauses which I have seen would need to be printed in red ink on the face of the document with a red hand pointing to it before the notice could be held to be sufficient."

ARGUMENT NO. 2: *"OK, I put my hands up. I knew about it but you can't legally exclude liability for **that**"*

Businesses cannot rely on an exclusion clause which purports to excuse them from liability for death or personal injury resulting from negligence or which purports to restrict that liability. The clause will be null and void.

PASSENGERS TRAVEL AT THEIR OWN RISK. NO LIABILITY FOR DEATH, PERSONAL INJURY OR LOSS DUE TO OUR NEGLIGENCE OR OTHERWISE	= Void

NO CLAIMS FOR DEATH OR PERSONAL INJURY DUE TO ALLEGED NEGLIGENCE WILL BE ENTERTAINED UNLESS WRITTEN NOTIFICATION IS GIVEN TO US WITHIN 14 DAYS OF LAST HEART BEAT OR FIRST PAIN OR REGAINING OF CONSCIOUSNESS (WHICHEVER SHALL FIRST OCCUR)	= Void

Nor can businesses (although auctioneers are an exception) rely on an exclusion clause which suggests the customer is without redress when the goods are not of merchantable quality, reasonably fit for their purpose or in correspondence with their description or sample.

You know—all that Sale of Goods Act stuff. Well, the clause is void. Not worth the paper or cardboard it is written on. And, generally, the clause will even be void when the customer is a business provided the purchase (same rules for HP too) is not one of a regular number by the business and made as part of the business actually carried on. What's all that about? Give you an example. The Court of Appeal has recently held that where a company which operated as shipping brokers and freight forwarding agents bought a car for the use of a director, an exclusion clause which tried to do away with the requirement for merchantable quality was void: the company had not made its purchase in the course of its business.

Some sellers carry on trying to con their customers into believing that they can exclude Sale of Goods Act liability. In an effort to deter them, the law makes it a crime to stick into order forms and ads and on to notices on the business premises a void clause excluding or pretending to cut down those Sale of Goods Act rights we have mentioned.

NO REFUNDS	×	CREDIT NOTES ONLY ON REJECTED SALE GOODS	×	MONEY CANNOT BE REFUNDED ONCE GOODS REMOVED FROM PREMISES	×
NO RETURNS CAN BE ACCEPTED AFTER USE	×	NO WARRANTIES WHATSOEVER	×		

Sorry—look at clause 479 sub-clause 12!

But

NO EXCHANGES ON SALE GOODS

√ probably valid because, sale goods or normal stock goods, the customer can never compel an *exchange* although he may have right to the return of the price or damages—that's not an exchange!

and

BOUGHT AS SEEN

√ will probably be valid in an order form where the buyer has actually inspected the goods but it does not mean that he cannot rely on the Sale of Goods Act requirements that they are of merchantable quality and reasonably fit for their purpose.

Dear Mr Trader
Have you read the Consumer Transactions (Restrictions on Statements) Order 1976? I suggest you do so and remove the notice behind your till which falls foul of it. I also suggest you refund the £10.50 price I paid for the "Soir de Scunthorpe Toilet Water" which I purchased from you yesterday. My husband believes the name may describe its origins more accurately than was intended. I will return the bottle when in town tomorrow afternoon and expect my money in return. Should you not be prepared to let me have it, I will let you have it in the form of a county court summons.

I am reporting the offending notice to the Trading Standards Department of the council. I had a photograph taken of it this morning which will show you standing close by. The notice looks better than you but it still offends. I thought the photograph would be helpful in case somebody steals the notice between now and the arrival of the council's representative at your premises.

Yours faithfully

V. Sentoff

Violet Sentoff

These automatic guarantees about merchantable quality, fitness for the purpose and correspondence with description and sample don't apply when the duff goods were bought from a private individual—and that's one good reason to go to a dealer! Of course, if a private seller tells a pack of lies on which the buyer relies to his detriment, the court should be as quick to enter judgment against him as against a dealer. Apart from some mild sales puff, prudent private sellers keep their mouths shut. And tricky seller masquerading as untricky private sellers hope to persuade the complaining customer that he has as much hope of proving a breach of contract as being invited to a Buckingham Palace tea party.

"Don't you give me the Sale of Goods Act bit, sir. You tell citizens' advice, trading standards and your lawyer that they can stuff their consumer law manuals up their fully guaranteed and extended warranty drain pipes, mate. I ain't no business man, guvner. I'm just a private bloke selling a bit on the side. Oops!"

It isn't cricket for the masquerading trader to tell porkies after the contract—nor is it a crime. But the trader—full time, part time, tax paying, tax dodging, on the side, off the side—must come clean when he advertises and make it reasonably clear that he is a trader. This requirement does not apply to ads concerned with the sale of flowers, fruit or vegetables, eggs or dead animals, fish or birds which have been gutted, produced or taken by the advertiser. You know it makes sense!

Dear Mr Flashman

I've a few hours on my hands as I wait for motorway call-out to come, so I thought I'd drop you a line. I realise there's a limit to what I can expect for £750 but an engine which seizes up after twelve miles isn't much of a buy, is it? The car should have been of merchantable quality. It was not. Before you tell me you're a private seller and so no guarantees about the standard or condition of the car were implied, let me tell you something. My neighbour says you work at the garage in Lord Street and you're always advertising in The Argus which makes you a trade seller. If I have to, I'll take a look at some back numbers. The Sale of Goods Act does apply and you've broken the Business Advertisements (Disclosure) Order 1977 because you said nothing in the advertisement for my wreck about being in business. The wreck is coming back to you. The £750 is coming back to me and you can compensate me for my out of pocket expenses as well.

Yours faithfully

M. Heap.

Martin Heap

PS See you in the magistrates' court for the Business Advertisements prosecution.

ARGUMENT NO. 3: *"You can exclude liability if it's reasonable and this ain't reasonable"*

In many situations the exclusion clause must be fair and reasonable. The reasonableness test has to be satisfied when the customer is a private person or is a business which has not entered into the transaction in the course of that business (see under Argument 2). And it also has to be satisfied when the customer *is* a business and the transaction has to do with that business but the exclusion clause is in the other party's written standard terms which apply to the transaction.

It's for the party relying on the clause to prove its reasonableness. In practice, among the considerations will be—

- The strength of each side's bargaining position. For those who need to travel by train, for example, there's not much they can do if they don't like the look of BR's conditions of carriage. "Mr. Ticket Clerk, clause 13 is quite ridiculous. Get me your chairman on the phone immediately and hold the 12.05 stopping train to Waterloo, my good man!" Not a strong bargaining position.
- Whether the customer received an inducement to agree to the exclusion clause.
- Whether the customer had an opportunity of transacting with another business without the exclusion clause.
- Whether the customer knew or ought reasonably to have known of the existence and extent of the clause: previous dealings with the same business will be taken into account.

It will probably count against the business that the customer had little or no option to accept; that the business adopted a "take it or leave it" attitude; that the clause was in small print; that the clause was expressed in legal mumbo jumbo which would be over the head of most normal customers or that the clause was too wide, seeking to give the business an escape for much more than was really required. But against the customer will count the fact that he chose the deal with the clause because that was the cheaper option.

In a 1981 case the claimant took photos at his friend's wedding which he intended to give to the bride and bridegroom and then passed them to a chemist's to be forwarded to the film processors. On the side of the envelope into which the film had been placed was an exclusion clause which restricted the processors' negligence liability to having to refund the price of the film. In the event, only thirteen out of thirty six prints were returned. The processors failed to prove that the exclusion clause was reasonable and the claimant was awarded not just the cost of the film but £75 damages for distress and disappointment. It was common for processors to offer a two tier system under which the customer could pay more and not be saddled with the clause, but the claimant had not been given this option.

And again in 1981, BR lost a case having lost a case! They should have delivered the claimant's suitcase from Stockport to Haverfordwest but it was lost. Their exclusion clause which attempted to saddle the claimant with the job of showing they were to blame for the loss was held unreasonable.

How to avoid rent and service charges without really trying

Or when did you last see your landlord?

A landlord may be adept at extracting rent, service charges and insurance premiums payable under the tenancy agreement, but hopeless when it comes to turning up for a leaking roof and dangerous electric wiring inspection. The tenant will be at a disadvantage in litigation when he knows neither the landlord's address nor who the landlord is: the landlord who let to the tenant may have passed his interest on to someone else. By courtesy of Her Majesty the Queen and her Parliament, we present a brand new game devised for the residential tenant with an anonymous or reticent landlord. It's the Landlord and Tenant Act 1987 Game and it applies to rented homes which came on the market on the 1st February 1988. Until the landlord has done what the game requires of him, the tenant can refuse to pay over certain money which would otherwise be due and he would have a complete defence to court proceedings brought by the landlord because of non-payment.

Rules of the game

What does the landlord have to do? In every *written* demand for rent, service charges or any other sum payable under the tenancy, he must put in his name and address (even if the tenant already has them). If the address is in Scotland, Outer Mongolia or anywhere else other than in England and Wales, he must include an address in England and Wales at which he may be served by the tenant with notices, including court papers. And if the landlord won't play? Then any service charge included in the demand—note only *service* charge—is pretended to be not owing until the landlord has given the necessary information in writing. This is section 47 of the 1987 Act at work.

There's more under section 48. And this time the landlord who won't play comes a cropper over not just service charges but rent as well. The landlord must furnish his tenant with an address in England and Wales at which the tenant may serve him with notices, including court papers. The address need not necessarily be the landlord's own address: it could be that of his solicitors or managing agents. And the landlord is caught even though the tenancy agreement does not require a written demand in relation to a particular payment: rent, for example, is normally payable without prior demand by the landlord. Unless and until the notice is given, the tenant can keep his money to himself. Any landlord who has yet to comply would be well advised to go ahead and serve his notice now.

The requirements we have been looking at do not apply to councils and certain other authorities; to an "approved" landlord (the old "assured tenancy" landlord); to residences which are part of business premises, and to money which should be paid to a receiver or manager under court order. In the vast majority of cases the requirements apply be the accommodation a house or a flat or the tenancy long, short, fat or thin.

NOTICE TO TENANT under section 48 of the Landlord and Tenant Act 1987

In accordance with section 48 of the Landlord and Tenant Act 1987 and as your landlord of 15 Drainpipe Place, Maidstone, Kent, I Jim Malvern-Rachman hereby give you notice that the address at which notices (including notices in proceedings) may be served on me by you is "Malvern-Rachman House", Ardunby Street, Maidstone, Kent.

Dated the 14th day of July 1988

(Signed) J. Malvern-Rachman......

To Cherrie Brandy
15 Drainpipe Place
Maidstone Kent

HEALTH WARNING: Landlord is recommended to prepare two copies of the notice, to serve one and to retain one, which, ideally, should be receipted by the tenant.

Sue two

In its mission to ensure that the tenant can identify from one day to the next who happens to be his landlord, the 1987 Act makes the old landlord who has transferred his interest jointly responsible for the sins committed by the new landlord—committed, that is, right up until the time the tenant is given written notice about the new landlord. Useful for the tenant, and worrying for the old landlord. If he's got any sense, the old landlord will ensure the new landlord has given the tenant notice or will get on and give the notice himself. When sections 47 and 48 of the 1987 Act do not apply, these other provisions also do not apply.

Notice of assignment

TAKE NOTICE that by a transfer dated the 14th day of July 1988 made between myself of the one part and Harry Cement of the other part I Jim Malvern-Rachman of "Malvern-Rachman House", Ardunby Street, Maidstone, Kent transferred to the said Harry Cement my interest in 15 Drainpipe Place, Maidstone, Kent and that the last known address of the said Harry Cement is H M Prison, Romsey Road, Winchester, Hants. The rent and other monies payable under your tenancy should in future be made to the said Harry Cement.

Dated the 14th day of July 1988
(Signed) J. Malvern-Rachman....
To Cherrie Brandy
15 Drainpipe Place
Maidstone Kent

HEALTH WARNING: Landlord is recommended to prepare two copies of the notice, to serve one and to retain one which, ideally, should be receipted by the tenant.

The job interview

Questions

1. QUESTION ASKED: HAVE YOU EVER BEEN IN TROUBLE WITH THE POLICE?

Question in interviewer's mind

Have you been done for theft or indecent assault in which case our stamps and our Amanda in reception are in for some pinching (especially Amanda when bending down in that tight mini manufactured from denim with orange stitching and a zip to the side which I glanced at as I flew by this morning)?

Answer guidelines

The answer should depend on the sentence for the offence, how long ago the offender was convicted and the job applied for. The Rehabilitation of Offenders Act 1974 wipes out criminal convictions after periods of crime-free living: the more severe the sentence, the longer the period needed:

Sentence	*Wiping out period*
over 2½ years imprisonment, youth custody or detention in a young offenders institution	never
6 months—2½ years imprisonment, youth custody or detention in a young offenders institution	10 years
6 months or less imprisonment, youth custody or detention in a young offenders institution	7 years
borstal	7 years
6 months—2½ years detention	5 years
6 months or less detention	3 years
fine	5 years
absolute discharge	6 months
conditional discharge, bind over, probation order, care order, supervision order	1 year or life of discharge or order (if longer)
disqualification	life of disqualification

If the offender was under seventeen when convicted, the wiping out period is halved. And if the offender had another bash at crime, the wiping out period for the first offence is generally that period (for all but low class offences) extended till he gets forgiveness for the second offence. Provided the conviction is wiped out, the job applicant can place his hand on his heart, balance a religious article on his head and solemnly and sincerely declare that his record is as clean as his underpants. That's unless he is applying for one of certain specified jobs and has been told of his legal obligation to own up. The specified jobs include those of police officers, traffic wardens, local authority social workers and teachers and welfare workers dealing with the under eighteens.

2. QUESTION ASKED: DO YOU HAVE ANY HOBBIES?

Question in interviewer's mind

So Mr. Know-All, I suppose you reckon you'll take the job and then tell me you've been accepted as a magistrate and want one day off a fortnight?

Answer guidelines

It is essential that the applicant demonstrates a broadness of mind, an ability to switch off from the job and an energy by reference to some interest which is not work-orientated. But under no circumstances must he hint at a mission to perform good deeds. That's because the law usually entitles an employee to a reasonable amount of unpaid time off to perform certain public duties. How long does an employee have to be in his job before he qualifies? There's no minimum qualifying period of employment—someone in his job for five minutes and even part-timers working at least sixteen hours per week (or just eight hours per week provided they have been doing so for at least five years). And what of the public duties? Magistrate, councillor, maintained school governor and a tribunal, health authority or water authority member.

The particular business in which the employee works and the affect his absence will have on the business will be relevant as to what is reasonable. The employer cannot be forced to give the time off but refusal to do so may result in the employee dragging him to an industrial tribunal for a declaration that the complaint is well-founded and for compenstion for any loss suffered by the employee and his "insult or injury". It is dangerous for the employee to insist on time off until he has clocked up two years' continuous service: then he would be able to claim for unfair dismissal if the employer sacked him on account of his public spiritedness. Of course, an employer with eleven points on his driving licence might conceivably welcome a beak among the work force to put in a good word on the employer's next motoring offence appearance. The applicant could ask the employer to produce his driving documents at the start of the interview. There is also a statutory time off entitlement for trade union activities.

3. QUESTION ASKED: THERE'S NOTHING DOWN HERE ABOUT A REFERENCE, IS THERE?

Question in interviewer's mind

You're going to tell me that you had to leave because you exposed the general manager as a fraudulent drunk and it became too embarrassing for you to stay on and absolutely nobody in management will be prepared to say a good word about you so it is a waste of my time contacting them but that one of the secretaries you were friendly with would verify everything you have told me, aren't you?

Answer guidelines

The applicant should not tell the interviewer that he had to leave because he exposed the general manager as a fraudulent drunk and it became too embarrassing for him to stay on and absolutely nobody in management will bc prepared to say a good word about him so it is a waste of the interviewer's time contacting them but that one of the secretaries he was friendly with would verify everything he has told him—unless the general manager had defrauded his employers of not less than a £¼m and his alcohol capacity exceeded one litre of whisky a day, as the interviewer will have an inherent hostility towards sneaks. The law does not *compel* an employer or former employer to provide a reference and anyone who shows a false reference might be charged with obtaining or attempting to obtain the job by deception or with forgery or under the swinging Servants' Characters Act 1792. It is true that the employer or former employer who comes up with an incorrect reference may find himself sued for libel or slander by his employee or former employee (it would be necessary to show he had acted out of ill-will or spite or with some indirect or improper motive in his mind). And a new employer who relied on the reference to his detriment would probably obtain damages against the author for negligent misstatement: last year a High Court judge went as far as saying that the author would also be liable to the employee even though the referee did not libel him. But, generally, the employee's position reference-wise is weak and so, wherever possible, no job should be left without a glowing "to whom it may concern" reference in the employee's grubby hands and the provision of such a reference should always be made a condition of a termination of employment package. A suspicious interviewer may convince himself that the truth is more likely to be elicited by an off the record telephone chat with the former boss. This should be borne in mind by the applicant who is invited to confirm at which site the former boss is based and the best time of day to catch him.

4. QUESTION ASKED: I TAKE IT YOU WOULD NOT HAVE ANY OBJECTION TO A MEDICAL EXAMINATION?

Question in interviewer's mind

Are you suffering from AIDS?

Answer guidelines

No applicant can be legally forced to submit to a medical examination. And no prospective employer can be legally forced to take on an applicant! An applicant who is aware that he is suffering from a disease or other illness and dishonestly denies it to be so could be charged with obtaining his employment by deception. It has actually happened to a man suffering from a heart condition. But note the dishonesty requirement: his belief that he was within his legal rights to deny would extricate him from criminal liability. An employer who has been misled may be justified in dismissing when he discovers the truth.

And say an AIDS victim gets into a job without deception on his part? Can the employer dismiss when he finds out? Possibly yes if he is unable to perform the job for which he was engaged, and even if he can perform it quite adequately, the behaviour of other employees may entitle the employer to dismiss the AIDS victim. In a recent case an industrial tribunal was persuaded (though the parties later agreed that the decision could not stand on technical grounds) that a cinema projectionist had been fairly dismissed where his two colleagues refused to work with him. They feared AIDS contamination knowing him to be homosexual and following his conviction for insulting behaviour in a public toilet. And in a previous case, an employer was again vindicated for dismissing the employee because her colleagues were outraged by what they considered to be immoral conduct of her private life about which she spoke freely at work and they refused to work with her. It was an exceptional case, the employee was senior to two disapproving females and it was felt that the employer had been faced with the choice of dismissing her or dismissing the two other females.

If an applicant who was asked to submit to AIDS testing does not get the job, he may wish to satisfy himself that testing was sought for female as well as male applicants. Otherwise, he will probably be able to establish sex discrimination.

5. QUESTION ASKED: SO YOU LEFT SCHOOL IN 1955, WORKED AS AN AU PAIR FOR THREE YEARS AND THAT TAKES US UP TO 1960 . . .

Question in interviewer's mind

She'll cost us a bomb under this blasted new law if she can't add up and subtract.

Answer guidelines

The Wages Act 1986 got employers worried: garage forecourt managers have actually been crying into their pumps. For a start, an employer cannot now dock the wages of an employee because of cash or stock shortages unless the employee has agreed to it when he took the job or subsequently. And the agreement can only be for shortages happening after the agreement, not before. The till is short for five consecutive days and the employer then extracts an agreement by the employee to make up the shortage out of her wage packet. Unlawful: the agreement has come too late.

Almost all employees have this protection. There's

even greater protection for people in retail employment —that's anyone involved in carrying out transactions involving supply of goods or services to the public; other work colleagues; or other individuals in their personal capacities. Roundsmen and cashiers in shops, garages and works canteens will be included. Deductions from wages for shortages must not exceed 10% of the gross wage and the deductions must start within twelve months from when the employer discovered the shortage or when he ought reasonably to have discovered it, whichever is the earlier. So an employer who has his eyes closed may pay the price. The shortage can be made good by instalments from the wage packet: the first instalment must be deducted during the twelve months mentioned. An aggrieved employee could claim back money unlawfully deducted through an industrial tribunal or he may be able to sue the employer in the county court for breach of contract.

An employer cannot get round the legislation by agreeing to pay a wage of £200 per week provided there are no shortages but £150 per week if there are shortages. Nor by fining the employee for allowing the shortage to arise instead of making a deduction of up to 10% from his wage packet!

So the employer knows he risks frightening off an applicant at interview by seeking a deduction-from-wage-packet-agreement and if he does extract an agreement the business could be stuck with a slow and painful pay-back procedure should the applicant go on to bestow double change on every alternate customer. The applicant should attempt to impress the interviewer with his numeracy. "I have a GCE in maths, my hobbies are dominoes and counting, I love the *Stocks and Shares Show*, I've been in my current job for thirty-two months, five hours and sixteen seconds" etc.

Power to the attorney!

Hold up the 'plane—I'm just signing me power

There's one good reason why the taking of a holiday abroad and the loss of marbles may be contemplated without too much anxiety—the power of attorney. A person may authorise someone else of his choice to act for him and in his name and the authority is given in a deed called a power of attorney. It can be as wide or restrictive as is required. Under the power, documents may be signed, property may be bought and sold, money may be lent and borrowed. Virtually anything can be authorised to be done under it except for the making of a Will, the serving on a jury and the performance of various acts of a personal and intimate nature.

Double dealing

The extent of the authority given could depend on how far the person granting the power—the donor—trusts the person to whom it is being granted—the attorney. It may suit the donor to give wide powers but appoint not one but two attorneys so that they can spy on each other.

The power of attorney must be in the form of a deed and signed by the donor. It is desirable for it to be witnessed: an independent witness should be used and not the donor's spouse. The Powers of Attorney Act 1971 sets out a form of power which can be used and operates to grant the widest powers available. A different form should be used if the attorney's powers are to be limited or some special conditions are required. We have shown later on the form from the 1971 Act and another form which might be suitable and can be appropriately adapted.

"I am Lobby Lud's attorney and I claim his pools winnings"

Stamp duty is no longer payable on a power and there's no place at which it needs to be registered. The document is drawn up, signed and witnessed, dated—and that's that. It is produced to whoever needs to be satisfied that the attorney has the authority he claims and they will almost certainly want to keep a copy of it. The power will last for any stated period; otherwise it generally lasts until it is revoked by the donor or he becomes mentally incapable.

Joint owners watch out

If a couple own a property in their joint names they must usually appoint a third party as attorney to sign a deed relating to it; for example, a husband could not appoint his wife where they jointly owned. And the form set out in the 1971 Act would not be appropriate when the couple—or any person who is a trustee—were granting a power of attorney.

Marbles, loss of

There's also what is called an enduring power of attorney which hasn't been with us for long. It's an ordinary power of attorney and more. Whilst the donor remains mentally normal it operates as an ordinary power. But it has considerable value should normality cease, and then it does not expire as would an ordinary power of attorney. The enduring power obviates the formal procedure of applying to the Court of Protection for the appointment of a receiver to take over the patient's affairs. But the attorney under an enduring power must register it at the Court of Protection as soon as possible on having reason to believe that the donor has become or is becoming mentally incapable. There's a £30 registration fee which will usually come out of the donor's money, although the Court may postpone or waive payment in cases of hardship. It's when the registration application is made that the donor's relatives may swoop in and allege that the attorney is an unsuitable representative for the donor on account of the fact that he blindfolded her, tied her up and threatened her with a shotgun and an entire week's offerings of *Neighbours* (blindfold removed!) before she signed the enduring power of attorney. Notice of intention to apply for registration has to be given to the donor and prescribed relatives (extending to uncles and aunts); and objection may be taken on the grounds of fraud or undue pressure or unsuitability of the attorney having regard to all the circumstances and, in particular, his relationship or connection with the donor; invalidity of the power; or prematurity in that the donor is still sitting as a Member of Parliament or High Court judge and is not mentally incapable. The Court of Protection will settle the objection or any dispute.

"But the book said you would supply up to twelve enduring powers—free!"

An enduring power *must* be in a prescribed form (prints available from law stationers), unlike an ordinary power and part of it must be completed by the attorney, again unlike an ordinary power. Provided the donor understood its nature and effect, an enduring power would still be valid though the donor was incapable of managing his property and affairs when he made it.

Any person may search at the Court of Protection to see whether an enduring power has been registered (search fee is £5) and will be supplied with a copy if he can satisfy the Court that he has good reason for requesting one and that it is not reasonably practicable for him to obtain one from the attorney. Contact may be made with the Court of Protection, Staffordshire House, 25 Store Street, London WC1E 7BP for a leaflet on the Enduring Powers of Attorney Act 1985—you guessed right, it deals with enduring powers of attorney —and for forms of notice of intention to register, application for registration and application for search. The Court will not supply prints of the prescribed form of enduring power of attorney.

STANDARD POWER OF ATTORNEY—WIDE POWERS, SHORT AND SIMPLE

THIS GENERAL POWER OF ATTORNEY is made this 14th day of July 1988 by FRANK TRUSTING of 33 St Valerie Road Gosport Hampshire
I appoint ROBIN GOODFELLOW of 2 Chorley Grove Bournemouth Dorset (and MEL PRACTICE of 38 Coke Road Bristol Avon jointly) to be my attorney(s) in accordance with section 10 of the Powers of Attorney Act 1971
IN WITNESS whereof I have hereunto placed my hand

```
and seal the day and year first before written
SIGNED SEALED AND DELIVERED )
by the said FRANK TRUSTING  )
in the presence of:         )
```

Frank Trusting

Millie Combes
147 Abbeywood Drive
Catisfield
Housewife.

Health warnings

- This gives wide powers.
- You can have just one attorney in which case omit the details in the brackets
- If you have two attorneys, you may want them to both do what is required (for example, both sign deeds in your name). The wording in our form will cover this. If, however, you are appointing two attorneys but remain happy for either of them to do what is required, you should substitute "jointly and severally" for "jointly".
- You can buy a red wafer seal from a stationer, or artists can draw in (LS). It is desirable to have your signature witnessed by one person.
- Enjoy your holiday and do not soak up too much sun too quickly, especially if you are fair skinned.

POWER OF ATTORNEY—TO BUY AND SELL HOME

```
THIS POWER OF ATTORNEY is made this 14th day of
July 1988 by FRANK TRUSTING of 33 St Valerie Road
Gosport Hampshire
1. I appoint ROBIN GOODFELLOW of 2 Chorley Grove
Bournemouth Dorset (and MEL PRACTICE of 38 Coke
Road Bristol Avon jointly) for the period of nine
months from the date of this deed to be my
attorney(s) and in my name on my behalf and as my
act and deed or otherwise to do all or any of the
following things -
(a) To sell my property 33 St Valerie Road
    Gosport Hampshire ("the property") by private
    treaty for a gross price of not less than
    £100,000
```

(b) To sell the fittings carpets and curtains at the property or any of them for any price or to include them or any of them in the said price for the property
(c) To buy any freehold land or any leasehold land having an unexpired term of not less than sixty years by private treaty or auction for such consideration and subject to such covenants restrictions and other matters as he (they) shall think fit
(d) To borrow money upon such terms as he (they) shall think fit in connection with the purposes set out herein including mortgaging or charging the land referred to in clause (c)
(e) To execute in my name and on my behalf any conveyance assignment assurance lease mortgage charge grant or other deed and any contract or other document in connection with the purposes set out herein
(f) To engage and pay such estate agents brokers solicitors or other persons or agents as he (they) shall think fit in connection with the purposes set out herein on such terms as to remuneration and otherwise as he (they) shall think fit.
(g) To withdraw money whether now standing or hereafter to be credited to my current account numbered 1212456 with the Smile Save Bank plc High Street Catisfield Hampshire in connection with the purposes set out herein provided that the said bank shall not be concerned as to the application of any money so withdrawn.
(h) To effect or cause to be effected on my behalf such insurance against such risks or liabilities as he (they) shall think fit on the land referred to in clause (c) and to pay all premiums and other monies which shall be payable in respect thereof.
(i) To do any other act matter or thing which he (they) shall consider to be necessary or expedient for carrying out any of the purposes set out herein and as fully and effectually in all respects as I myself could do.

2. I hereby undertake with my attorney(s) at all times to ratify and confirm each and every act done by my attorney(s) in under or by virtue of this deed

```
SIGNED SEALED AND DELIVERED)  Frank
by the said FRANK TRUSTING )  Trusting
in the presence of:        )
```

Willie Combes
147 Abbeywood Drive
Catisfield
Housewife

Health warnings

- Don't forget those exquisite red wafers or your own artistry (see page 186) and one witness.
- Remember that if your home is in joint names, both you and the co-owner will need to sign legal documentation. Will your co-owner be available to sign? If not, a power of attorney will be needed for her too (and see page 183 for an alternative power of attorney where a property is jointly owned).
- Please see *Joint owners watch out* (page 183).
- What the attorney can do may be increased or reduced but it is vital to ensure that he has the minimum authority to achieve what you want. At the very least, a solicitor should cast his eye over a power of attorney which you draw up for some particular purpose, like this one.
- If you appoint two attorneys and you are happy for either of them to do what is required, you should substitute "jointly and severally" for "jointly" towards the start of clause 1.
- The life of the power does not necessarily have to be nine months: it can be whatever period you wish or unlimited in time.

Power to the attorney!

THE JOINT HOME-OWNER POWER OF ATTORNEY

THIS POWER OF ATTORNEY is made this 14th day of July 1988 by FRANK TRUSTING of 33 St Valerie Road Gosport Hampshire ("Mr Trusting")

BACKGROUND:

(1) Mr Trusting and Heather Trusting hold 33 St Valerie Road Gosport Hampshire ("the property") on trust for sale

(2) Mr Trusting is desirous of appointing ROBIN GOODFELLOW of 2 Chorley Grove Bournemouth Dorset ("Mr Goodfellow") to be his attorney

NOW THIS DEED WITNESSES as follows:-

1. In exercise of the power conferred by section 25 of the Trustee Act 1925 as amended and of all other powers Mr Trusting hereby delegates to Mr Goodfellow for the period of six months from the date of this deed the execution of the trusts powers and discretions in the property including all trusts and powers implied or conferred by statute in relation to the property

2. Mr Trusting hereby appoints Mr Goodfellow to be his attorney and on his behalf and in his name or in the name of Mr Goodfellow where the law otherwise requires to execute all deeds and instruments and sign all other documents and do all other things which in the opinion of Mr Goodfellow shall be required to be executed signed and done in or about the execution of the said trusts powers and discretions whether statutory or otherwise

3. Mr Trusting hereby undertakes at all times to ratify and confirm each and every act done by Mr Goodfellow as his attorney in under or by virtue of this deed

SIGNED SEALED AND DELIVERED)
by the said FRANK TRUSTING) Frank Trusting
in the presence of:)

Millie Combes
147 Abbeywood Drive
Catisfield
Housewife.

Health warnings

- Don't forget the seal!
- See Joint owners watch out, page 183.

Enduring Power of Attorney

Part A: About using this form

1. **You may choose one attorney or more than one.** If you choose more than one, you must decide whether they are to be able to act:

   - Jointly (that is, they must all act together and cannot act separately) or
   - Jointly and severally (that is, they can all act together but they can also act separately if they wish).

   On the form, at the place marked **1**, show what you have decided by crossing out one of the alternatives.

2. **If you give your attorney(s) general power** in relation to all your property and affairs, it means that they will be able to deal with your money or property and may be able to sell your house.

3. **If you don't want your attorney(s) to have such wide powers,** you can include any restrictions you like. For example, you can include a restriction that your attorney(s) must not act on your behalf until they have reason to believe that you are becoming mentally incapable; or a restriction that your attorney(s) may not sell your house. Any restrictions you choose must be written or typed on the form in the place marked **2.**

4. **Unless you put in a restriction preventing it** your attorney(s) will be able to use any of your money or property to benefit themselves or other people by doing what you yourself might be expected to do to provide for their needs. Your attorney(s) will also be able to use your money to make gifts, but only for reasonable amounts in relation to the value of your money and property.

5. **Your attorney(s) can recover the out-of pocket expenses** of acting as your attorney(s). If your attorney(s) are professional people, for example solicitors or accountants, they may be able to charge for their professional services as well.

6. **If your attorney(s) have reason in the future to believe** that you have become or are becoming mentally incapable of managing your affairs, your attorney(s) will have to apply to the Court of Protection for registration of this power.

7. **Before applying to the Court of Protection for registration** of this power, your attorney(s) must give written notice that that is what they are going to do, to you and your nearest relatives as defined in the Enduring Powers of Attorney Act 1985. You or your relatives will be able to object if you or they disagree with registration.

8. **This is a simplified explanation** of what the Enduring Powers of Attorney Act 1985 and the Rules and Regulations say. If you need more guidance, you or your advisers will need to look at the Act itself and the Rules and Regulations. The Rules are the Court of Protection (Enduring Powers of Attorney) Rules 1986 (Statutory Instrument 1986 No 127). The Regulations are the Enduring Powers of Attorney (Prescribed Form) Regulations 1987 (Statutory Instrument 1987 No 1612).

9. **Note to Attorney(s)**
   After the power has been registered the attorney(s) should notify the Court of Protection if the donor dies or recovers.

You can cancel this power at any time before it has to be registered

Form F1702 November 1987

Part B: To be completed by the 'donor' (the person appointing the attorney(s))

Don't sign this form unless you understand what it means

Please read the notes in the margin	
Donor's name and address	I FRANK TRUSTING
	of 33 St. Valerie Road Gosport Hampshire
Donor's date of birth	born on 3rd June 1931
Attorney(s) name(s) and address(es)	appoint ROBIN GOODFELLOW
See note 1 on the front of this form. If you are appointing only one attorney you should cross out everything between the square brackets	of 2 Chantry Grove Bournemouth Dorset
	• [~~and~~
	~~of~~
Cross out the one which does not apply (see note 1 on the front of this form)	1. • ~~jointly~~ • ~~jointly and severally]~~
	to be my attorney(s) for the purpose of the Enduring Powers of Attorney Act 1985
Cross out the one which does not apply (see note 2 on the front of this form)	• with general authority to act on my behalf • ~~with authority to do the following on my behalf:~~
If you don't want the attorney(s) to have general power, you must give details here of what authority you are giving the attorney(s)	
	in relation to
Cross out the one which does not apply	• all my property and affairs • ~~the following property and affairs:~~

Part B: continued

Please read the notes in the margin

If there are restrictions or conditions, insert them here; if not, cross out these words (See note 3 on the front of this form)

2 ● subject to the following restrictions and conditions:
the said Robin Goodfellow shall not be entitled to act as my attorney hereunder until he has reason to believe that I am becoming mentally incapable of managing my own affairs the said Robin Goodfellow shall not be entitled to dispose of any of my property by way of gift except with my prior consent

I intend that this power shall continue even if I become mentally incapable.

I have read or have had read to me the notes in Part A which are part of, and explain, this form.

Your signature

Signed, sealed and delivered by me Frank Trusting (L.S.)

Date

on 14th July 1988

Someone must witness your signature

Signature of witness

In the presence of N. Parker

Your attorney(s) cannot be your witness. If you are married it is not advisable for your husband or wife to be your witness

Full name of witness Nosie Parker

Address of witness 29 Woodbine Park
Catisfield
Hants
Civil Servant

Part C: To be completed by the attorney(s))

Note ● This form may be adapted to provide for sealing by a corporation with its common seal

● If there are more than two attorneys attach an additional **Part C**

Don't sign this form before the donor has signed Part B

I understand that I have a duty to apply to the Court for the registration of this form under the Enduring Powers of Attorney Act 1985 when the donor is becoming or has become mentally incapable.

I also understand my limited power to use the donor's property to benefit persons other than the donor.

I am not a minor

Signature of attorney — Signed, sealed and delivered by me Frank Trusting (L.S.)

Date — on 14th July 1988

Signature of witness — in the presence of N. Parker

Full name of witness Nosie Parker

Address of witness 29 Woodbine Park

Catisfield, Hants

Civil Servant

Each attorney must sign the form and each signature must be witnessed. The donor may not be the witness and one attorney may not witness the signature of the other

---

To be completed only if there is a second attorney

I understand that I have a duty to apply to the Court for the registration of this form under the Enduring Powers of Attorney Act 1985 when the donor is becoming or has become mentally incapable.

I also understand my limited power to use the donor's property to benefit persons other than the donor.

I am not a minor

Signature of attorney — Signed, sealed and delivered by me ______ (L.S.)

Date — on ______

Signature of witness — in the presence of ______

Full name of witness ______

Address of witness ______

______

______

Each attorney must sign the form and each signature must be witnessed. The donor may not be the witness and one attorney may not witness the signature of the other

Stamping on duty

Expensive pelmets

It is the purchaser of a house or flat who pays stamp duty on the price—where the price is over £30,000, that is. Once £30,000 is exceeded, duty is payable on the lot and at the rate of one per cent. Price = £55,000. Duty = £550. Often the property price includes fittings like carpets, curtains and blinds and items like the fridge or furniture. They do not attract stamp duty and so by splitting in the contract the price for the property and fixtures from the price for the fittings and other bits and pieces, stamp duty can be saved. It might even be avoided. Total price £32,000. Property price = £30,000. Furniture price = £2,000. No duty. But anyone after a high mortgage, watch it! It's unlikely that the lender will take the fittings and other bits and pieces into account in putting a value on the property. The 100 per cent mortgage seeker paying that £32,000 would only obtain a £30,000 loan based on the property price.

Backfire

Thinks: "I'll inflate the value of the fittings and bits and pieces, reduce the value of the property and save a nice few bob." Not a good idea. To start with, that would be criminal and, in theory at least, the seller and buyer could be charged with conspiring to defraud the Inland Revenue of the duty. And if the buyer had to sue the seller for damages for misrepresentation or breach of contract, the court might decline to help him though he had a valid claim because the transaction was tainted with illegality over the duty. In a 1987 case which went to the Court of Appeal, a couple who had a valid claim over the seller's misrepresentation that the roof terrace was part of the London flat he was selling when, in fact, it was not, almost lost the case in view of their fraudulent evasion of £300 stamp duty by inflating the price of chattels they had bought.

So long as the price for everything apart from the property and fixtures is a reasonable one, there is seldom any reason why the seller should object to the split for which the buyer asks.

Joint point

For joint homeowners

When two (or more) people own a freehold or leasehold house or flat they do so as joint tenants or tenants in common. The deed by which it was transferred to them will usually make it clear—to their lawyers if nobody else!—which basis of ownership applies. If they are joint tenants and one of them dies during ownership, his interest automatically passes to the survivor even though by his will he had purported to leave it to somebody else. But if they are tenants in common, this does not happen: each is free to will their interest to the other, to someone else, to the other but to someone else should the other die first, to someone else but with the other being allowed to stay put so long as he wishes to do so, to Maharashi Mahesh Yogi or to you.

Joint tenants can become tenants in common in a relatively painless way. The owner who wants to change the basis of ownership needs to prepare a statement to this effect called a notice of severance, ensure that the co-owner receives a copy—should the co-owners be married it is permissible for this to be handed over in the matrimonial bed—and to put the statement with the deeds. Where the property is registered, the joint owners or one of them should apply to the Land Registry to take account of the new basis of ownership by registration of a restriction; the Land Certificate should accompany the application if possible, although the application can proceed without it. The Land Registry fee is £25:

Notice of severance

```
To Minnie Mouse, Cheese Cottage, High Street,
Titchfield, Hants
   I hereby give you notice of my desire to
sever the joint tenancy in equity of and in
Cheese Cottage, High Street, Titchfield now held
by us as joint tenants at law and in equity.
Dated the 14th July 1988
(Signed) ...C...Mouse... (Charles Mouse)
```

Health warning: Minnie Mouse should be asked to sign one copy of the notice which Charles Mouse should take back as proof she has received the notice. Her signature under the words "I hereby acknowledge having on the 15th July 1988 received the notice of which this is a true copy" would be ideal.

With these shears I do assign

Notice to the Swinging Gardener

Christmas, birthdays, engagements and weddings are times for clearing the attic. The cherry stoner, purple dinner service, automatic mushroom peeler, yellow and orange set of bedding may be dusted off, placed in a fresh-looking Fortnum & Mason's carrier bag and gifted "with all my love and earnest wishes for much happiness". Such articles have probably come into the attic as unwelcome gifts to the donor and so there is little legal comfort for the donee should the articles fall to pieces when an attempt is made to put them to some practical use.

Very occasionally, a gift will actually be *purchased* by the donor from a retail outlet and given direct to the donee! Really! There's a legal problem attached to this. The contract for the purchase is made between the donor and the retailer, which means that the donee is not a party to the contract and so has no legal right to return the article to the retailer or to claim damages if it was under legal standard. Of course, the retailer may be quite willing to do the proper thing but if he is not, the donee is faced with the embarrassment of asking the donor to do a bit of litigating for him or passing on the article to some other sucker when he has to acknowledge Christmas, a birthday, engagement or wedding.

Why not an assignment by the donor of his rights when he gives the article? That ought to be legally effective and enable the donee to sue the retailer (or press his claim without suing if the retailer is simply refusing to talk to him on the ground that he has no legal standing) in his own name. The retailer should be notified of the assignment.

Assignment

To Auntie Vera Mavison
A Happy Xmas and All the Best for '89.
Please accept the enclosed gift of a pair of shears purchased from the Swinging Gardener, Southsea on the 1st December 1988. As a supplemental gift, I hereby assign to you the benefit of all my rights and remedies under the contract for sale and purchase of the shears and in particular my rights and remedies under the Sale of Goods Act 1979.
Love
Nephew Stephen
XXX
PS I attach copy of the notice of assignment which I have given to the sellers. Keep it in a safe place

Notice of assignment

To The Swinging Gardener
Green Road
Southsea
TAKE NOTICE that by an assignment in writing dated the 20th December 1988 I assigned to Vera Mavison of 32 Victoria Gardens Southsea the benefit of all my rights and remedies under the

contract for the sale by your firm and purchase by me on the 1st December 1988 of a pair of shears at the price of £23 (inclusive of VAT) and in particular my rights and remedies under the Sale of Goods Act 1979.

Dated the 20th December 1988.

Signed ....S. Gold........ (Stephen Gold)

16 Mill Road

Hayling Island   Hants

Insolvent abuse

Here today, there tomorrow

The great appeal of a limited company for anyone wanting to run a business is that, as a general rule, if the company collapses, they do not collapse with it be they director, secretary or purveyor of massage services to the chairman during the luncheon break. They walk away and start up somewhere else. We do not forget that a director cannot for five years start up or be concerned with a new company which has the same or similar name. *Flash Harry Glazing Co. Ltd.* won't be allowed five minutes after *Flash Harry Double Glazing Co. Ltd.* has gone into liquidation owing £2m and with three hundred customers still awaiting delivery of their paid-for windows. And we do not forget that an unscrupulous director may be disqualified from having anything to do with another company for between two and fifteen years after he has been grassed on by the liquidator or official receiver in a report to the Secretary of State for Trade and Industry. Nevertheless, in the vast majority of cases there is a walking-away-and-starting-up-again with a vengeance, and the creditors are left to whistle (and if featured in *That's Life*! it will probably be in harmony with a dog).

Company directors personally vulnerable

But the court can order a director of a company which has been trading fraudulently to dip into his own pocket and produce something of a blue and crinkly kind to go towards the company's debts. Fraud is difficult to prove.

There's more hope for the unpaid creditor in provisions which originally came into force on April 28 1986 (applying to insolvencies on or after that date) and are now contained in the Insolvency Act 1986. To take advantage of the provisions, the creditor needs a company which has gone into liquidation because of insolvency. Then he needs a liquidator who reads his letters and reckons it can be proved in court that one or more of the directors knew before the winding-up commenced that there was no reasonable prospect the company would avoid going into liquidation but that trading continued. The liquidator can apply to the court to order the culpable directors to dip into their own pockets. The court will not make an order if it considers the director concerned took every step he ought to have taken with a view to minimising the potential loss to creditors. *Every* step, please note—trying to borrow, selling assets which wouldn't put the company out of business, getting rid of the chairman's masseuse and the rest. The director's conduct will be judged on the basis of what a reasonably diligent person would have done having the general knowledge, skill and experience that might reasonably have been expected of a person carrying out the director's job *and* the general knowledge, skill and experience which the particular director *did* possess. So it's hard luck on crackpots, half wits, dreamers and the really switched on.

Insolvent abuse

Dear Mr Director,

On the 14th July I ordered from your company the supply and installation of double glazing throughout my property at the price of £3,000 (inclusive of VAT) and I have paid all but £100 of the price, your surveyor having informed me that this would give me priority in your installation diary. My order form number is 2468U-A-MUG. I subsequently telephoned your offices on twelve hundred and forty-two occasions to enquire when I could expect installation. Among the excuses for non-installation were that your fitter had been wrongly arrested by the metropolitan police, the order was lost in the system and you were awaiting the delivery of a new wonder sealant which had been secretly invented and so I was not to mention it to anyone (and, in particular, to "That's Life" if they contacted me which you did not think they would do and anyway you had never heard of Esther Rantzen). On my final call you asked if I was interested in having my roof re-tiled at a discount price.

Mr A. Scrooge who has been appointed as your company's liquidator informs me that the liabilities are such that I have no prospect of recovering any part of the £2,900 with which I have parted. However, I believe that there are grounds for an order being made by the court under section 214 of the Insolvency Act 1986 for you to contribute towards the company's assets on the ground of wrongful trading by you prior to the commencement of the winding-up. Therefore, I claim the £2,900 from you personally and, in default of settlement within seven days of the date of this letter, it is my intention to make representations to the liquidator to apply to the court for a section 214 order. If you settle with me I am prepared to keep our settlement confidential. Strictly without prejudice, I am also prepared to consider any instalment or other proposals for settlement you may wish to put forward.

Yours faithfully

A.F. Creditor

A Friendly Creditor

P.S. I wish you well with your new venture.

Mouldy covenants

Getting rid of them

The purchaser with intent and so as to bind the property hereby conveyed into whosoever hands the same may come and so as to benefit the retained land of the vendor hereby covenants with the vendor that he the purchaser and his successors in title will at all times hereafter observe and perform the restrictions and stipulations set out in the schedule hereto.

THE SCHEDULE ABOVE REFERRED TO

1. Not to use any building erected on the said property for any purpose other than as a private dwellinghouse in the occupation of one family
2. Not to carry on any trade or business in any building erected on the said property
3. Not to alter the external plan or elevation of the building now erected on the said property or to construct any other building on the said property without the written consent of the vendor or his successors in title and to pay the costs of the vendor or his successors in title and his or their surveyor in considering any application for consent whether or not such consent shall be granted
4. To maintain the fences on the boundaries of the said property marked inwards with a "T" on the said plan
5. To pay a fair proportion according to use of the cost of keeping in repair the common driveway coloured brown on the said plan
6. Not to obstruct or cause to be obstructed the said common driveway.

The deeds to most freehold properties are littered with covenants like this. Tough on an owner who one hundred years on would like to turn his house into a betting shop, stick up a block of flats in his two acres back garden or tell his neighbour to "get lost" when he demands that he reinstate the wall at the side which was brought down by The Hurricane. Tough but not fatal. He must play the Mouldy Covenant Game.

Can the covenant be ignored?

Some covenants, possibly so. These are positive covenants, covenants to do something—repair a fence or not allow a fence to fall into disrepair, which amounts to the same thing—where the covenants were given by a former owner but not by the present owner personally. Positive as opposed to negative covenants —not to use the property for a business is an example of a negative covenant. One point to be watched on positive covenants before deciding to ignore them—if the present owner and everyone else who has owned the property since the covenant was given by the original purchaser has promised to obey the covenant, the owner of the property who would benefit from the covenant could sue the original purchaser for damages (exhumation for the purpose of serving court papers is positively prohibited) and the original purchaser could get his money back from his purchaser and his purchaser could get his money back from his purchaser and his purchaser could get his money from his purchaser and his purchaser could . . . So, you see, not too much to worry about with old positive covenants. Incidentally, when there's a lease—even one for 999 years—different rules apply: positive covenants can be enforced against the current lessee direct.

Ignoring the negative covenants—and they are the more needling—is dicier. The present owner won't get locked up if he ignores: he may find that if the neighbouring property owner in whose favour the covenant was given years ago is no longer around and he is on good terms with the other residents who may have the benefit of the covenant in their deeds, he will hear nothing more about it. Damned inconvenient, though, to be served with a temporary injunction when the footings are already in; and whilst he may have been prepared to take a chance, the purchaser from him of the house or one of the flats he may be developing—and the purchaser's mortgagee—won't!

Creeping

The would-be developer finds the person in whose favour the covenant was originally given or, if that person has sold on, the present owner of the property and any other neighbours whose deeds entitle them to enforce the covenant, and he tries to do a deal. It is open to whoever has the benefit of the covenant to effectively discharge or modify it by deed. "Now look here, chaps, times have changed and we want to attract fresh blood to the neighbourhood—and, if you ask me, a bit of fresh female flesh wouldn't come amiss, what! I'll put up these flats, shouldn't take longer than a couple of months: builders I am using do a lot of church work, you won't know they're around. About time they brought back Botham, eh? Could you sign here, chaps. Jack, you first. Fill up Jack's glass, will you Mary?"

Insurance

"Mary, I always said that Jack was a b . . . . He must have got through two bottles of my vintage champagne." It may well be possible to insure against the risk of the covenant to be breached being successfully enforced; the premium will range from a few hundred pounds to a few thousand pounds depending on such factors as the degree of risk and the amount to be insured. Often, the premium will be .25% of the amount insured and the leading insurers in the field are the Sun Alliance, Norwich Union, Eagle Star and Commercial Union. The benefit of the insurance policy will pass on automatically to all subsequent owners.

The Lands Tribunal

If a willing insurer cannot be found, or the premium quoted is punitive, consideration should be given to an application to the Lands Tribunal to discharge or modify a *restrictive* covenant under section 84 of the Law of Property Act 1925. The application may be made by the freeholder or a lessee under a lease originally granted for more than forty years where there are at least another twenty five years to go. The Lands Tribunal can oblige if, for example, the covenant is obsolete because of changes in the character of the property or the neighbourhood, or simply on the ground that the person entitled to the benefit of the covenant would not be injured by its discharge or modification. Compensation in that person's favour can be awarded. Fewer than one hundred people a year go to the Lands Tribunal for discharge or modification of a restrictive covenant but the success rate is high for those who do. About three quarters are legally represented. There's a £90 application fee and a further £155 fee for any hearing and the drawing up of the Tribunal's order. The Tribunal gets as close to the property as possible: not on the pavement outside but, if possible, to the nearest court or town hall which can be hired. It might welcome a bit more business. The Tribunal is to be found at 48-49 Chancery Lane, London WC2A 1JR (telephone 01–936 7200). Please don't mention our name.

Who keeps the housekeeping?

The proceeds of thrift

```
Date:  14th July 1988
   We Joe Thrift and Mavis Thrift of 2 Caution
Cottages Tightely, Hants hereby agree that the
money saved by Mavis Thrift from any allowance
made to her by Joe Thrift for the expenses of the
matrimonial home or similar purposes and any
property purchased by Mavis Thrift out of such
allowance shall belong to us as to three quarters
for Joe Thrift and one quarter for Mavis Thrift.
Signed ..J..Thrift........... (Joe Thrift)
Signed .M...Thrift.......... (Mavis Thrift)
```

Any money which the wife saves from her housekeeping allowance along with property she may buy with that money belongs to the wife and husband *equally*. That's the general rule—section 1 of the Married Women's Property Act 1964 says so, and the same general rule applies to engaged couples who are living together. But the general rule can be displaced by some other agreement which the couple may make. There's nothing to stop the couple signing a document along the lines of the one we have devised and putting in whatever sharing arrangement they settle on. That should eliminate the risk of either alleging a sharing other than that specified and it will well cater for the wishes of the man who is after more than the one-half which the 1964 Act would give him. Still, the woman ought to have some reward for her economical management or she'll have little incentive to shop around for the broken biscuits and smoked salmon off-cuts.

Before the man rushes into proferring a sharing agreement to the woman for signature he should first consider whether he might be better off keeping quiet, allowing her to accumulate a fortune in a surreptitious account and then swooping in for his one half!

Any dispute between husband and wife or formerly engaged cohabitees over the housekeeping or property bought with it can be dealt with by the county court under section 17 of the Married Women's Property Act 1882 and the engaged couple have three years from the termination of the engagement to bring proceedings under the swinging 1882 Act. If it's a husband and wife and they are divorcing or judicially separating, a housekeeping allowance fiddle can be taken into account by the court when it deals with the overall carve-up.

Wot-a-load-o-rubbish!

Getting rid of it

Refuse collector hasn't called for two months or won't take away the refuse because the house occupier insists on leaving his dustbin at the bottom of the garden and the garden is long and Groucho the lovable pet Alsatian who likes leg flesh has a habit of lurking in the bin's vicinity. In the good old days the neglected occupier could serve notice on the local authority requiring his house refuse to be removed. If the cabbage and left over curry meals still continued to spill out he could go off to the magistrates' court and recover a penalty of twenty five pence a day from the authority. That remedy was murdered on June 6 1988 when a new rubbish—sorry, waste—regime contained in the Control of Pollution Act 1974 was, somewhat belatedly, brought into force.

Reincarnation?

It is possible that an aggrieved occupier could claim damages from the non-collecting collection authority for breach of statutory duty under the 1974 Act. The point would have to be tested. We suggest there is an evens chance of success. Provided the damages claim was limited to £500, the county court would have power to deal with the claim under the small claims arbitration procedure where the claimant with a reasonably arguable case ought to escape an order for costs against him if he loses. But the authority might well ask for the open court procedure to apply with judge, paraphernalia and the usual loser-pays-winner's-costs rule applying on the ground that the claim involves a difficult question of law. Such a request would be made to the county court registrar who normally acts as the arbitrator. It should be countered this way:

> Sir,
>
> I am quite confident that you could more than adequately deal with the law involved yourself. However, if you came to the conclusion that there was some merit in the authority's request, I would ask you to direct that the arbitration be by a judge before whom the same practice and procedure would apply as if the arbitration was by you. The case can continue to be a "small claim". It would not have to lose its "small claim" status. I understand you have power to direct arbitration by a judge under rule 2(3) of Order 19 of the County Court Rules 1981.

And here is how the claim is made:

<u>IN THE MUCKLEAVE COUNTY COURT</u> <u>Case No 88/6148</u>
<u>BETWEEN</u>

SUE ERR <u>Plaintiff</u>

\- and -

MUCKLEAVE DISTRICT COUNCIL <u>Defendants</u>

<u>PARTICULARS OF CLAIM</u>

1. At all material times -
   (a) The Plaintiff has been occupier of the dwellinghouse known as "Sweet Violets", Aroma Lane, Muckleave ("the property") and
   (b) the Defendants have been under a duty imposed by section 12 of the Control of Pollution Act 1974 to arrange for the collection of household waste from the property ("the duty").

2. Between on or about the 1st day of June 1988 and the 31st day of July 1988 and in breach of the duty, the Defendants neglected or refused to arrange for the collection of household waste from the property. Notwithstanding persistent demands during the said period by the Plaintiff to the Defendants both orally and in writing to arrange for the collection of household waste from the property no such waste was collected.

3. By reason of the matters aforesaid, the Plaintiff has suffered annoyance, discomfort, inconvenience, loss and damage.

<u>Particulars of annoyance, discomfort and inconvenience</u>

Over the said period a huge quantity of household waste accumulated at the property such waste having been generated by the Plaintiff and her seven children all of whom resided at the property. The stench from such accumulation became progressively worse; the property was shunned and avoided by roundsmen and post and newspaper delivery persons; and rats and mice were attracted to the property.

<u>Particulars of loss and damage</u>

	£
Cost of postages and telephone calls in respect of communications by the Plaintiff to the Defendants	5.00
Cost of private collection of refuse and deposit at Defendants' public tip (inc.VAT)	23.00
Fresh air sprays	13.00
	41.00

And the Plaintiff claims:-

(1) Damages limited to £300;

(2) Such interest as shall be just pursuant to the provisions of section 69 of the County Courts Act 1984; and

(3) Costs

Dated this 15th day of August 1988

(Signed) Sue Err.............

Sue Err of "Sweet Violets", Aroma Lane,Muckleave who at this address will accept service of all pleadings and documents on her own behalf. Plaintiff.

To: The Registrar and

To: The above named Defendants

As an alternative or addition to suing, the aggrieved occupier can make a complaint to the Department of the Environment. The Secretary of State there can get heavy with the collection authority.

Rubbish notice

An authority is empowered to serve notice on an occupier requiring him to place waste for collection "in receptacles which are of a kind and number reasonably specified in the notice". And here's the rub. The notice may make provision for "the placing of the receptacles on premises for the purpose of facilitating the emptying of them and access to the receptacles for that purpose." Stick your dustbin one metre from the front gate or you've 'ad it, mate!

Rubbish appeal

There's no prescribed form of notice; it could be typed out on to a bin liner. The notice can be appealed against, though, to the local magistrates' court on the ground that—

- any requirement specified in the notice is unreasonable or
- the receptacles already available are adequate.

The time for appealing is twenty-one days from getting the notice, or, where appropriate, from any date specified in it for the occupier to enter into an agreement to pay for further receptacles to be provided. The notice is then frozen pending the appeal being dealt with. Failure to comply with the notice is an offence which attracts a maximum fine of £400.

Money for old rubbish

What is this household waste which must be collected, usually free of charge? Basically it is waste from a private dwelling (including a garage or store used *wholly* in connection with the dwelling), but that doesn't mean the occupier can insist on the free collection of a tank from his garage and a tree from his back garden. The authority can make a charge—only a reasonable one—for the collection of, (amongst others)—

- any article exceeding 25 kilogrammes in weight;
- any article which cannot be fitted into a dustbin provided by the authority;
- garden waste;
- dead domestic pets.

Love is the sweetest thing, but . . .

Promises, promises

Since they abolished breach of promise of marriage actions Mr. & Miss Jilted have had limited scope on the litigation front. Unless he agreed to do so in advance Mr. Jilted is not legally obliged to pick up the expenses incurred by Miss Jilted and her family for the wilting flowers, empty hall, unopened champagne or empty negligée—and (sort of) *vice versa*. The law presumes that the engagement ring was an outright gift so that Mr. Jilted cannot have it back, but if, as is unlikely, there is evidence to show that the ring was to be returned should the marriage not take place, Mr. Jilted does get it back. The same principle applies to personal gifts by one to the other. Engagement and wedding presents will normally be presumed to belong to the one whose relatives or friends gave them although it could well be possible to prove the couple intended an equal sharing.

Homely argument

And then there is the intended marital home. If it is in joint names this will usually mean an equal split (with the lady entitled to her share in the value as at the date of sale or as at the date of her being bought out rather than as at the date she left), but where one has put in much more money than the other, the court could decide that something other than equal ownership was intended and give effect to the intention. The deeds may spell out the portions in which the property was to be owned. If the property is in the sole name of Mr. or Miss the other may still be able to collect by showing that they both intended the other should have an interest and that the other acted to her detriment reasonably believing she was getting an interest by, say, ploughing in money or carrying out substantial work to the place.

Engaged couples and married couples—different law

One thing is quite clear. The law does not put engaged couples on a par with married couples in relation to property. Anyone who had doubts about that recently saw the doubts eliminated by the Court of Appeal. It appeared that the fiancée had lived with her man for four years in a house in his sole name and had not provided any of the purchase money. There was no suggestion that the couple had intended she should have any interest in the property. When the relationship broke up the fiancée sought to persuade the court that she should have a fair share in the property bearing in mind some of the factors which would have been taken into account if the couple had been married. NO! It was not on.

Bricks through the window, scratched eyes . . .

If an engaged couple just cannot agree over who owns and who is to get what, the court can decide. It is open to Mr. or Miss to bring proceedings within three years of the termination of the engagement—there are other remedies if the three years are up—under section 17 of the Married Women's Property Act 1882. And don't pay too much attention to the Married Women's bit. However, the court cannot vary what it declares to be the basis of ownership. Now if the couple had been married. . . .

. . . and joint savings accounts

What did the couple intend about the savings account? If the intention is clear, the court will give effect to it. Otherwise, the court will look to see how the couple contributed. Pooling will probably mean equal shares although the contributions have been unequal. But items bought with money withdrawn from the account will belong to the purchaser solely unless there is evidence that the couple intended to the contrary.

"I've been meaning to mention to you that it might be a good idea if . . ."

Couples prepared to put the romance to one side for an hour or so may be able to agree what should happen in the most, most, most remote, tiny, microscopically small ("Oh I know this is ridiculous but") . . . event of match abandonment. We have devised an engagement contract for them. Daddy-in-law elect will be most impressed. Alternatively, he will kick the suitor out of the door:

THIS AGREEMENT is made the 14th July 1988 BETWEEN ERNEST HART of 31 Woodbine Park Catisfield Hampshire ("Mr. Hart") and MISTY EYED of 6a Navigators Walk Gosport Hampshire ("Ms. Eyed")

BACKGROUND:

(1) The parties have for some time past been close friends and are desirous of intermarrying.

(2) Mr. Hart and Ms. Eyed are both legally free to intermarry

(3) The parties have agreed that in the unhappy event of such intermarriage not taking place the distribution of property now or hereafter belonging to them and other matters shall be dealt with as hereinafter mentioned

(4) The parties have both obtained or been aware of their right to obtain legal advice on the terms of this agreement and have carefully read and understood its contents

NOW IT IS HEREBY AGREED AND DECLARED as follows:-

1. The parties shall upon the making of this agreement be engaged to be married to each other

2. This agreement shall terminate upon the intermarriage of the parties

3. The remaining clauses of this agreement shall apply upon one of the parties for whatever reason notifying the other in writing that he or she wishes to terminate the said engagement

4. The interest of Ms. Eyed in the engagement ring delivered by Mr. Hart to her shall be extinguished and Ms. Eyed shall forthwith return the ring to Mr. Hart OR

The engagement ring given by Mr. Hart to Ms. Eyed shall remain the property of Ms. Eyed and any interest of Mr. Hart in the ring shall be extinguished

5. (a) All articles which shall have been given to Mr. Hart and Ms. Eyed or either of them on the occasion of or in contemplation or arising out of the engagement or their intended forthcoming intermarriage and which shall not be reclaimable by the donor by virtue of the said termination shall belong to such of Mr. Hart and Ms. Eyed whose friends relatives or otherwise gave them

(b) For the purpose of sub-clause (a) where the donor was a friend of both Mr. Hart and Ms. Eyed he shall be treated as the friend of the party with whom such friendship had prior to the said notice to terminate lasted for longer

6. Each party shall indemnify the other for one half of such sums as the other shall have

reasonably expended or incurred in connection with the wedding ceremony celebrations or honeymoon whether by way of food beverages clothing entertainment accommodation travel or otherwise

7.Any freehold or leasehold dwelling which the parties or either of them shall have purchased with the intention that it should become the matrimonial home upon the said intermarriage (whether or not the parties shall have cohabited in such dwelling in the meantime) shall be forthwith sold at the best price reasonably obtainable on the open market and with vacant possession and the sale price after deductions in respect of the aggregate of the amount required to redeem any mortgage on the said property as at the date of sale legal conveyancing costs and disbursements on sale and estate agents' commission (if any) shall belong to the parties in equal shares provided that in the event of either party having made payments under or in respect of any such mortgage or in respect of rates poll tax or sewerage charge on such dwelling as from the date of the said notice of termination which payments are in excess of similar payments made by the other the party who has made the excess payments shall be reimbursed for one half of such excess by the other party upon division of the said proceeds and out of his share in such proceeds.

8.Any furniture or articles of household use or ornament which shall have been purchased by either of the parties since the date of this agreement shall belong to the party who paid for the same and where such furniture or such articles were paid for jointly by the parties the same shall be shared between them so that each of the parties shall have furniture and/or articles equal so far as is practicable in market value as at the date of the said notice of termination to one half of the total market value at that date of the furniture and such articles so jointly paid for.

9.Neither party shall represent himself as still being engaged to be married to the other

10. Neither party shall make any claim against the other or the estate of the other except as may be provided for under this agreement

IN WITNESS WHEREOF the parties have hereunto placed their hands the day and year first before written.

SIGNED by the said ERNEST) E. Hart
HART in the presence of)
Millie Combes
147 Abbeywood Drive
Catisfield. Housewife.

SIGNED by the said MISTY) Misty Eyed
EYED in the presence of)
Millie Combes
147 Abbeywood Drive
Catisfield. Housewife.

How to gain land without really trying

At last, the truth about squatters' rights

Land cannot be stolen. That is why those who move their fences forward do not appear before the local beaks charged with theft. As it happens, the law rewards them because, having used the extra land as their own for twelve years, the law says it then belongs to them, and the right of the original owner to get it back by returning the fence to the former boundary or through the court will have disappeared along with any right to claim damages for being deprived of the land during the twelve years. And so it is that we must write of land trespassers rather than land stealers.

Waiting—for twelve years

Land trespassers go about their business quite openly for this is essential to get the law to work for them. They make it obvious that they are using the land as their own and that is why the fencing is so important. They might move the fence at the bottom of the garden three hundred metres into the adjoining field and erect extended fencing to the sides. They will probably also cultivate the new land. Never will they seek approval from the original owner; it is crucial for them to be doing something which is without his consent. Should the original owner ask them to desist—even in writing—they will ignore him unless and until they are convinced that he will otherwise punch them on the nose or take civil court proceedings against them. Positively never, ever as the twelve years are being clocked up will they sign an acknowledgment in writing that the original owner has any right to the land, for they would then have to start counting the twelve years over again.

It is unlikely that the trespassers will sell the land until the twelve years are up because its value to the purchaser would be nominal. But should they sell and the purchaser continue the trespass then the purchaser's trespassing period can be added to their own trespassing period in order to score the twelve years needed. The purchaser will obtain a statutory declaration from them—a written statement signed before a solicitor—setting out the trespass history in lurid detail. That's what happened when Mr. Christopher Moran bought a house in Dolphin Place, Amersham in 1971. His sellers in the conveyance deed transferred "all such estate right title and interest as the vendors may have in or over . . ." a plot which had belonged to Buckinghamshire County Council and which it intended to use at some time in the future for a proposed diversion of the A404. Since 1967, you see, the sellers had cultivated the plot to the extent of cutting the grass and trimming the hedges and had from time to time parked a horse box on it: in short, they had treated it as part of their garden although it was unfenced on one side.

A statutory declaration was made explaining the history and Mr. Moran carried on where his sellers had left off and he padlocked the gate to the plot and kept the key. In February 1988 the county council failed in its High Court action to recover the land from Mr. Moran. It now belonged to him. He had had an intention to *possess* the land, which was sufficient. It was unnecessary to prove he had had an intention to *own* it.

Buildings too

Sometimes there are buildings on the land on which the trespasser operates. These buildings would go the same way as the land after twelve years. And things can work out in a similar fashion where a landlord who owns property stops demanding his rent from the tenant; after twelve years the tenant may well take over ownership from him, as has happened in the case of a Gosport couple whose landlord disappeared. They are now the proud owners of a £50,000 plus house for which they had once paid a weekly rent.

Land watch

Landowners need to be alert and, preferably, not take holidays abroad for thirteen consecutive years:

Dear Mr Trespasser,

I have noticed over the past twelve months that the length of my back garden has been gradually decreasing and your rear fence has been getting closer and closer to my living room window. As much as I am impressed by the quality of the woodwork I would prefer it in the position it was originally intended to be. Unless it is put there within the next one week I shall without further notice instruct contractors to remove the fence and return it to you and I shall also institute proceedings for damages for trespass (to include the contractors' charges) and an injunction to restrain you from further trespass in the future.

Yours in neighbourliness

Minnie Land

Minnie Land

Accidents will happen

The dreaded motor insurance claim

No claim bonus, alcohol on the breath, witnesses, hire of another car. Such are the topics which flash through the motorist's mind as he careers across the carriageway and then, moments later, checks that his limbs are in the same position as when he dressed that morning. Satisfied that all is intact, he must decide whether or not to call the police.

999 or not 999—that is the question

A motorist involved in an accident is not under a legal duty to call the police to the scene. He is under a legal duty to stop and give his particulars to others involved who want them. He is also under a legal duty to report to the police as soon as practicable and within twenty-four hours (he breaks the law if he reports within twenty-four hours but it was practicable for him to have gone to the station before he did so) if either:

- he has not exchanged particulars at the scene; or
- there has been injury to someone other than himself and he has not produced his insurance

certificate at the scene (and so good idea, son, to always carry the certificate on you).

Whether or not the driver does call the police may depend on whether or not he is likely to be worse off than he already is by their appearance. He may be worse off *if*—

- he was wholly or partly to blame for the accident, because he then runs the risk of being prosecuted for careless driving—or worse! Unfortunately, no driver ever considers himself remotely to blame for an accident. For some objectivity, he should consult his spouse and assess whether the witnesses are standing close to him or his adversary;
- he has been drinking, because a police constable—in uniform—can require a roadside breath test from anyone who he has reasonable cause to believe was driving or attempting to drive or in charge of a vehicle which has been involved in an accident;
- he has an invincible fear of going to court because if the other driver is prosecuted by the police for a traffic offence and contests the case, he'll almost certainly have to go to the magistrates' court to give evidence against him;
- he is married and could be embarrassed by disclosure of his passenger's identity:

The Argus July 14 1988 23

BLACK SPOT ACCIDENT

The tenth accident this year occurred last night in High Street, Southsea at its junction with Gobstopper Road. A motor cycle ridden by John Bushy, 24, of Haircut Road, Southsea was in collision with a Daimler driven by Mark Tyme, 52, of Wade Court Emsworth. Both motorists escaped unhurt as did the Daimler passenger Thelma Rigby, 21, of Railway Cuttings, Fareham. The police attended the scene.

Sometimes, it will be of positive benefit to the motorist to call the police. Satisfied that he is blameless and as sober as a judge, he may still find that the other driver, between vulgarity and abuse, is denying negligence. The police could well be persuaded to fully investigate with a view to prosecuting the other driver (they may not be all that keen in the absence of personal injury and some encouragement may be needed). A conviction will raise the presumption in civil proceedings that the other motorist was negligent; once any traffic offence proceedings have been concluded or a decision has been taken not to prosecute, the chief constable's office will supply a copy of the police report on the accident, including statements from the motorists involved and witnesses, and will grant facilities for any officer concerned in the investigation to be interviewed. The fee for a full report is £29.10 and for interviewing an officer the fee is £30.20. No fee is charged for supplying particulars of the names and addresses of those involved and of their insurance cover.

"I beg of you. Don't call the cops. I've got nine points on my licence already. I'll lose my job if I get disqualified. My wife is pregnant with our twelfth child. I have a weak heart. My father was killed in the war. I was once forced to watch an episode of *Neighbours*." A plea of this passion and nature should only be acceded to in exchange for a written admission of liability in the other driver's handwriting and signed by him—

```
I am making this statement voluntarily.  I admit
that the accident which occurred on the 13th July
at approx. 7.30 p.m. in Southsea High Street at
the junction with Gobstopper Road was caused by
my sole negligence.
John Bushy
14 Haircut Road
Southsea
13th July 1988
```

But wouldn't Bushy's insurers go berserk if they knew about that? Probably, but it is most unlikely they would seek to wriggle out of indemnifying him. Nevertheless, an admission of this kind should be kept up the claimant's sleeve. Bushy knows he has made it and, that being so, it would be surprising if he told his insurers anything about the accident which would justify them denying liability and so make it necessary for the admission to be relied on by the claimant.

The claim

Anyone involved in a traffic accident should report the accident to his insurers immediately, even though he may not intend to make a claim under his own policy. If cover is comprehensive, the motorist's own insurers will pick up the repairers' bill less any uninsured excess and, provided that excess or other uninsured losses are recovered in full from the other driver or his insurers, the motorist's no claim bonus will not be affected. The great advantage to the motorist in claiming under his own comprehensive policy is that his insurers give the instructions to the repairers instead of leaving it to him to give the instructions and claim reimbursement later as happens when a claim is made against the other driver. And in claiming against his own insurers, the motorist avoids the uncertainty over whether it will be alleged that he was wholly or partly to blame.

It may happen that the repair bill is modest and there is some doubt that the motorist will be able to prove the other driver was wholly to blame and, hence, some doubt about whether uninsured losses can be recovered in full and so preserve a no claim bonus. The value of the bonus could exceed the value of the claim. In this sort of situation, the motorist may prefer not to claim under his policy (though he should still report the accident). Any suggestion by the other insurers that he has failed to mitigate his loss by not going to his own insurers would be legally misconceived. Should the motorist prefer to test the prospects of success against the other driver by seeing their reaction to notification of a claim, he ought to report the accident to his insurers giving them just qualified notice of a claim at that stage:

> I enclose accident report form with estimate as referred to in it. I consider myself blameless for the accident and although I have comprehensive cover with you, I would prefer to claim the entire cost of repairs and other losses from the third party's insurers. For the moment, I formally reserve my right to claim under my policy but will confirm whether or not I need to pursue such a claim as soon as possible after I have established contact with the third party's insurers.

A claim against another motorist or his insurers will not fail simply because the claimant was partly to blame. The law operates a system of *contributory negligence*. The claimant's damages are reduced by the proportion of negligence for which he was responsible. Take this situation. A disregards give-way signs in minor road and comes out when it is unsafe. B is driving along the main road. A and B collide. Had B been travelling at 30 instead of 90 mph a collision would have been avoided. A is 70% to blame. B is 30% to blame. A's claim is worth £1000 so he only recovers £700. If B has suffered some losses he can claim against A and will be entitled to 30% of their value.

Some motorists are so obsessed with their dented wing that they forget about their dented body. If a motorist can collect compensation for damage to his property or other losses due to negligence, there is no earthly or legal reason why he should not collect compensation for injuries to his body, pain and suffering and loss of amenity. A bit of shock, a sleepless night and headaches for two days can be converted into £ and p. It's wise for the claimant to visit his GP to get his symptoms on record (and, who knows, a bit of medical treatment to boot) and receipts for tablets and prescriptions should be kept.

If the claimant recovers some compensation from the other motorist's insurers then the charges of any solicitor who has been acting for him will normally be paid on top. But a lot of insurers refuse to pay solicitors' charges where the amount recovered does not exceed £500. In all cases, the claimant may qualify for help from a solicitor under the legal aid scheme which will be free or subject to a contribution by instalments, depending on the loot situation. And there's also ALAS (for the uninitiated, that's the Accident Legal Advice Service). Under the service a solicitor will give a FREE (yes, FREE, folks so HURRY to a solicitor today AND DON'T BREAK A LEG DOING SO) interview to an accident victim about a compensation claim at which he will get preliminary advice. The scheme was devised because it was reckoned that up to seventy per cent of accident victims who could claim compensation did not bother to do so. Citizens' Advice Bureaux, advice centres and libraries keep regional legal aid directories and these show the solicitors who participate in the scheme. Any claimant who suffers from the screams upon entry into an advice bureau, centre or library can get help from The Law Society on finding a solicitor to help them under the scheme, by 'phoning 01–242–2430.

How to handle the other motorist's insurers

Anyone who believes he has pushed himself to the ultimate by reaching the top of Everest or sitting through an episode of *Neighbours* could never have attempted to get a claim for accident damages settled by the other motorist's insurers. The claimant must constantly set deadlines and act as he has threatened when the insurers fail to meet them. We recommend that, whenever it is feasible to do so, proceedings be instituted at the very start against the other driver who can be proved to be at fault. These proceedings, which can be conducted concurrently with negotiations, should induce the other driver's insurers to give priority to the claim. In most insurers' claims departments, writs and county court summonses speak volumes. And if they fail to give priority, it is open to the claimant to enter judgment against the other driver in default of putting in a defence or taking some required procedural step. Proceedings also establish the claimant's entitlement to interest on his damages. Without the proceedings, neither the other driver nor his insurers is liable to pay interest in the absence of an agreement to do so.

Be there proceedings or be there not proceedings, some negotiations between the claimant and the other motorist's (he'll be called the third party although we have never been able to fathom out what became of the second party) insurers are unavoidable. The attitude of those insurers will be determined by who they are: insurers vary in degrees of meanness and lack of co-operation. Many take the view that delay on their part will save them money—frustrate the claimant into dropping his claim or into settling for less than the claim is really worth. They are there to save money, not give it away.

Showing the other driver was to blame

The other driver's insurers will ask what allegations of negligence are being made against him:

10 Acious Road
Southampton
14th July 1988

To The Claims Manager
The Really Tightfisted Insurance PLC
Penny Pinching House
Mean Street
Southampton

WITHOUT PREJUDICE

Dear Sir

Your claims reference BX 492C1-94218362-22-AXB-90909-69-212511111982272: LMB4

Your insured was fully to blame in that he:

- ☐ drove at an excessive speed.
- ☐ failed to keep any or any proper lookout.
- ☐ drove on the wrong side of the road.
- ☐ failed to give any or any sufficient warning of his intention by way of signalling or otherwise.
- ☐ moved off without checking that it was safe to do so.
- ☐ moved off when it was not safe to do so.
- ☐ emerged from the minor road without checking traffic on the major road.

- ☐ emerged from the minor road when it was unsafe to do so.
- ☐ drove into the rear of my motor vehicle when it was stationary and unattended and although I can clearly establish negligence, the legal maxim <u>Res Ipsa Loquitor</u> (the facts speak for themselves) applies with the result that I am home and dry unless you can come up with a pretty good reason for your insured's unorthodox driving.
- ☐ failed to take any or any proper action so as to avoid colliding with my vehicle.

Further, your insured was convicted at the Wecanholdem Magistrates' Court on the 14th July 1986 of driving without due care and attention, contrary to section 3 of the Road Traffic Act 1972 and driving with excess alcohol, contrary to section 6 of the Road Traffic Act 1972. Both convictions arose out of the accident and are relevant to the question of your insured's negligence.

Yours faithfully

A. Riverthreat

Andy Riverthreat

A read through the Highway Code may inspire other allegations of negligence. The failure of a driver to observe some part of the Code can actually be used in civil proceedings to prove that he was negligent: section 37 of the Road Traffic Act 1972 says so. And the fact that a driver has been convicted of some motoring offence arising out of the accident can be prayed in aid in the civil claim. Whilst the conviction is not conclusive and does not automatically prove the claimant was entirely blameless it does raise the presumption that the other driver was negligent.

Damaged car! No money!

If a claim is made against the other motorist's insurers it should be borne in mind that, unlike one's own insurers, they will not give instructions to the repairers to get on with the work and they will not ask them to send the receipted invoice on to them for settlement. They will simply approve the estimate (or say it is too high and only approve a lesser amount) and leave it to the claimant to give repair instructions, pay the bill and then claim it back. This practice can make many claimants nervous.

"Crikey, Moses. Will I ever get my money back? Can I prove the other bloke was fully to blame? Maybe I did glance down to check on the runners and riders for the three o'clock at Uttoxeter—but only very quickly! And the garage will never give me the car back till I've paid them and I can't pay them until the insurers have paid me and the insurers won't pay me till I've shown them a receipted invoice. I'm going to kill myself."

Suicide is quite unnecessary. It is legally possible for a claimant who intends to instruct a garage in accordance with an estimate to demand to be paid out for the estimate total (he'll have to find out the list prices for parts because they are seldom spelt out) and for such other losses which he can prove he will suffer (like hire charges). And it is legally possible for a claimant who is then met with silence or argument on the part of the other driver's insurers to sue the other driver on the same basis.

You may find it hard to believe that some claimants produce to the other driver's insurers an estimate from the Big and Expensive Boy without any intention of going to the aforesaid Boy but with the intention of going to a Backstreet Banger-Outer at one-third the price. No insurance company would fall for that one (except, possibly, the morning after the department Christmas party the night before). But insurers do realise that, within reason, a claimant can cost them more by going to the Bigger Boy and by extracting every minute of alternative vehicle hire to which he is entitled if he really wants to. A cash settlement in lieu of repairs could suit both sides. The claimant settles for a fixed sum on the strength of the estimate he has produced and before giving repair instructions to anyone. The settlement can reflect the potentially heavy repair charges which could conceivably be incurred:

10 Acious Road
Southampton
14th July 1988

To The Claims Manager
The Really Tightfisted Insurance PLC
Penny Pinching House
Mean Street
Southampton

WITHOUT PREJUDICE

Dear Sir

Your claims reference BX 492C1-94218362-22-AXB-90909-69-212511111982272: LMB4

I enclose estimate for repairs to my damaged vehicle. Strictly without prejudice, I am prepared to accept the estimate total in satisfaction of my claim against your insured provided I receive your settlement cheque within the next seven days. In default, I will sue for the estimate total in addition to the cost of hiring alternative transport during the repair period, or, in the alternative, damages for loss of use plus out of pocket expenses.

Yours faithfully

A. Riverthreat

Andy Riverthreat

This ought to be met by settlement or an offer to pay something on a cash in lieu of repairs basis.

The inspection

The claimant should always give the other driver's insurers the opportunity to inspect his vehicle before it is converted into a very small cigarette box or it is repaired. Otherwise, it may make it difficult for the claimant to challenge any attempt to down-value the vehicle where it has been written off or any attempt to argue that the repair charges were too high. And an expert inspection might be important to the insurers in concluding how the accident occurred: they might say that an inference adverse to the claimant should be drawn from the fact that he has eliminated the evidence before their expert could get to it. Any loss suffered by the claimant in waiting a reasonable period for the other driver's insurers to inspect can be added to his claim. But because the claimant has no guarantee that the insurers will come up with the loot until he sees the colour of their cheque (and statement accompanying it to the effect that liability is not admitted) he would be daft to wait indefinitely:

10 Acious Road
Southampton
14th July 1988

To The Claims Manager
The Really Tightfisted Insurance PLC
Penny Pinching House
Mean Street
Southampton

<u>WITHOUT PREJUDICE</u>

Dear Sir

<u>Your claims reference BX 492C1-94218362-22-AXB-90909-69-212511111982272: LMB4</u>

You have requested an inspection of my vehicle. I have agreed to one and asked that your engineer contact me to make the necessary arrangements. I have since heard absolutely nothing from him or you or anyone else about an inspection. Hire charges are mounting up. Unless I am contacted about an inspection within seven days of the date of this letter and arrangements are made for an inspection to take place within seven days of the contact, I propose to give instructions to the repairers without further notice to you or your

insured to carry out repairs in accordance with the estimate you have seen.
Yours faithfully
A. Riverthreat
Andy Riverthreat

Write off or repair?

The claimant cannot make the most of his misfortune. So if the market value of his car in its pre-accident condition is less than the cost of repairs, he will only get paid out for the pre-accident value although it may be possible to show that repairs are reasonable because of the vehicle's unique character. The claimant will have one hell of a struggle to show that and an expert to back him will be essential. It is open to the owner of a common or garden type banger which just ain't unique though he is really attached to it, to collect the pre-accident value from the insurers and pay the difference between that and the repair bill out of his own pocket:

10 Acious Road
Southampton
14th July 1988

To The Claims Manager
The Really Tightfisted Insurance PLC
Penny Pinching House
Mean Street
Southampton

WITHOUT PREJUDICE

Dear Sir
Your claims reference BX 492C1-94218362-22-AXB-90909-69-212511111982272: LMB4
I enclose estimate for repairs. I acknowledge that the amount of the estimate exceeds your pre-accident market valuation of my vehicle in its undamaged condition but because of its unique character (about which I have my own expert's report) it would not be reasonable to expect me to replace the vehicle and I shall insist on being paid the repair bill. My legal authority

is O'Grady v Westminster Scaffolding [1962] 2 Lloyd's Reports 238.

Yours faithfully

Andy Riverthreat

THE REALLY TIGHTFISTED INSURANCE PLC
Registered in England No 4287290473810
Penny Pinching House Mean Street Southampton

Our claims reference BX 492C1-94218362-22-AXB-90909-69-212511111982272: LMB4 Date as postmark

WITHOUT PREJUDICE

Dear Sir

Accident: 1.1.88

Thank you for your letter dated the 14th July 1988. Our own engineer has now inspected your vehicle. We do not accept that there was or is anything unique about it except for the cigarette burns to the front passenger seat, the Elvis Presley bust on the bonnet and the orange, green and mauve body work. The cost of repairs would be £2,429 (inc. VAT). Our engineer places the pre-accident value at £75. Strictly without prejudice, we will be prepared to agree a value of £100 and pay you this sum in full and final settlement of your claim and with a denial of liability.

Yours faithfully

P Face,
Claims Department

Thou shalt mitigate—hiring another vehicle

To get his money back, the claimant needs to be ready to justify the principle of hire, the type of vehicle hired and the length of the hire period. On principle, there is not usually an argument, although some of the tighter insurers may contend that the hire of a vehicle for unexceptional social and domestic use only was unreasonable: there is the possibility of the argument succeeding if it had to be thrashed out in court. Generally, the requirement to have a vehicle to get to and from work or in connection with a business will be sufficient justification for hiring so long as more than trivial mileage is likely to be undertaken.

Type of vehicle hired? If the claimant replaces like with like or goes slightly downmarket and has done some shopping around and gone to the cheapest hirer, he should be O.K. The High Court has allowed twenty five weeks' hire of a Jaguar XJ6 to replace a Rambler Ambassador at a £25 per week discount to an "old customer". But the Court of Appeal has upheld a county court judge who ruled that the claimant company had failed to mitigate its loss in hiring over a seven and one half weeks period in substitution for a damaged Jensen, first a Rover 100 and then a Jaguar 3.8. The company had failed to enquire in advance what the hire charge would be and whether it could get the vehicles cheaper elsewhere. A Ford Zephyr 6 would have done them! If hire is reasonable, the claimant isn't compelled to go to a commercial hire company. His mate or his dad may have a spare runner or be prepared to go without. He can pay a reasonable sum, get a receipt and claim away.

There's this cursed rule which says that a claimant cannot recover losses which have been incurred because of his impecuniosity. So, strictly speaking, he can't call on the negligent driver or his insurers to foot the cost of hiring another vehicle when his own has been written off until his insurers have paid him out (where he is comprehensively insured) or the other driver's insurers have paid him out (where he has third party cover only). But he is allowed a reasonable time to fix up another vehicle and so hire for, say, up to one week should normally be in order. He can pre-empt any suggestion that the hire period was too long by pressing the garage to start repairs, drawing the garage's attention to the fact that a vehicle is on hire and bombarding the garage with progress enquiries. A few letters with carbons on file for production to the other driver's insurers (and, if need be, a friendly judge in due course) will never go amiss.

10 Acious Road
Southampton
14th July 1988

To The Claims Manager
The Really Tightfisted Insurance PLC
Penny Pinching House
Mean Street
Southampton

WITHOUT PREJUDICE

Dear Sir
Your claims reference BX 492C1-94218362-22-AXB-90909-69-212511111982272: LMB4
I enclose estimate for the hire of another vehicle during the repair period.
Yours faithfully
A. Riverthreat
Andy Riverthreat

THE REALLY TIGHTFISTED INSURANCE PLC
Registered in England No 4287290473810
Penny Pinching House Mean Street Southampton

Our claims reference BX 492C1-94218362-22-AXB-90909-69-212511111982272: LMB4

Date as postmark
WITHOUT PREJUDICE

Dear Sir

Accident: 1.1.88

We thank you for your letter dated the 14th July 1988. We have the following observations on your estimate for the hire of another vehicle:-

- ☐ You are under a common law duty to mitigate your loss and we do not consider it is reasonable for you to hire another vehicle for the short repair period.
- ☐ The proposed hire vehicle is a larger, more powerful, more prestigious and more expensive vehicle than your own. We do not consider it is reasonable for you to incur the greater expense of hiring such a vehicle.

- The estimate includes a period after repairs have been completed during which your vehicle will be retained by the repairers pending settlement of their charges. We assume from this that you are unable to settle the repairers' invoice until we have settled with you. We cannot be held responsible for your unfortunate impecuniosity and so we will not agree to reimburse you for the extra period in question.

Yours faithfully

P Face,
Claims Department

10 Acious Road
Southampton
21st July 1988

To The Claims Manager
The Really Tightfisted Insurance PLC
Penny Pinching House
Mean Street
Southampton

<u>WITHOUT PREJUDICE</u>

Dear Sir

<u>Your claims reference BX 492C1-94218362-22-AXB-90909-69-212511111982272: LMB4</u>

Thank you for your observations on my estimate for the hire of another vehicle. My own observations are as follows:-

- I accept I am under a common law duty to mitigate my loss. Nevertheless, it is reasonably necessary for me to have the use of a motor vehicle. That I need one is borne out by the fact that I used my own vehicle extensively until your insured chose to inflict grievous bodily harm upon it. I shall use the hire vehicle to travel to and from work and for various social engagements to which I am already committed and on which my family will be joining me.
- Fair cop! I accept that, as a general rule, like should be temporarily replaced with like and that there is some disparity between a Mini and a Roller. However, I have so far refrained from making any claim in respect of other losses and if you are insistent on arguing about the hire, I shall have to claim every new pence to which I am entitled, and interest on top. As your insured's accident report form to

you will probably disclose, and as will be obvious from the extent of the damage to my Mini, the impact of the collision was considerable and my neck was thrown back and then forwards. I have since counted five twinges in my neck, have had some disturbed sleep and can no longer stomach my wife's steak and kidney pies. I am thinking of seeing my doctor.

□ I accept that, as a general rule, a claimant cannot recover losses which have been incurred because of his impecuniosity. However, in my case, the impecuniosity is not due to culpability on my part and so I suggest the general rule will not apply. Further, should you be unwilling to capitulate, I shall claim interest on damages for which purpose I realise it will be necessary for me to commence civil proceedings even though you will settle them and you will be alive to the fact that the commencement of proceedings will involve expense, most of which will have to be borne by you on your insured's behalf. Touché.

Yours faithfully

A. Riverthreat

Andy Riverthreat

THE REALLY TIGHTFISTED INSURANCE PLC
Registered in England No 4287290473810
Penny Pinching House Mean Street Southampton

Our claims reference BX 492C1-94218362-22-AXB-90909-69-2125111111982272: LMB4 Date as postmark

WITHOUT PREJUDICE

Dear Sir

Accident: 1.1.88

Thank you for your observations on our observations. We are arranging for our claims representative Mr. Poe Face (he is so mean that he was recently charged with burglary for breaking into a £5 note but they gave him a conditional discharge because it was a first offence) to contact you in order to arrange a meeting at which your claim can be discussed.

Yours faithfully

P. Face

P. Face
Claims Department

Betterment

Accidents can occasionally be blessings in disguise. Say the claimant's vehicle was previously damaged and the claimant gets that previous and non-urgent damage put right when his vehicle goes in for repairs arising from the later accident. He can still recover his hire charges in full from the negligent second accident driver so long as the repair period is not extended.

And repairs may well result in the renewal of a part which had seen better days. In an extreme case this might enable the other driver's insurers to say they should be given some credit for what is called betterment: where, for example, only a few days or months of working life of the part were left when the accident occurred. In a 1982 High Court case called Bacon v Cooper (Metals) Ltd a rotor was halfway through its seven years' life on accident date. The claimant got a new rotor. Did the opposition have to pay the full cost —a cool £41,500? Yes! The claimant had been forced to repair damage involving a new rotor which he would not otherwise had to replace for several years. The opposition had placed a burden on him which was entirely their fault. For this and other reasons, the betterment argument failed. Insurers who raise it should have Bacon v Cooper (Metals) Ltd bellowed into their earholes.

Worsement

10 Acious Road
Southampton
14th July 1988

To The Claims Manager
The Really Tightfisted Insurance PLC
Penny Pinching House
Mean Street
Southampton

WITHOUT PREJUDICE

Dear Sir

Your claims reference BX 492C1-94218362-22-AXB-90909-69-212511111982272: LMB4

I enclose a schedule in which I have set out my heads of claim, including the cost of repairs to my vehicle and damages for its diminution in value. My own expert advises me it will always be apparent that the vehicle has been involved in an accident and that has reduced its value. My legal authority is Payton v Brooks [1974] RTR 169 CA where the claimant lost in the Court of Appeal as the evidence was against him, but the principle I have mentioned was given judicial blessing.

Yours faithfully

A. Riverthreat

Andy Riverthreat

THE REALLY TIGHTFISTED INSURANCE PLC
Registered in England No 4287290473810
Penny Pinching House Mean Street Southampton

Our claims reference BX 492C1-94218362-22-AXB-90909-69-212511111982272: LMB4

Date as postmark

WITHOUT PREJUDICE

Dear Sir

Accident: 1.1.88

We reject your claim for damages for diminution in value. We have never recognised such a claim and do not intend breaking with a good tradition. In fact, we consider that your claim for the repair damage should be reduced by £250 at the least to take account of the betterment you will enjoy by virtue of some of your old and badly worn parts being replaced by new parts.

Yours faithfully

P. Face

P. Face
Claims Department

No car hired—much suffering

A claimant who chooses not to hire a replacement vehicle until his own has been repaired or he has been paid out for his wreck may still be able to claim damages from the negligent driver's insurers for "loss of use". Something for inconvenience: out of bed one hour earlier than usual, impossible to get home at lunch time twice a week for a bit of nookie, back at night one hour twenty minutes later than usual and having to walk to and from the match on Saturday afternoon. The claimant should go after around £20 per week. And he can claim the difference between his public transport fares and (where reasonably necessary) his taxi fares *and* what it would have cost him in oil and petrol had he made the journeys in his own motor.

No claim bonus

To many motorists, the prospect of the loss of a no claim bonus is just marginally less appalling than genocide and a pint of flat brown ale. The bonus will be in jeopardy if the claimant's own insurers have settled the cost of repairs or the write off value of his vehicle. To preserve his bonus the claimant must demonstrate to his own insurers that he was blameless. He does this by recovering his uninsured losses in full from the other driver's insurers. There may just be an excess to claim for (the first £25 or whatever of the claim against his own insurers which he has had to bear). If not, some uninsured loss can be found: inconvenience suffered during the repair period would do. The loss in question may be small. The saving in bonus will probably be considerable. The same course should be taken even where the claimant and the other driver are insured by the same company.

Pals . . .

I wonder if you could do me a favour . . .

One of the problems about buying a used car from a dealer is that by the time you are ready to sue him he has gone bankrupt for a few years or gone to Bermuda for good. The problem can be solved by getting a clever dick friend to undertake the purchase of a suitable vehicle on your behalf or, at the least, by taking him along when you inspect. Upon the vehicle falling to pieces you may be able to sue the friend for damages for negligence whether or not you also make a claim against the seller. If you are short on friends, a relative will do.

"No previous accident. Geddit?!"

Consider the case of accountant Miss Nazma Chaudhry. The twenty-six year old lady wanted a second-hand car. What better way of going about acquiring one than to ask her friend Mr. Kamal Prabhakar to try and find her something suitable. She knew nothing about the mechanical side of cars herself and whilst Mr. Prabhakar was not a mechanic, he had had quite a lot to do with cars and, not infrequently, he had bought and sold them at a profit. Miss Chaudhry stipulated to Mr. Prabhakar that she would not buy a car which had been involved in an accident. Out of friendship and without payment, he agreed to help her. Subsequently, he found a car which was up for sale by Mr. Bhupinder Singh Jandoo, trading as Jandoo Autocrafts. He was a car sprayer and panel beater and a stranger to Mr. Prabhakar. It was known by Mr. Prabhakar that the bonnet had been crumpled and either straightened or replaced. But he did not ask Mr. Jandoo whether the car had been involved in an accident.

Oh, dear

To Miss Chaudhry the car was taken by Mr. Prabhakar. He told her it was in very good condition and he highly recommended it. He said the seller was a friend of his—not quite right—and had a garage. Miss Chaudhry asked if the car had been involved in an accident and he said it had not and assured her that she need not have it examined by a mechanic. She relied on Mr. Prabhakar and bought the car.

Altogether now: The car had been involved in a serious accident and had been bought as salvage and repaired by Mr. Jandoo. It was worthless and Miss Chaudhry had a claim for £5526 damages plus interest.

Miss Chaudhry sued Mr. Jandoo—and Mr. Prabhakar. On May 20 1988 the Court of Appeal ruled that Mr. Prabhakar was liable to her in negligence. He owed her a duty of care. The duty was to do that which might reasonably be expected of him in all the circumstances. He had shown a remarkable degree of naiveté over his dealings with Mr. Jandoo. He had not asked Mr. Jandoo whether the car had been involved in an accident and he had told Miss Chaudhry it had not been involved in one.

The extra factor

Without the existence of a duty of care, there can be no hope of a successful claim against the friend or relative, however reckless he may have been. Indeed, the likelihood is that the giving of advice which has been sought in the context of family, domestic or social relationships will often not create a duty. It will depend on each case: some extra factor will normally be required, like the high degree of trust obviously placed by Miss Chaudhry in her friend, her strong reliance on his advice and the fact that he was being sent out to find the vehicle.

A tame disclaim

Similar principles apply when a friend or relative carries out work as a favour. After all, if you knew that your car was going to hit a brick wall after Fred had serviced it or the elements were to join you in the front room after Jack had double glazed it, you would have paid to have the job done by a professional, wouldn't you? Mr. Prabhakar, Fred and Jack might in future try and prevent a duty of care arising in the first place by a disclaimer—

> I am prepared to undertake the task you have set for me but on the clear understanding that I shall not be legally responsible to you in any way whatsoever.
> P.S. Two lumps and not too much milk, thank you.

Keeping it in the family

When a person drives his friend or relative and, as a result of his negligence, the passenger is injured in a traffic accident, there is no legal difficulty in the passenger making a claim for damages against the driver whose insurers will have to dish out the lolly. It is not uncommon for a wife to sue her husband on account of his negligent driving. In fact, a serious matrimonial dispute after a Sunday afternoon bump in the Forest has been averted on a number of occasions by the fast production of a High Court writ and an undertaking that the wife can keep the damages for herself.

Out for a walk

A searching subject . . .

Some find it a pleasurable experience to engage in conversation with a police officer in a street. They could well be flattered if, not content with conversing, the officer seeks to search their person. Others will watch in envy, hoping that the officer will turn his attention to them. Housewives have been known to watch and hope in similar fashion as market researchers go about their interrogations outside supermarkets. Police officers tend to be on more serious business than market researchers and a lack of co-operation could lead to a detention for the purpose of search or even arrest. The only sanction legally available to a rebuffed market researcher is to withhold the free sample of washing powder and affect a sickly smile.

"Excuse me, sir"

How Mr. Citizen responds to the police officer's advance will depend on what the officer wants, who Mr. Citizen is with and whether or not he is on his way to or from a crime. Should the officer require directions to the nearest station, he is likely to be obliged. Should

Mr. Citizen be up to no good or in the company of a young lady on their first date he will wish to stand or sit on his rights. Mr. Citizen is under no legal duty to talk to the officer, not even to supply his name or address. But Mr. Driving Citizen may be required to give his name and address to a police officer under section 162 of the Road Traffic Act 1972. He offends if he refuses and he could find himself arrested.

Out with a bulge

A police officer can stop Mr. Citizen and, without arresting him, detain him whilst he briefly tries to get him to talk and then, if he wishes, searches him. To do this lawfully he must have reasonable grounds to suspect that Mr. Citizen has stolen goods on him or other prohibited articles: these are offensive weapons and articles made or adapted for use in connection with burglary, theft, taking a motor vehicle without consent or obtaining property by deception. The officer, for the same reason, can search a motor vehicle. Basically, the power given by the Police and Criminal Evidence Act 1984 can be exercised in a street or public place. Separate powers exist in relation to other property. For example, there is power to stop and search Mr. Citizen and his vehicle under the prevention of terrorism and drugs legislation and to do so anywhere, public place or private place. Special rules apply to the police forces of statutory undertakings like docks, harbours and railways and to searches at airports.

Suspicious mind

Mr Citizen is black and a number of black males in the vicinity have been suspected of going about with knuckle dusters.

Mr. Citizen has a conviction for theft.

Mr. Citizen is seen to whisper something to his girl friend when sighting a police officer in close proximity.

Mr. Citizen's right overcoat pocket has a distinct bulge.

None of these factors alone would entitle a police officer to stop and search, for none of them would amount to *reasonable* grounds to suspect. Police officers are told in their own code of practice that a hunch or instinct will not do. They may justify the officer continuing to watch or even attempting to get the suspect to voluntarily chat to him—"Hello, Ronnie, can I interest you in tickets for the Police Benevolent Fund Barn Dance next month?"—but the officer must suspect, and do so on reasonable grounds, before he pounces and exercises his powers to which Mr. Citizen might well object. In the first nine months of 1987, fourteen thousand two hundred Messrs. Citizen were stopped and searched by police in England and Wales. The top reason for suspicion was that they had stolen property on them: suspicion of drugs was runner-up. The statistics strongly suggest that around five out of six searched had nothing on them and they were allowed to go on their way peeved, humiliated, embarrassed or, possibly, looking for a market researcher to ask them whether they could tell the difference between an edition of *Neighbours* and *The Flower Pot Men*.

"Are you comfortable? Then we'll begin."

Before he starts his search, the police officer must do his best to inform Mr. Citizen of his name and station; the object of the search; his grounds for making it; and Mr. Citizen's right to a copy of the search record (the officer must complete this on the spot or, if this is not practicable, as soon as it becomes practicable) within twelve months. If the officer is in plain clothes, he must also produce documentary evidence that he is a police officer. The officer may require Mr. Citizen to remove his outer coat, jacket and gloves. He can ask for more but he cannot compel more. If he wants the lot off, he must arrest. But an officer will be vulnerable to a civil action for wrongful arrest and false imprisonment should he arrest without reasonable grounds to suspect Mr. Citizen of an offence, as opposed to reasonable grounds to suspect possession of stolen goods or other of the prohibited things we have mentioned. For detaining and searching without sufficient legal grounds or without following the statutory rules, the officer could look forward to prosecution for criminal assault as well as a civil claim for damages.

That was my job, that was

Reducing the pain

Unemployment is an unhappy state. It can be made less unhappy by obtaining compensation from the employer. Occasionally, an employer will be prepared to negotiate a package with an employee under which, for example, the employee takes a capital sum and the company car and tenders his resignation. Such a package normally owes something to the employee's intimate knowledge of the personnel director's private life or a propensity by the employee to sell trade secrets to competitors, which the employer cannot prove. More often than not a reasonable compensation payment is a direct result of the employee being in a strong legal position and knowing how to use it to his advantage.

"Honest, loyal, punctual and giving every satisfaction."

But the employee who is a realist appreciates that a prospective new employer will award a black mark for the compensation tussle and a blacker mark for an industrial tribunal application by the applicant which went the whole way though it culminated in an award to him. "What is this troublemaker I see before me? Them last time. Us next?" So the employee who is a realist and wants to work again will seek a settlement which provides for withdrawal of the dismissal notice and a termination by the employee. And he will go for the reference, which no industrial tribunal or court of law can compel the employee to hand over.

For most prospective employers the reference has a place in the selection process, and wise prospective employers will want to go behind the reference in writing to 'phone the author. If the old employer and the prospective employer are aggressive rivals and the employee was quite dreadful at his job, there will be an inclination to persuade the prospective employer to hire him fast. ("Sorry to lose him, I was, Ted. Just didn't have room for him here at the top where he deserves to be. He should be flying as high as a kite. Meet you for a jar at the Bear tonight?"). But nothing is certain. So an undertaking is needed from the employer to answer verbal or written questions from a prospective employer in the same vein as the written reference and to keep confidential any specific matters about which the employee may be concerned. And no coughs and telephone nods and winks should the prospective employer phone up. Perhaps even a settlement like this —£X compensation payable as to £Y forthwith and £Z six months later unless the employee is then in fresh employment earning no less than he was earning under his terminated job in which event the payment of the £Z shall be waived. An incentive then to the employer to do all he can to get his former employee re-employed by some other mug.

Man from ACAS

Whatever settlement is arrived at, the employer will want ACAS to play some role. Provided a conciliation officer has poked his nose in—"has taken action" in the promotion of the settlement —the employee cannot collect and then press ahead with his industrial tribunal application. Ideally, the conciliation officer will organise the completion of a form which records the settlement and which both sides sign. Then the form is sent to the industrial tribunal and some record is made of what has happened. The employee is best off with the tribunal directing that the employee can go on with an application should the employer default in his obligations under the settlement.

Long enough . . .

So how does the dejected and rejected employee get himself in a position to negotiate hard? He needs to be able to complain to an industrial tribunal that he was unfairly dismissed. As with redundancy, he must have been continuously employed for at least two years. And remember that an employee made redundant can still increase his compensation potential by alleging that the redundancy amounts to an unfair dismissal if the employer has acted unreasonably by, for example, unfairly selecting him for the chop as against other employees who have been kept on, or by failing to give a warning of impending doom when one could reasonably have been given. That's why it's useful for an employee to obtain a fixed term contract for at least two years when he is taken on—though such contracts don't grow on trees—for then, he has the guarantee that he'll be around for long enough to complain of unfair dismissal should his contract not be renewed when the two years are up. True that this would preclude him from giving notice should he find the employer and his work colleagues lacking in good manners, but it would offer him security. The employer could always provide for a probationary period to be satisfactorily completed and reserve his right to dismiss if it were not: such provision would not legally prevent the contract from being classed as fixed term. Incidentally, whilst as a general rule any agreement by the employee in his contract to abandon his rights on unfair dismissal or redundancy are void, there are certain exceptions in relation to fixed term employees. Unfair dismissal rights can be abandoned in writing by an employee on a fixed term of at least two years (so he could not complain of unfair dismissal if the fixed term was not reviewed). And redundancy rights can be abandoned in writing by an employee on a fixed term of at least one year. Abandonment may come during the employment but it must be before the fixed term expires.

An employer cannot deprive an employee of his right to go to a tribunal by dismissing without notice as the two years is about to be clocked up. The minimum statutory notice to which the employee was legally entitled is added to his employment. After one month the employee must have a minimum of one week's notice. Once an employee has been in his job for two years or more he should have one week's notice for every full year of employment up to a maximum of twelve weeks: so for two years, he gets at least two weeks, for eleven years, he gets at least eleven weeks.

. . . and young enough

And to complain of unfair dismissal to a tribunal (or of redundancy) the employee must be under "normal retirement age", which usually will now be sixty-five for both men and women unless there was some other normal retirement age, being the same for men and women, and which applied in the business concerned. Part-timers may also be able to have a go—that's provided they've worked at least sixteen hours per week. But a part-timer who has worked for between eight and sixteen hours per week for at least five years is also eligible.

Reverse dismissal

Nasty employer thinks to himself: "I won't throw him out. I'll make his life such a misery that he'll beg of me to accept his resignation. He can clean the lavatories for a start. Fetch my fags. Move in with the secretaries and watch *Neighbours* on the office box. Managing director, my eye!" It won't work. If the employer behaves so diabolically, the employee is entitled to walk out immediately or give notice and walk out when it expires and then claim for unfair dismissal. Constructive dismissal it's called. But it's vital for the employee to make his walk out fairly quickly. If he carries on working for too long under the new regime designed specially for his misery he may be taken to have accepted it. Should the employee wish to refrain from the drastic step of a walk-out until he has given the employer a final chance to put the clock back, he might write him a note (with a copy for his file)—

MEMO

14th July 1988

To: BP
From: MD

Re: My employment

Over the last few years you have subjected me to a succession of industrial indignities from which I can only conclude that you wish to be rid of me. I have remained under protest. Unless my previous conditions of employment are reverted to, I shall have no alternative but to cease the employment and make an application to an industrial tribunal for relief on the ground of constructive dismissal.

Take an unfair dismissal, add a request for reasons . . .

It is prudent for the employee to fire on as many cylinders as possible. He should start with a request to the employer for a written statement giving reasons for the dismissal. That's whether he's been dismissed with or without notice, or the employer has simply declined to renew a fixed term contract. And that's whether or not the employer has already informed him of the reasons, or the employee is convinced he is aware of the reasons anyway. The employer is given an opportunity to fall into a trap, to state reasons which may be in conflict with what he later says when the unfair dismissal application comes along. If the employer fails to comply with the request within fourteen days, or gives reasons which are inadequate or untrue, the employee can complain specifically about that to an industrial tribunal—along with the unfair dismissal complaint—and if the tribunal is with him it must award him the equivalent of a fortnight's pay (but subject to a maximum of £164 per week—this maximum is normally increased every April). And this right is available to an employee who has been continuously employed for at least six months and so could be open to an employee who was ineligible to go for unfair dismissal as less than two years' employment had been clocked up:

88 High Street
Somewhere
14th July 1988

To: The Secretary
Turnover-Fast, Quickfire & Co. Ltd.

I hereby require you to provide me within the next fourteen days with a written statement giving particulars of the reasons for you dismissing me on the 13th July 1988. I make this requirement under section 53 of the Employment Protection (Consolidation) Act 1978.

Yours faithfully
Joe Foreman
Joe Foreman

. . . and mix with a "no particulars" complaint

There's a sporting chance that the employer has failed to comply with section 1 of the Employment Protection (Consolidation) Act 1978. In short, this generally requires the employer to give the employee a written statement about the main terms of employment with an additional note on disciplinary and grievance procedures. It has to be done within thirteen weeks of the employee starting the job. The statement may be incorporated in the contract which the employee accepted when he started the job: changes should be notified in writing within one month. Even the biggest and best organisations have a habit of falling foul of this obligation. That they have done so will not entitle the dismissed employee to compensation as with a failure to supply a written statement of reasons for dismissal. But it will entitle the employee to ask the tribunal to rule what the terms of employment were (particular terms could have a bearing on an unfair dismissal application), and it has even been suggested by one judge that where a particular term was just not agreed, the tribunal could invent one, but there's doubt about that. A complaint that the employer is in breach is likely to embarrass him and suggests some inefficiency which could be helpful on the main allegation of unfair dismissal: to that extent the complaint has its tactical use. Here's a statement which complies with the law and shows the particulars which must be covered—

MAIN TERMS AND CONDITIONS OF EMPLOYMENT

Employer's name: Turnover-Fast, Quickfire & Co. Ltd

Employee's name: Joseph Foreman

Date employment began: 2nd February 1986

Job title: Department Manager

Whether paid weekly, monthly, etc: Weekly in arrear

How payment is calculated (eg piece rate, with overtime rates etc): £3 per hour

The hours agreed to be worked (including any terms and conditions about normal working hours and whether overtime is compulsory):
8 a.m. - 12 noon and 1.30 p.m. - 5.00 p.m. Monday - Friday inclusive. Overtime (if available) is voluntary.

Holiday entitlement and holiday pay (if any agreed): After working a continuous period of six months you will be entitled to paid holiday at the rate of 15 working days per annum. If you wish to take a holiday during the first 6 months of employment, consideration will be given to your request but the days taken will be unpaid. Further this and other absence from work for any reason will not be included in the calculation of the original period of 6 months leading to entitlement for paid holiday. Paid holiday dates are to be agreed with the general manager and each absence for holidays is not to exceed two weeks consecutively.

Details of pension schemes (but not statutory pension schemes) and whether or not a certificate as to contracting-out is in force: Your employment does not carry separate pension rights.

Details of notice of termination to be given by employer to employee:
Three weeks (subject to any increased statutory entitlement)

Details of termination to be given by employee to employer: Two weeks

Details of the disciplinary procedure and grievance procedure are set out in separate documents, a copy of which has been received by the employee.

```
Signed .Shorter.Fuse....... (Employer)
Signed .Joe..Foreman.... (Employee)
Date: 2nd February 1986
```

. . . simmer for a while

An application to a tribunal on the ground of unfair dismissal, failure to give reason and failure to give a proper written statement of employment terms must be made within three months before the dismissal took effect: the tribunal has power to extend this period in relation to the first two matters, but only if satisfied it was not reasonably practicable to comply (for example, the employee only came to hear of certain things which made him realise she might have a case after the three months had expired). It is not compulsory to make the application on a special form although such a form has been originated—the trendy IT 1 obtainable from all good Department of Employment offices and CAB's. But if the employee is feeling bloody minded or the three months are about to run out and he cannot conveniently get hold of an IT 1 he could write out the application on the back of a bus ticket and it would be valid provided it gave the minimum prescribed details. This would do—

> I Miss Marilyn Jones of Box Cottage, Raglan Terrace, Lumley Road, Emsworth, Hants claim against Turnover-Fast, Quickfire & Co. Ltd. of 1b High Street, Chichester, West Sussex on the ground that I was unfairly dismissed by them.

The application should be sent to the Central Office of the Industrial Tribunals (England and Wales), 93 Ebury Bridge Road, London SW1W 8RE: in urgent cases, it can be sent to the regional office—there are twelve of them. Wherever possible, IT 1 should be used. Miss Marilyn Jones has been a good girl and used one. Paragraph 13 of IT 1 invites the employee to give his opinion for the reason for his dismissal. We see no advantage to the employee in doing so: leave it to the employer to dig as many holes for himself in which to fall in his "notice of appearance", which is effectively the defence.

Application to an Industrial Tribunal

Notes for Guidance

Before filling in this form please read:
- **these GUIDANCE NOTES**
- **LEAFLET ITL1 which you were given with the form**
- **the correct BOOKLET for your type of case**

Information: There are many things you can complain to a Tribunal about. LEAFLET ITL1 tells you what they are, which law (an Act of Parliament) covers your complaint, and which booklet you should get. Each of the BOOKLETS explains the law in simple terms. You can get the booklets free from any employment office, Jobcentre, or Unemployment Benefit Office. If you are in doubt, your Trade Union or a Citizens' Advice Bureau may be able to give you further advice or information.

Time limits: You must send in your application form so that it arrives at the Central Office of the Industrial Tribunals within the time limit. The time limit depends on which complaint you are making; for example, for unfair dismissal complaints it is three months beginning with the date of dismissal. So if you were dismissed on 10th January, the form must arrive by 9th April.

Qualifying periods: There are rules about how long you have to work for an employer before you can bring a case to a Tribunal. These rules are explained in the BOOKLETS.

If you are in any doubt about the time limits or qualifying periods, please contact your local employment office, Jobcentre, or Unemployment Benefit Office; or get in touch with the Advisory Conciliation and Arbitration Service (ACAS) - see the LEAFLET ITL1 for addresses and telephone numbers.

Representatives: You can present your own case at the Tribunal. If you want someone else to present your case, try to consult him or her before you complete your application form, but remember your form must arrive within the TIME LIMIT. If you name a representative, all future dealings will be with him or her and not with you. If you name a representative, you should ask him or her any questions you have about the progress of your case and when the Tribunal hearing will be.

If your complaint concerns EQUAL PAY or SEX DISCRIMINATION, you may wish to contact the Equal Opportunities Commission for advice or representation. If your complaint is about RACIAL DISCRIMINATION, you may wish to contact the Commission for Racial Equality for advice or representation.

FOR OFFICIAL USE ONLY

Received at COIT	Case No.	Code
	Initials	ROIT

Application to an Industrial Tribunal

Please read the notes opposite before filling in this form.

1 Say what type of complaint(s) you want the tribunal to decide *(see note opposite).*

(a) Whether I was given a written statement of my employment terms;
(b) whether I was unfairly dismissed;
(c) whether I was given a written statement of reasons for dismissal

2 Give your name and address etc. in CAPITALS *(see note opposite).*

Mr/Mrs
Miss/Ms JONES Marilyn

Address
Box Cottage
Raglan Terrace
Lumley Road
Emsworth
Hants

Telephone 07056 5986723

Date of birth 1/2/64

3 Please give the name and address of your representative, if you have one.

Name

Address

Telephone

4 Give the name and address of the employer, person or body (the respondent) you are complaining about *(see note opposite).*

Name TURNOVER-FAST QUICKFIRE & CO LTD

Address
1b High Street
Chichester
West Sussex

Telephone 30965 4783952

Give the place where you worked or applied for work, if different from above.

Name

Address

Telephone

5 Please say what job you did for the employer (or what job you applied for). If this does not apply, please say what your connection was with the employer.

Receptionist

IT 1 (Revised August 1986)

Please continue overleaf

6 Please give the number of normal basic hours you worked per week.	
Hours	38 per week

7			
Basic wage / salary	£ 102.00	per	week
Average take home pay	£ 89.00	per	week
Other bonuses / benefits	£ 250.00	per	year

8 Please give the dates of your employment *(if applicable)*	
Began on	3/9/84
Ended on	1/7/88

9 If your complaint is **not** about dismissal, please give the date when the action you are complaining about took place (or the date when you first knew about it).

Date

10 Give the full details of your complaint *(see note opposite).*

1. The Respondents never gave me a written statement of my employment terms. I repeatedly asked for one but my requests were always ignored.
2. On the 30th June 1988 I was in the stationery room at work when the office manager Mr. Henry Wiggins came in. He asked me whether I was wearing stockings and suspenders and went to kiss me. I moved out of the way and then ran from the room. Next day the 1st July 1988 Mr. Wiggins told me to pack up my make-up bag and leave. He said I was creating an unpleasant working environment and was rude to him and other staff.
3. On the 2nd July 1988 I sent a recorded delivery letter to the Respondents requiring them to state the reasons for my dismissal in writing. I have not been given the reasons in writing and my letter has not even been acknowledged.

11 Unfair dismissal claimants only (Please tick a box to show what you would want if you win your case).

- [x] Reinstatement: to carry on working in your old job as before OR
- [ ] Re-engagement: to start another job, or a new contract, with your old employer
- [x] Compensation: to get an award of money

You can change your mind later. The Tribunal will take your preference into account, but will not be bound by it.

Signature: M. Jones Date: 22/7/88

Dd 8040082 100m 11.86 H.D.B. Ltd. 3657

Employer hits back

Paragraph 5 of the employer's notice is the one that really matters. There the employer should give reasons for the dismissal:

Industrial Tribunals

Case number:

Notice of Appearance by Respondent

1 Please give the following details

Mr ☐ Mrs ☐ Miss ☐ Ms ☐

Other title

(Or give the name of the company or organisation)

Name TURNOVER-FAST QUICKFIRE & CO LTD

Address 1b High Street
Chichester
W Sussex

Telephone 30965 4783952

2 Do you intend to resist the application made by

Miss M Jones

YES ☑ NO ☐

3 Was the applicant dismissed?

YES ☑ NO ☐

If 'YES', what was the reason?

The applicant's conduct

4 Are the dates of employment given by the applicant correct?

YES ☑ NO ☐

If 'NO', please give the correct dates

Began on

Ended on

5 If a representative is acting for you, please give his/her name and address (NOTE *All further communications will be sent to him or her, not to you)*

Name

Address

Telephone

Reference

6 Are the details given by the applicant about wages/salary or other payments or benefits correct?

YES ☑ NO ☐

If 'NO', or if details were not given, please give the correct details:

Basic wage/salary

£ per

Average take home pay

£ per

Other bonuses/benefits

£ per

7 Maternity rights cases only

When the applicant's absence began did you have more than five employees?

YES ☐ NO ☐

8 If you answered 'YES' to question **2**, please give below sufficient details to show the grounds on which you intend to resist the application: ***(continue on a separate sheet if there is not enough space for your answer)***

Miss Jones persisted in flaunting herself in front of customers, the Company's officers and members of staff. She was warned about her conduct on several occasions and told she was giving the Company a bad reputation and causing ill-feeling and offence to the officers and staff, especially the females.

On the 30th June 1988 Mr. Wiggins had occasion to enter the stationery room where he unexpectedly encountered Miss Jones. On seeing him, Miss Jones closed the door and asked Mr. Wiggins if he could adjust her bra straps as they were digging uncomfortably into her flesh. Of course, he showed no interest whereupon Miss Jones tried to rub herself against him. When Mr. Wiggins ordered her to stop, Miss Jones struck his face and ran out of the room. Mr. Wiggins considered the situation with the directors at a meeting that evening and instantly dismissed Miss Jones the following day.

We accept that Miss Jones was not given a written statement of her employment terms but she was fully aware of the terms which were explained to her verbally by Mr. Wiggins himself before she started work and on numerous occasions subsequently when Mr. Wiggins had discussions with her.

9

Signed Shortie Fuse

Date 8th August 1988

10 Please send this form to:
The Assistant Secretary

Regional Office of the Industrial Tribunals
London South
93 Ebury Bridge Road
LONDON SW1W 8RE

For official use

Date received ____________ Initials ____________

Putting on the pressure

It is open to either side to ask his opponent for further particulars of the written allegations made in the application and appearance, and to be sent copies of any documents referred to which the other side has in his possession or which he could get hold of and which have some relevance to the issues. And if the request is turned down or ignored, an application can be made to the tribunal for an order to compel the giving of the particulars, or supply of the document or supply of a full list of what documents the other party has available. It is right that both sides should have reasonable details of what the other is saying so that it can be countered at the ultimate hearing, and that both sides should be able to see those of the other's documents which have some bearing on the case and not be taken by surprise at the hearing: certain documents, such as correspondence which the employer exchanges with his solicitors after the dismissal about his legal position, are excluded, but the importance of documents should never be under-estimated. The tribunal will be reluctant effectively to order one side to give away his evidence to the other side—that would go beyond allowing the opponent to know the allegations to be faced—but you don't get what you don't ask for!

Box Bottage
Raglan Terrace
Lumley Road
Emsworth
14th August 1988

The Secretary
Turnover-Fast Quickfire & Co. Ltd
1b High Street
Chichester
West Sussex

Dear Sir

Myself v Your Company

I refer to your company's notice of appearance. Please supply me with the following particulars under paragraph 5:-

Of "Miss Jones persisted in flaunting herself in front of customers, the company's officers and members of staff" -

(a) the date and place (and if in a building, the precise part of the building) of each and every incident relied on and the name of each and every customer, company's officer and member of staff before whom I allegedly flaunted myself in each and every such incident;

(b) precisely what I allegedly did and/or said by way of flaunting and the full nature of the case relied on in relation to each and every incident.

Of "She was warned about her conduct on several occasions" -

(a) the date and place of each alleged warning;

(b) whether the warning was in writing or oral and, if oral, the identity of the person who allegedly administered such warning and precisely what was allegedly said.

Of " ... she was giving the company a bad reputation and causing ill-feeling and offence to the company's officers and staff, especially females" among precisely whom I was allegedly giving the company a bad reputation and in precisely what way such reputation was allegedly bad, in precisely what way the feeling I was allegedly causing was ill and allegedly to whom, in precisely what way I was allegedly giving offence and the name of each and every officer of the company and member of staff who was allegedly offended.

Of "Mr. Wiggins had occasion to enter the stationery room" what the occasion allegedly was and the alleged location of myself in the room when Mr. Wiggins entered.

Of " ... On seeing him, Miss Jones closed the door" the alleged location of Mr. Wiggins in particular reference to myself when I allegedly closed the door.

Of "Miss Jones tried to rub herself against him" what allegedly prevented the completion of the act, whether Mr. Wiggins's trousers were allegedly up or down as the attempt was allegedly made by myself and what part or parts of my body I was allegedly trying to rub against what part or parts of the body of Mr. Wiggins.

Of " ... Miss Jones ... was fully aware of the terms which were explained to her verbally by Mr. Wiggins himself ... on numerous occasions ... when Mr. Wiggins had discussions with her" who allegedly initiated such discussions, precisely when, where and at what time they occurred and the alleged nature of each and every discussion concerned.

Of " ... we simply forgot to post the statement having written it out" when and by whom the statement was allegedly written out, whether it was allegedly placed in an envelope and stamped and, if so, allegedly by whom and, if not, why allegedly not, who allegedly had possession or control of it after it had allegedly been written out, when, by whom and from where it was allegedly intended to be posted and the date, by whom and circumstances in which it was allegedly discovered that the statement had not been sent.

Further, I require you to supply me with a list of the documents relating to the matters in question in my application which are or have been in your company's possession, custody or power and also to supply me with copies of the following:

1. All written warnings to me (if any) on which you rely
2. Minutes of the meeting which was allegedly held on the evening of 30th June 1988 which is referred to in paragraph 5 of your notice of appearance.
3. All notes of discussions between myself and Mr. Wiggins and letters and/or memoranda passing between the company's officers and Mr. Wiggins and/or other members of staff relating to myself and my employment.

4. The written statement of reasons for dismissal.

Should the above particulars, list of documents and copy documents not be supplied to me within ten days of the date of this letter, I intend to apply to the tribunal for an order that they be so supplied.

Yours faithfully

M. Jones

Marilyn Jones (Miss)

The one great factor which stops so many people going to law is *costs*: the threat of having to pay the opponent's legal and other expenses if the case is lost. Industrial tribunal cases (except those relating to industrial levy and safety) are different. True that in May 1988 the Department of Employment suggested that some applicants to tribunals might be required to pay a deposit of £150 which they could lose if the complaint was ill-founded. For the moment, this is the law—the loser will only be condemned to pay the winner's costs (and nothing else) if it is reckoned that the loser has acted "frivolously, vexatiously or otherwise unreasonably" in relation to the application: behaviour before or over the dismissal (in unfair dismissal and redundancy cases) will be an irrelevance to costs. If the employee has lost, his financial circumstances would have to be taken into account and, in practice, the order against him would almost certainly be limited to a contribution. And, again in practice, it would be a rarity for an order to be made against an employee (or employer) without a nod and a wink beforehand—a warning of what may happen on costs if he persists.

The warning is usually administered at a pre-hearing assessment, which can be arranged by the tribunal at its own initiative or at the request of either side, and is designed for the giving of a nod and wink (at the least) where the case is patently hopeless: where, say, the employee cannot get into work because he has been sentenced to seven years imprisonment for defrauding his employers of a few million, or the employer maintains that a voice from Heaven directed him to dismiss without notice and he felt constrained to obey. So whilst we do not advocate a frivolous, vexatious or unreasonable application, the fact is that the unemployed employee has little or nothing to lose (except the vote of a prospective new employer) by pushing an application until nod and wink time, as against the employer for whom time spent on resisting the application is money down the drain and if, as often happens, the employer is legally represented, there will be a legal bill to be paid too. The employer will bear the inconvenience and expense in mind when he comes to decide whether or not to try and resist and he will also bear heavily in mind whether he can afford to allow his existing work force to come to know he has settled. If the word gets round that he's a soft touch, everyone will have a tribunal go at him, whenever they can. But the employee should remember that a settlement offer may come on the morning of the hearing—when the employer sees the array of witnesses, any legal adviser and maybe the reporter from the local paper—and not before.

Legal aid

Full legal aid is not available for the tribunal hearing. But an applicant may well qualify for free or limited contribution legal help from a solicitor under the "Green Form Scheme" in connection with advice on whether he's got a case, help in drawing up the application and on preparing the case. And the solicitor may even be able to go along to the tribunal to advise during the hearing on how the applicant should conduct his case. Very often, the solicitor will be allowed to do the whole thing and speak for the applicant, despite the fact he's there only under Green Form and he isn't being properly paid by the legal aid people.

Bouncing back

It is open to the employee to state in his application form that he wants to go back: he wants reinstatement (old job) or re-engagement (comparable job with old employer). Miss Jones has done so because somebody told her that if the tribunal ordered reinstatement and the employers refused to comply, this would increase her compensation. They were right. Reinstatement or re-engagement are rarely ordered but it does happen and, at the least, the thought of having to take back the employee may be yet a further factor which persuades the employer he must settle. In deciding whether to order reinstatement or re-engagement the tribunal will need to declare the employee the winner, and take into account whether it would be practicable for the employer to comply, and whether the employee was partly to blame for what has happened. The chances of securing a reinstatement or re-engagement order will be virtually wiped out if the employer shows he had to hire a replacement and there was delay in the employee asking for his job back. It's wise for the employee to pen a letter to the employer the moment the employer's front door has slammed behind him to the effect that he intends to apply to an industrial tribunal for reinstatement on the ground that he was unfairly dismissed.

How much?

In unfair dismissal cases there's a basic award which is equal to the redundancy payment: an employee will not be able to collect both. The employee collects the award without having to prove any loss: if he has been unfairly dismissed or made redundant, the award is his though he starts a job as chairman of a nationalised industry the following day. The award is calculated according to a formula based on the employee's age and his length of service. The maximum basic award is currently £4,920. Then there's the compensatory award which is intended to cover the earnings the employee has lost and will lose in the future, loss of fringe benefits, the expenses incurred in looking for another job and so on. The maximum here currently stands at £8,500. And there's an additional award which will be made when the employer fails to comply with an order for reinstatement or re-engagement of between thirteen and twenty six weeks' pay (the actual net, or £164 per week, whichever is the lesser). The award may be higher in trade union cases. The basic and compensatory awards may be reduced by any contributory fault by the employee: for example, employer did not follow disciplinary procedure, but employee had been pinching the paper clips.

Full boards

Another go at estate agents

A parade of estate agents "For Sale" notices jostling for attention at the same property is a joy for never and an irritation to neighbours. An estate agent's "Sold" notice standing erect in the front garden three weeks after the new owner has moved in is a joy for never, an irritation to neighbours and an embarrassment to the new owner as his visitors enquire why he has decided to go so quickly. It is an offence for more than one board to be displayed outside the house or flat concerned without specific planning consent. The offence is committed by all the agents concerned and by the property owner. It matters not that any of the agents thought that their board was the only one. And in a prosecution against a Richmond-upon-Thames firm of agents who claimed they had not offended because their board was the first to go up, magistrates decided they were still guilty and became so as soon as another board from the second agent was displayed. As this book goes to press, the case is in the House of Lords on appeal.

And not too big

In the absence of consent for anything bigger from the planning authority, there are restrictions on the size of the board too. The maximum area allowed is 0.5 square metre (or 0.6 square metre for two boards joined together) and if actually displayed on a building the board must not project from the face of the building by more than one metre. Better still, a "Sold" notice will only be allowed without permission provided a board was displayed before, and better, better still, a board must be removed within a fortnight of completion of the sale.

Blind eye

If you wonder whether you must have been dreaming when you last took a look at a property for sale, we can put you straight. You weren't dreaming and the probability is that the law was being broken—unless you were in Richmond, for the council there is showing the way and prosecuting agents who anywhere else may well have escaped even a caution by the mayor. The law became stricter in October 1988 and councils should be encouraged to enforce it.

```
To: Dwellingsagogo
    Bricks Anonymous
    Honesty, Trust, Integrity & Co.
    The House of Bargains
    The Rackman Property Shop
    Swift Home Selling Service
    Instant Flog Centre
    Maximilian Pressure & Co.
    Haggle, Deception & Complete
    and Mr. Smith, the owner
```

Ladies and gentlemen:

I live at No. 31 Acacia Avenue, Ambiance, Newtown. You know No.29. Certainly, Mr. Smith knows it because he owns it and lives there. The rest of you know it remotely from rushing around it to produce your particulars and stopping by to erect a "For Sale" board. Acacia Avenue used to

be a pleasant place to live in. You have collectively made it unpleasant. I intend to make it pleasant again. Unless, within two days of the date of this letter, all but one of the boards is removed and the remaining board is replaced by a smaller one, I shall request Ambiance Newtown Council to institute proceedings against all of you for offences contrary to the Town and Country Planning (Control of Advertisement) (Amendment) Regulations 1984 (as amended by the Town and Country Planning (Control of Advertisement) (Amendment) Regulations 1987 and the Town and Country Planning (Control of Advertisement) (Amendment No. 2) Regulations 1987) and to section 109(2) of the Town and Country Planning Act 1971.
A Gent-Hayter

The litigant's dilemma

Being sued?—come on down!

You will have heard of *Winner Takes All*, *Lucky Ladders* and poker. Here's another—*Payment Into Court*. To play, you need High Court or county court proceedings in which there is a claim for money: it may be for a fixed sum—£7,500 for building work carried out by the plaintiff to the defendant's house—or it may be for an unfixed sum—damages for personal injuries which are never quantified by the plaintiff in court papers, although he may specify a fixed amount in negotiations with the defendant's insurers.

Once you've got the proceedings, this is how *Payment Into Court* is played. The defendant starts. First he puts in a written defence: he may deny he has done anything to the plaintiff which was civilly wrong; he may admit he has done something which was civilly wrong but deny the plaintiff has suffered any loss as a result; he may admit he has done something which was civilly wrong but allege the plaintiff is claiming too much. Or he may say the lot, pleading his case in the alternative.

A defendant to criminal proceedings would seldom plead in the alternative—

> "Members of the jury, my client cannot be guilty because he was just not there when the stabbing took place. This is a case of mistaken identity. If, however, you come to the conclusion he was there, then my client says that these wounds were self-inflicted by a man with a grudge towards the casualty department of the local hospital. Now, you may (we hope you won't, but you may) come to the conclusion that my client was present and that these wounds were not self-inflicted. Then, it is obvious, in my most respectful submission, what happened. This is a classic case of a young, frightened defendant, acting in self-defence."

That could hardly be expected to go down well. But it is different in civil proceedings:

1988-D-No. 426

IN THE HIGH COURT OF JUSTICE
QUEEN'S BENCH DIVISION
OXFORD DISTRICT REGISTRY
BETWEEN

ARNOLD DRUNKYARD	Plaintiff
-and-	
HORACE FANCY TWIT	Defendant

DEFENCE

1. The defendant admits that on the 1st January 1988 the plaintiff agreed to deliver to the defendant twenty five cases of champagne and that the said champagne was so delivered on the 5th January 1988. The defendant denies the other particulars alleged in paragraph 1 of the statement of claim.
2. The defendant avers that the said champagne was a gift by the plaintiff to the defendant and that there was no intention between the parties to create any legal relationship.
3. Further and alternatively, at the time of the said agreement and delivery the defendant was a minor.
4. Further and alternatively, if (which is denied) the defendant was to pay for the said champagne, it was implied that the price would be a reasonable one and not the sum claimed. A

reasonable price was £1,800 plus value added tax.

5. Further and alternatively, if (which is denied) there was a binding agreement between the parties it was an implied condition of the said agreement that the said champagne would be delivered to the defendant by the 3rd February 1988. Upon delivery of the said champagne on the 5th January 1988 the defendant rejected the said champagne as he was entitled to do provided that without prejudice to his right to reject he sampled the contents of one bottle of the said champagne.

6. Further and alternatively, if (which is denied) there was a binding agreement between the parties conditions were implied that the said champagne should be of merchantable quality and also reasonably fit for the implied purpose for which it was allegedly being bought namely capable of consumption by human beings. The said champagne was neither of merchantable quality nor reasonably fit for the said purpose in that it was corked. The defendant rejected the champagne save and except for the contents of one bottle thereof as is set out in paragraph 5 hereof.

7. Save as hereinbefore expressly admitted, the defendant denies each and every allegation of fact in the statement of claim as if the same were set forth herein and specifically traversed.

(Signed) H. F. Twit......

Horace Fancy Twit

Served this 14th day of July 1988 by Horace Fancy Twit, "Intoxicanto", The Sanctuary, Oxon.

Tempting

So, the defence in, the plaintiff begins to worry. "Perhaps, I am going mad?" The defendant then follows up with a payment into court. This involves him lodging money with the court (credit facilities not available) which ostensibly represents what, with interest, he is prepared to have paid over to the plaintiff to get rid of the claim. The plaintiff is given notice of the amount paid in. He can accept that amount which will generally mean he can also collect his legal costs from the defendant up to that stage. Or he can do nothing about the payment and fight on.

This is the question—to accept or not to accept?

If he does not accept and fights on and ultimately is awarded by the judge a sum which is equal to or less than what was paid in, the plaintiff will still be paid the award but, generally, he will have to bear both his own legal costs and the defendant's legal costs from the date of the payment in. Say the defendant pays in £10,000. The plaintiff declines to accept, fights on and is awarded £9,000. The plaintiff will be able to take the £9,000 but out of it will have to pay his legal costs and the defendant's legal costs from the date of payment in, which will eat heavily into the £9,000: in fact, it is not beyond the realms of possibility, if the payment in was made promptly and the lawyers on both sides had much to do subsequently, that the entire £9,000 will be spent on these costs and the plaintiff will end up plunging into his own pocket. And so it is that a tantalisingly calculated payment in will present the plaintiff with a very real dilemma. Does he dare decline it and risk ending up with nothing? Can he be sure he will score more at the trial? Will a particularly mean judge be inflicted on him? Will his witnesses falter under cross-examination? Might the defendant pay in a bit more if he fights on? Why did he start the case in the first place? Why is litigation such a lottery?

If you don't at first succeed . . .

The defendant who miscalculates his plaintiff on the size of the payment in could lose the game badly and be restricted to playing "snap" for the next three years. After all, if the plaintiff does fight on, the defendant has increased his potential liability for legal costs. The defendant may always top up the amount he has paid in where the plaintiff does not bite.

Counterclaim

It is possible the defendant, in addition to defending, has put in a counterclaim: "I don't owe you any money because the accident was not my fault and since I ended up with a broken leg and you were to blame, you can pay me damages." In that situation, the defendant must make it clear that, if it be the case, he has taken the counterclaim into account and satisfied it. Thinks: "I suppose you might get £25,000 out of me and I might get £15,000 out of you. That means I could end up owing you £10,000 because I secretly reckon we were each one half to blame. I'll pay into court £5,000 and say I have taken the counterclaim into account and satisfied it and sit back and see what you do." If the plaintiff accepts the payment in, the defendant will still have to pay the plaintiff's legal costs up to that stage, but he can offset his own legal costs on the counterclaim which the plaintiff is liable to bear.

Seconds out

Where the game reaches the final round—money in court but a trial before the judge as the plaintiff has declined to accept—secrecy prevails. Nobody tells the judge whether money has been paid in and, if it has been, how much. He doesn't find out details of any payment in until he has given judgment on all matters except who pays whose legal costs. Should some big mouth accidentally blurt out the secret information, the judge may abandon the match and order a retrial, judge on regardless, or pretend he didn't hear. Therefore, the defendant who wants to be able to deny in court that he should pay anything to the plaintiff can still do so though he has made a payment in. The payment in does not imply that the defendant admits he is liable to the plaintiff!

The plaintiff has twenty-one days from the date he is notified of it to accept the payment in. After that he will effectively need the agreement of the defendant to take his money before trial. A defendant who has gone to a lot of trouble to prepare his defence genuinely believing that the plaintiff would never capitulate may only be prepared to agree to a late payment out if there is an acceptable arrangement over his legal costs.

Interest

Money paid into court will earn interest from the court once twenty-one days have been clocked up from when it was paid in, assuming of course, it is not accepted in the meantime. The interest will eventually be paid out to one of the parties: when the plaintiff accepts the payment in but does so belatedly it is practice for the defendant to have the interest, and he will certainly get it when the plaintiff has fought on and failed to secure an award from the judge exceeding the amount paid in.

Notice of payment in

The defendant must complete a notice of lodgment form available from the court, and also give the plaintiff written notice that he has paid in:

1988-D-No 426

IN THE HIGH COURT OF JUSTICE
QUEEN'S BENCH DIVISION
OXFORD DISTRICT REGISTRY
BETWEEN

ARNOLD DRUNKYARD <u>Plaintiff</u>
-and-
HORACE FANCY TWIT <u>Defendant</u>

<u>NOTICE OF PAYMENT INTO COURT</u>

Take notice that -
The Defendant Horace Fancy Twit has paid £1500 into court. The said £1500 is in satisfaction of the causes of action in respect of which the plaintiff claims (add where appropriate and after taking into account and satisfying the above-named defendant's causes of action in respect of which he counterclaims).

Dated the 14th day of July 1988

In the county court, a similar form should be completed and be lodged with the court which will itself notify the payment in to the plaintiff.

Tick tock

Food rotten—jailer miserable—wish you were here

The police are now bound by strict statutory rules on how long they can detain a suspect without charge and on the rights he can exercise whilst they are entertaining him. Doubters should grab an eyeful of the Police and Criminal Evidence Act 1984 and the Codes of Practice made under it. There cannot be detention without charge for longer than four days, and any such detention beyond thirty-six hours will require sanction by a magistrates' court at which the suspect can have his shout. But the clock does not generally begin ticking until the suspect arrives at the police station, assuming he has been arrested before he gets there. If he has gone to the police station voluntarily and is arrested there later, the clock begins ticking only later when he is arrested.

"I'm off."

Except for relatively harmless offences, a police officer can arrest anyone he has reasonable grounds to suspect of breaking the law. If the police have little or nothing to go on, there will be a strong reluctance to arrest because that will start the clock and also render them liable to an action for damages by a disenchanted suspect who is keen on his civil rights should they subsequently release him without charge. So the suspect may be invited to go to the station for a chat, to assist the police with their enquiries. But there is absolutely no legal obligation on him to go or, in the absence of arrest, to stay. Of course, if the suspect has done no wrong and is confident that he can persuade the police they should be sniffing elsewhere, he might prefer to be at the station as a volunteer rather than as an arrestee, but could change his mind if told that the police would like him to take a rest in a locked cell whilst they check out his story. The suspect then can effectively force the police to arrest or let him go. The Code of Practice made under the 1984 Act which deals with detention, treatment and questioning says this:

> "Any person attending a police station voluntarily for the purpose of assisting with an investigation may leave at will unless placed under arrest. If it is decided that he should not be allowed to do so then he must be informed at once that he is under arrest and brought before the custody officer. If he is not placed under arrest but is cautioned . . . the officer who gives the caution must, at the same time, inform him that he is not under arrest, that he is not obliged to remain at the police station and that he may obtain legal advice if he wishes."

"I think you should have gone left at the lights, officer."

Since, for the suspect arrested before he gets to the police station, the clock starts ticking on arrival, he will wish to ensure the police do not lose their way or take some obscure route: a road map could be kept on his person. The police should take the suspect to the police station as soon as practicable after arrest, although there is power to delay if the presence of the suspect elsewhere is necessary "in order to carry out such investigations as it is reasonable to carry out immediately". But if there is delay, the reasons for it must be recorded when the suspect eventually reaches the station. Special rules apply when the suspect is arrested in one police area and is taken to another area for questioning.

"Tell me mum I'll be late for tea."

A detained suspect is entitled to have one person known to him, or who is likely to take an interest in his welfare, informed about where he is. If that person cannot be contacted, the suspect can choose two alternatives. If the alternatives are also out at the boozer, the police have a discretion to allow others to be tried. The police may postpone allowing the right to be exercised where it is reckoned that the contact could lead to other suspects at large being alerted, the recovery of property being hindered or interference with evidence or interference with or physical injury to people. But that right cannot be postponed beyond thirty-six hours from when the clock started ticking.

"I want my brief."

There's an important and fundamental right as well for the suspect to consult privately with a solicitor. It can be postponed in exactly the same circumstances as the right to have someone informed of the arrest but, again, only for thirty-six hours. But the courts do not like a solicitor being kept away from the suspect who wants to see him. In one case which was before the Court of Appeal in December 1987 a robbery conviction and ten years' imprisonment with it went down the drain because the police had denied the suspect legal advice. The suspect had been arrested and interviewed twice on the same day. It was during the second interview that he had asked to see a solicitor. Two further solicitor-less interviews followed and during the second on the next day, the suspect confessed to two burglaries but continued to deny the robbery. After yet another interview that day he confessed to the robbery. Then the police let in the solicitor. The Court of Appeal ruled that the judge at the suspect's trial should have refused to allow evidence of the confession to be heard by the jury because the suspect had not seen his solicitor when he wanted to see him.

In January 1988 at Leeds Crown Court the judge refused to allow the police to give evidence about statements allegedly made by the suspect who had been interviewed whilst detained but without the solicitor he wanted. The jury were directed to acquit him of murdering a police sergeant and attempting to murder a police constable. And in February 1988 at Manchester Crown Court a man who had been denied access for "an appreciable period of time" was acquitted of two murders to which he had allegedly confessed in police interview.

The denial to the suspect of access to a solicitor would not *automatically* rule out any confession which the suspect gave in the absence of his solicitor being heard by the jury. The trial judge will have a discretion about whether or not to let the confession be heard. The Lord Chief Justice recently decreed that there would have to be investigated a variety of matters including the degree of sophistication of the suspect and, in some cases, the conduct of the solicitor himself or his clerk. It might also be necessary to discover from the solicitor the advice which he would have been likely to give to the suspect if he had been allowed to see him earlier.

"I keep telling you, Rumpole is a barrister"

Wise suspects ensure that they become the object of suspicion in relation to an offence allegedly committed in an area close to the home of their ace criminal law solicitor; otherwise there will be a solicitor under a duty scheme or panel prepared to burst into action at three in the morning. But whether it be a duty or other solicitor who falls dishevelled into the police interview room, or recites good advice over the phone (he'll turn up at the station personally if he thinks this is necessary for the protection of the suspect's interest), it's all free. Yes, the Government which put up health scheme prescription contributions and reduced housing benefits for those having more than £6,000 capital provides utterly free legal advice to the banged-up. Now that can't be bad, can it?!

Quiet

Most police officers putting their hands on their hearts would admit to regarding the interview of the suspect as a means of getting him to confess. It is now practice for interviews about more serious offences to be tape-recorded: that fact virtually guarantees the police will play according to the rules, although, as we have seen, these rules can be misinterpreted insofar as they relate to solicitor access. Before he is questioned, the suspect must generally be told: "You do not have to say anything unless you wish to do so, but what you say may be given in evidence."

It is still the law that a suspect may remain silent. Whether or not it is wise for a suspect to keep his mouth shut in the face of police interrogation is something on which a solicitor will need to advise in the light of the particular circumstances. Whilst neither the judge nor prosecuting lawyer at any trial which followed will be allowed to make any criticism of a mouth shut (though watch for a change in the law here), it would take a remarkable member of the jury or magistrate to exclude from his mind the fact that the suspect had said nothing when the allegations screamed out for him to say something. But if the suspect is being interviewed during the first thirty-six hours following the start of the clock tick without his solicitor being allowed in, he may well wish to restrict each answer to "I'm not prepared to say anything until you permit me to obtain legal advice." Nobody trying the case could reasonably draw an adverse inference from that.

The invitation

Aggro at Bollinger Towers

A few hundred years ago there was this dad. He promised £100 to the brave man who, with his consent, married his daughter. This bloke obliged and when dad refused to cough up, the bloke, quite naturally, sued him. He failed. The promise, held the court, had not been legally binding: dad had merely spoken some general words to excite suitors. There had been no intention by dad to create any legal relationship. The absence of such an intention is fatal to a claim for breach of contract. So almost fatal, that, if a couple postpone a trip to Venice and fix up a babysitter so that they can accept the kind invitation to dinner by Mimi and Tom and it's called off the day before, they can't do a thing about it, because it is unlikely that either side had an intention to create a legal relationship. So a bit of legal relationship should be injected into social arrangements, and the cancelling host and hostess can then be sued for damages:

Bollinger Towers
14 VII 88

Mimi and Tom –

Thank you so much for your note. Oliver and I would love to come but we are mindful of your weakness for last minute changes. Remember the

Silver Wedding Concorde flight? We were actually on the runway when we heard about the cancellation. It was so, so embarrassing.

We are delighted to accept your invitation to dinner at Cloisters provided you confirm that you regard the invitation as legally binding and acknowledge that you will be liable to compensate us should the invitation be cancelled otherwise than on the ground of outbreak of war or the death of both or either of you.

Fondest regards

Diana and Oliver

I hate my building society

Another chapter which speaks for itself

Dear Mr Building Society Branch Manager

I refer to my complaint about -

- ☐ your failure to promptly cancel insurance cover under your block policy following the repayment of my mortgage as a result of which I did not receive the premium refund to which I would otherwise have been entitled.
- ☐ your refusal to allow me to withdraw from my account on the ground that I had not given at least seven days' notice of my wish to do so notwithstanding that you had a discretion to waive full notice.
- ☐ your failure to process my application for a home improvement further advance within a reasonable time as a result of which I did not qualify for tax relief under the 1988 Budget deadline.
- ☐ your imposition of a three months interest for early repayment penalty although you failed to take any or any reasonable steps to draw my attention to the penalty when I accepted the original mortgage offer.
- ☐ my allegations that the price your society obtained for my property when it was sold because of my arrears was not the best which could reasonably be obtained.

I am dissatisfied with your rejection of the complaint and refusal to make me any offer of

> compensation. I require you to arrange for my complaint to be considered under your internal complaints procedure until that procedure has been fully exhausted (unless, before exhaustion, you uphold the complaint and make me a compensation offer which I find acceptable). Should I remain dissatisfied I will follow up my complaint with the Building Societies Ombudsman.
>
> Yours faithfully
>
> O Pressed
>
> O Pressed (Mr)

The Building Societies Ombudsman works on very similar lines to the Banking Ombudsman (see page 107). He too offers a FREE service and can award up to £100,000. The internal complaints procedure of the society concerned must be exhausted before he will touch and although there is no specific time limit for the lodging of the complaint, he can refuse to investigate where the complainant has acted with undue delay in going to him. Generally, he will look at any complaint of infringement of legal rights, unfair treatment and maladministration—including inefficiency and undue delay—which has resulted in loss of money or inconvenience. The complainant must usually be a customer of the society. Out are complaints by companies and about credit-worthiness, although if the society has allegedly failed to use proper credit rating procedures, the Ombudsman may interest himself. The service can be of benefit in similar situations as we looked at in relation to banks.

Who plays?

All building societies who are members of the Building Societies Association participate, along with the Century, Ecology, Heart of England, Louth, Mablethorpe and Sutton Permanent Benefit, St. Stephens and Sun.

House of Ombudsman

Contact the Office of the Building Societies Ombudsman, 35–37 Grosvenor Gardens, London SW1X 7AW (telephone 01–931 0044).

Double sue

Section 75, I love you

Garage repairs car. Customer pays with Access or Barclaycard. Car conks out on way to Scotland on touring holiday. Garage *and* credit car people equally liable to customer for garage's cock-up.

What do you know!

Salesman persuades customer to buy compact disc system by falsely asserting that the production of vinyl records is about to be stopped nationwide. Customer pays with Access or Barclaycard. Salesman's employers *and* credit card people equally liable to customer for salesman's misrepresentation.

What do you know!

Householder signs agreement for new double glazing and salesman arranges a personal loan with a finance company so it can be paid for. Measurements negligently taken by double glazing surveyor and rain is admitted. Double glazing company *and* finance company equally liable to customer for double glazing company's negligence.

Equal liability

This is how equal liability works. The business supplies a customer with goods or with services which are to be paid for under a credit agreement, but the business is guilty of some breach of contract or misrepresentation. Not only is the business liable to the customer but so is whoever extended the credit. Good, eh? Equal liability for each of them and the customer can claim his damages and whatever else he is after from either or both, although he cannot end up with double compensation! But there must have been some prior arrangement between the business and whoever has extended credit. There's a sufficient prior arrangement where a business has agreed to accept a credit card. This means that, generally, every time the business is liable to the customer for breach of contract or misrepresentation so are the credit card people if they are Access or Barclaycard. And there's a sufficient prior arrangement where a finance company has agreed to grant personal loans to customers of the business who are introduced to them. There would not be a sufficient prior arrangement where a customer obtained an overdraft from his bank for personal expenditure and then went out and bought a new motor lawn mower: the bank could not be sued because the mower tore up the lawn and then passed out. This additional protection is not available when a charge card is used—American Express and Diners' Club, for example, although their merchant agreements give some indirect protection to the card holder.

"That will be £99.99, thank you."

Before equal liability can operate, though, the cash price for the item or service must be more than £100 (including VAT), but not more than £30,000. And the credit must be for not more than £15,000. With the credit card, the cash and credit price will be the same. All but a few types of agreement are covered provided the customer is an individual (and this will include business people and partners).

That will do nicely

For all this, section 75 of the Consumer Credit Act 1974 may be praised. Any attempt by small print, large print or fast talk to exclude the lovely section 75 will be null and void. Equal liability is just the thing where the business which supplied the goods or service has gone down the financial drain or looks like going that way; where the business has refused to respond acceptably to the customer's complaint; or where a credit card has been used abroad (after all, suing in the Cairo county court could prove a trifle inconvenient), but there may be legal complications which cannot be overcome on a lot of foreign transactions. With the credit card people the customer could actually settle his own claim by deducting the compensation he can show is due to him on the transaction in question from money he owes the credit card people on other transactions. That, however, is not a course which should be necessary. The credit card people are in an influential position over the business—if it is still there!—and will not be pleased with a complaint about an unremedied contract breach or misrepresentation.

Pre-July 1977 Blues

One important factor. The equal liability law came into operation on July 1 1977. Holders of credit cards whose accounts were opened before that date could probably not claim to be able to take legal advantage of it. In practice, Access and Barclaycard will accept responsibility in relation to pre-July 1977 card holders for the face value of the loss (for example, purchase price of useless article) but not for consequential loss (for example, damages for distress, inconvenience and expense suffered because the article did not work). Any pre-July 1977 card holder who wanted to put himself in the strongest legal position possible could settle up and close his credit card account and then apply to open a fresh one. As a post-July 1 1977 account holder he would then be a very happy credit card customer.

```
Dear Credit Card Company
   On the 14th July 1988 I had the misfortune to
purchase a law book by Stephen Gold from the
Legal Bookcage, Chancery Lane, London WC2 at an
extortionate price and I used the credit card
issued by your company.  The salesperson
represented to me that one reading of the book
would guarantee my success with a distinction
pass in the law examinations I was about to sit.
I relied on the representation which induced me
to buy the book.
   The representation was false.  I failed my
examinations dismally and I find the book to be
misleading and filled with trivial nonsense,
written in a style which would be better suited
to a school magazine.  You are equally liable
with the Legal Bookcage for their misrepresent-
ation under section 75 of the Consumer Credit Act
1974 and I claim from you the return of the
price.  If the price is not returned within seven
```

days I shall take proceedings against the Legal Bookcage and your company for my money and damages.
Yours faithfully

Des Appointed
P.S. I knew about section 75 before I bought the ruddy thing.
Copy to Legal Bookcage, WC2

HP OK

Separate laws govern the position of customers who take goods on H.P. There the goods are hired out (till payments are complete) to the customer by the finance company which owns them and grants the credit, and the customer has full protection against duffness and misrepresentation under these separate laws.

Don't drive them to sleep!

Or how not to score driving licence points

Motoring offences are dealt with alongside the burglaries and assaults and, apart from a couple of the most serious offences like reckless driving, they are always tried by magistrates. Sometimes, the motorist must turn up at a court in person as when, for example, he is charged with drinking and driving or when he is contesting a charge. But more often than not, the law permits him to stay away provided he is pleading guilty and has sent the court a form to say so. On the form he will have an opportunity to put forward factors he would like the court to take into account in fixing the sentence and to set out his financial circumstances if he wants time to pay the judicial bill. Credit card facilities, incidentally, are not available.

Eyes down and judging

The motorist should be economical with his written words. Intense concentration by the magistrates can lead to regrettable consequences. In 1981 the High Court quashed a criminal conviction against a defendant during whose trial at Weston-super-Mare magistrates' court the chairman closed her eyes and looked down rather than at a witness, leading to certain persons in court concluding she was asleep. Although the High Court was satisfied she had, in fact, been awake, it acted as it did on the principle that justice had not been seen to be done! Imagine how a bench of magistrates might respond to a batch of a few dozen written statements in mitigation from erring motorists read out by their clerk in monotone at three times the maximum speed limit for speech. They must be delivered from actual or apparent slumber.

Tell it to the marines

If the magistrates happen to be awake, listening and following what is read out from the motorist's statement, there's a good chance they will disbelieve it. Too many cars appear from nowhere. Too many motorists are strangers to the area and put their foot down moments before the police officers switched on their electronic equipment. Too much tread wears off overnight. On a guilty plea by post the magistrates will hear no more of the police allegations than is contained in the "statement of facts" sent out with the summons. The motorist should avoid answering allegations which are not in the statement. And he should refrain from putting forward points which suggest he does not accept he has committed the offence—"I am only pleading guilty because I have neither the time nor the patience to come to court"—for the magistrates will then almost certainly refuse to accept his guilty plea and will adjourn the hearing for witnesses to be called.

Speeding pleading

Traditionally, speeders were never going as fast as the police allege. It is idle to winge on about the alleged speed in the guilty plea form if it is admitted that the limit was actually broken. Should it be of sufficient importance to the motorist to show the police got it wrong (his fate over disqualification may hinge on the extent to which the speed limit was exceeded), let him plead not guilty at court. Then, the motorist may have more hope of persuading the magistrates that his account is the right one. Or he may care to suggest to the magistrates that if they cannot be sure he was doing 101 mph, they cannot be sure he was doing over 30 mph in the first place. The onus is on the police to prove the charge with the same standard as they would have to prove a charge of homicide, and the motorist can challenge their evidence in cross-examination and without going into the witness box himself. Indeed, if going into the witness box would oblige him to confess to the offence albeit to a lower speed than that alleged against him and the police evidence has been shaken, he may well do well to keep out. Realistically, speeding charges are difficult to defend and the chance of winning is about equal to the chances of lassoing an eel.

Discretionary disqualification dilemma

If the magistrates wish to consider disqualifying the motorist when he has pleaded guilty by post, they will adjourn the hearing and give him a chance of attending another day to argue against disqualification. This will *definitely* happen when the number of live penalty points on his licence, added to the number of penalty points which the latest offence attracts, comes to at least twelve, as then it is on the cards that he will lose his licence for a minimum of six months. And this will *probably* happen when the magistrates view the offence as a bad one of its kind—say, speeding at 104 mph or above on a motorway—and, as they can do for any offence which carries an endorsement, are proposing to exercise their discretionary power to disqualify, even for a first-time offender. So the motorist who is in jeopardy of discretionary disqualification like this has a dilemma. Does he go to court on the first hearing instead of pleading guilty by post and hope to win favour by demonstrating an acknowledgment of his culpability? Or does he stay away and not tempt fate by being at court, and hope the magistrates will not go to the trouble of adjourning to get him there?

"For the defendant who came, deux points"

Sometimes, there's a powerful reason for the motorist to turn up personally at court instead of pleading guilty by post. That's when there is a range of penalty points which the magistrates can order and the prospects of persuading them to stick to the lower end of the range are good. A range exists for using a motor vehicle without insurance (6 to 8 points), careless driving (3 to 9 points), failing to stop after an accident (8 to 10 points) and failing to report an accident (8 to 10 points). If two or more offences arose out of the same set of circumstances, the motorist will score the highest number of points to be allocated to any of the offences and the points will not be added together.

And if the motorist is after trying to avoid any endorsement of penalty points at all, he must attend court and give evidence. He will only escape an endorsement if he can show there is a "special reason". That means some reason special to the offence and not special to the motorist. Previous safe driving, or that endorsement would lead to disqualification and disqualification would lead to catastrophe, won't do because these are special to the offender. An obstructed 30 mph sign at the start of a speed restricted stretch and a "foreign" driver or an uninsured driver covering just three feet of road in an emergency might do. And in one case a motorist who drove 10 mph over the limit on a motorway escaped endorsement. He had been worried about his blind, incontinent eighty years old passenger becoming ill, and so anxious was he to reach the nearest service area that he was unaware of his speeding. That the offender was 1 mph over the limit could not of itself amount to a special reason.

Most irritatingly for police forces who see too many accidents from motorway U-turners, the High Court did a good turn for three motorway drivers in March 1987. The drivers had U-turned on a motorway to avoid a long stationary traffic jam, but when there had been no oncoming traffic in the opposite direction for a considerable time. The drivers escaped endorsement on the ground of special reasons with the High Court at pains to point out that if the motorway had been in normal use, special reasons would have been difficult, if not impossible.

Stress sufferers should not worry too much about a personal court appearance. True that on Friday February 13 1987 a self-proclaimed Evangelist preacher and rapist "collapsed" in the dock before he was due to be sentenced (but went on later in the day to collect sixteen years with no apparent discount for his medical attention). But this seems to have been a highly exceptional occurrence. Manchester consultant heart and chest physician Alan Bernstein tells us that a court appearance as a defendant or witness is very unlikely to actually kill. The stress could induce a faint in some people from which they could expect to be completely recovered within half an hour.

Stain removal

Most motoring convictions are alive for totting-up purposes for three years, but the motorist cannot get the endorsement removed from his licence until four years after the conviction. Drink-drive convictions are alive for the purpose of fixing the minimum period of disqualification on a later drink-drive conviction for ten years, but the offender cannot get the endorsement removed until eleven years after the conviction. Court clerks and magistrates may just see a dead endorsement which is still on the licence. This cannot help the defendant. A dead endorsement will be removed on application to DVLC, Swansea: a new licence will be issued.

Licence to sign

The law requires any person to whom a driving licence has been issued to forthwith sign it in ink with his usual signature. Failure to do so is an offence. Imperative, then, for a motorist who is to be sentenced for an endorseable offence to ensure his licence has been signed before tendering it to the court whether by post or on a personal attendance. When the licence issued to Judge Peter Greenwood was handed in to Chelmsford magistrates in January 1986 upon His Honour pleading guilty to careless driving (on the way to court to deliver a difficult summing-up about which he may have been thinking he had emerged from minor road when unsafe to do so and collided with a vehicle on major road), it was unsigned. The court clerk ventured the opinion that the police would probably not mind the missing signature. We think he was probably right.

MITIGATING STATEMENT IN CARELESS DRIVING CASE

This offence was due to momentary inattention OR mental aberration OR distraction caused by a small boy running on the offside pavement.

I had been doing my best to pay attention to the road. The car radio was switched off and I was driving alone. I am very sorry for what happened.

Although an accident occurred, the consequences of it were negligible. OR Although an accident occurred and the consequences were disastrous which I much regret, the degree of carelessness on my part was small.

Further, although I am the only party to the accident to have been prosecuted, the fact is that I was minimally to blame. OR I was not entirely to blame. I did not commit a flagrant breach of the law.

This prosecution blemishes my driving record. Over a driving career of twenty years, I have never been prosecuted let alone convicted for a motoring (or any other) offence (not even a parking offence). I drive an average of 25,000 miles a year and have never before been involved in a traffic accident. OR I have never been involved in a traffic accident for which I was in any way to blame. I have a full no-claims bonus from my insurers but the claims arising out of the recent accident will result in its forfeiture. OR I am not comprehensively insured and I will have to bear the heavy cost of repairs to my own vehicle out of my own pocket (subject to any contribution I may recover from the other driver).

I was fully co-operative with the other driver at the scene and with the police and I have pleaded guilty to the charge at the first opportunity. I ask that credit be given for this.

MITIGATING STATEMENT IN SPEEDING CASE

My speed was measured over a distance of just two-thirds of a mile. This speed was not typical of what was a long journey, as is borne out by the fact that I had left home two hours earlier and had only travelled approximately 40 miles when I was stopped by the police. I did so exceed the limit because my journey was taking me longer than I had estimated and I was late for an appointment. OR I have to confess that I deliberately drove over the limit because I felt under a moral duty to get to my destination as reasonably fast as I could as I was so concerned about the condition of my wife. OR I was nearly at my destination; it had been a long, arduous day; and other vehicles ahead on the road were going faster than they should have been and I allowed myself to imitate them.

Whilst I did speed, I had total control of my vehicle and the prosecution do not suggest otherwise. There is no aggravating feature about the case and no accident occurred. The traffic was light, the road surface was dry, the weather was fine and visibility was good. It was a long, straight road.

I drive extensively and have done so for the last twenty years but I am normally careful to keep within the speed limit. Whilst it will be seen from my licence that I have motoring convictions, I have never before been in trouble for speeding. I apologise for the inconvenience I have caused.

Business is business

Closet proprietors

The law says that anyone dealing with a business is entitled to know who is running the business show. That's whether the business is a corner shop owned by a humble down-trodden husband supplementing his income as a double glazing rep, or a hypermarket owned by a multi-national company. For a start, this information could be vital if the customer is dissatisfied with the treatment he has received and wants to complain or sue, or both. So there are various legal rules which businesses have to keep to when the identity of the show-runners is not obvious—and sometimes when it is! A customer wanting to resist a demand for money from the business he has dealt with would do well to check that the business has kept to the rules. If it has not, he may possibly have a defence to a civil claim: more likely, those running the business have committed an offence and may decide that embarrassment and prosecution could be avoided by calling off their chase of the customer.

Name check

The customer should start his check (for a way out) on the business *name*. It may have been necessary for the business to comply with the Business Names Act 1985. This applies when the business name does not consist of the surname of the sole trader, the surnames or company names of all partners in the business or the company name of a company running a business on its own. Phew!

- Harry Ball and Sammy Silver trade as "Ball and Silver". The Act does not apply to them.
- Harry Ball and Sammy Silver trade as "Harry and Sam" or "The Precious Teapot". The Act does apply to them.
- Crumpets and Muffins Ltd. trade as "Crumpets and Muffins Ltd". The Act does not apply to them.
- Crumpets and Muffins Ltd. trade as "House of Crumpets and Muffins". The Act does apply to them.

When the Act does apply, the business must include on its stationery the names of the business proprietors and an address in Great Britain to which documents for each proprietor—like a summons or a writ!—may be sent. Business stationery? That's letters, written orders, invoices, receipts and written demands for payment. There's a let-out for businesses with more than twenty partners, presumably on the basis that they don't make notepaper which would be long enough to accommodate the names of them all. And there's a bit more. The same information which should go on the stationery must be contained in a notice prominently displayed at the business premises—that's *any* premises where the business is carried on and to which customers or suppliers of any goods of services to the business have access, and not just the place to which our checking customer may have gone.

Naughty business

There are two consequences of non-compliance with the Business Names Act 1985. Firstly, an offence is committed by the business proprietor or proprietors. Secondly, the customer may be able to secure the dismissal of any civil proceedings which the business has brought against him. It won't be easy, but it could be possible. The customer will have to show that *he* had a claim against the business himself arising out of the same contract and that he has not been able to follow it up because of non-compliance. Or that, because of non-compliance, he has suffered some financial loss in connection with the contract. But, either way, the civil court could let the business off the hook if it reckoned it was "just and equitable" to do so.

Bad company

Generally, *companies* running a business have to go even further. Their business letters and order forms must state the place of registration of the company (for example "registered in England") and the registration number. Their business letters, if they contain the namcs of any of the directors—and director-naming is not obligatory—must state the *full* names (Christian and forenames as well) of *all* individual directors and the company name of every company which is a director (yes, one company may be a director of another). Non-compliance with these additional requirements is an offence by the company *and* its directors and secretary, but they may ask the court to excuse them on the ground that they acted honestly and reasonably. And if that's not enough, companies must conspicuously show their names outside offices and business addresses: defaulting companies may be prosecuted. When a business gets all that lot right, it deserves to be paid!

Fully baked letter

14 Stickler Avenue
Hartlepool
14th July 1988

The Secretary
Crumpets and Muffins Ltd
Bread House
Bin Road
Coleslore

Dear Sir

I refer to the invoice dated the 1st July 1987 and numbered 1468AZ issued to me by what I have now established to be your company's business "House of Crumpets and Muffins" in respect of a supply of stale cakes. I also refer to the threatening letter from the business dated the 1st July 1988. Before I consider my position further, I invite your observations on the following matters:-

(a) contrary to section 4(1)(a) and section 4(6) of the Business Names Act 1985, neither the invoice nor the letter stated your company's name;

(b) contrary to section 4(1)(b) and section 4(6) of the Business Names Act 1985, no notice containing your company's name at your Bread House premises was displayed in a prominent position or at all;

(c) contrary to section 348 of the Companies Act 1985, your company's name was not painted or

affixed on the outside of your Bread House premises in a conspicuous position and in letters easily understood or at all;
(d) contrary to section 349 of the Companies Act 1985, neither the invoice nor the letter mentioned your company's name in legible characters or at all; and
(e) contrary to section 351(1) and section 351(5) of the Companies Act 1985, neither the invoice nor the letter mentioned in legible characters your company's place of registration, its registration number or its registered office.

Yours faithfully

Gerry Hawkwood

Gerry Hawkwood

No sex please—we're married!

Including the no sex agreement

No sex, irregular sex, unsatisfactory sex. Assuming the complaint is being made by one spouse against the other, can the marriage be ended on account of it?

Nullity

Proceedings for nullity may be brought on the ground that the party who wants the decree, or his wife, is incurably incapable of consummating the marriage—yes, you do read correctly: the impotent party can rely on his own condition—or on the ground that the other party has wilfully refused to consummate the marriage. With nullity, the marriage is deemed not to have taken place as from the date of the final nullity decree and proceedings can be started immediately bags have been unpacked following the return from honeymoon. With divorce, the existence of the marriage can never be erased from the score book and proceedings cannot be started until one year after the wedding ceremony.

Incapacity

It is incapacity to have normal sexual intercourse which the law requires to justify a nullity decree. The husband will be legally incapable if he cannot manage an erection *and* penetration: penetration for a short period without emission will amount to incapacity, as will an inability on the man's part to consummate with his wife although he could make the earth move for his female secretary. And a wife who has an invincible repugnance to sexual intercourse with her particular husband, whilst she would be ready, willing and able so far as Englebert Humperdink is concerned, will be legally incapable. That one party is unable to conceive or to give satisfaction to the other is a legal irrelevance to the nullity law.

Wilful refusal

Wilful refusal means wilful refusal and not just neglect. But before long, the ritual of devouring the classified advertisements section of the local rag before lights out, or turning over for a quick nap before the frollicking, will look very much like refusal. In practice, a no-sex nullity petitioner who is not relying on his own incapacity will allege both the other party's incapacity and wilful refusal and leave it to the court to decide which it was. However, the court can refuse a nullity decree to a party if he knew it was open to him to bring nullity proceedings but carried on with the marriage in a way which led the other party to believe he would not try and end the marriage and the court reckons it would be unjust to grant the decree. The nullity defence, we'll call that.

Divorce

So if the nullity defence might apply or the marriage has been consummated but there are sexual difficulties of the none, insufficient or excessive variety, what else is on offer from her Majesty's courts? Divorce on the most common ground—unreasonable behaviour: the other party has behaved in such a way that the party petitioning for divorce cannot reasonably be expected to live with the other. Was the behaviour unreasonable bearing in mind that it was by this particular respondent towards this particular petitioner? That's what the court has to decide. The fact that, for whatever physical or mental reason, a husband cannot manage sex regularly or at all will not in itself amount to unreasonable behaviour, but if his particular wife has a sexual appetite and, over a period, finds that the sexual (or more precisely, non-sexual) side of the marriage is getting her down, she may well be able to secure her freedom from the marriage by a divorce decree. She will not have to prove that the husband intended to behave unreasonably and so the husband whose moral culpability is zero could find himself divorced against his will on the ground of unreasonable behaviour. But the ingredient of intention in unreasonable behaviour could convert what would otherwise be a borderline case into a strong one.

Journey through the cases

It's because the court has to decide whether there has been unreasonable behaviour on the facts of the case actually before it that makes consideration of decided cases of limited use only. Those decided cases, though, do give some guidance and show the occasional inconsistency and even discrimination against women. Some of the cases concern the old ground of cruelty; others the ground of unreasonable behaviour which replaced cruelty in 1971. It is no more difficult to prove unreasonable behaviour than it was to prove cruelty: if anything, it's a bit easier.

Wife fails

In a 1977 case involving an unreasonable behaviour divorce petition by a wife, she failed notwithstanding the husband had allowed the case to proceed as undefended. She alleged that throughout the marriage her sexual life had been unsatisfactory because the husband had been cold and indifferent to sexual intercourse. She said that intercourse took place about once a month and, when it did, the husband penetrated but withdrew very quickly. This led to upsets and quarrels between them and she left. The judge who heard the case refused her a divorce and so did the appeal court to whom she then went.

Another wife fails

And in a 1964 cruelty case which, again, was undefended, the parties had married when the wife was eighteen and the husband thirty-three. They had a child soon afterwards but sexual intercourse stopped about one year later. After fifteen years without sexual intercourse in spite of her requests, the wife left: she alleged her health had suffered. She was also refused a divorce by the court and her appeal was turned down. "I'm not satisfied," said the appeal judge, "that the husband was guilty of inexcusable conduct. In view of his natural disinclination for sexual intercourse, to find him guilty of cruelty is rather like beating a dog because it will not eat its food."

And again

In a 1965 cruelty case there was a similar story. Despite complaints by the wife of its effect on her health and the husband's admission after she had left him for a short period that he had been wrong and a promise that "it would be alright" if she went back, the husband refused to have sexual intercourse except at infrequent intervals of weeks or months. He was indifferent to the "whole business". Abstinence had a deleterious effect on the wife's health. The court held that the husband had not treated the wife with cruelty: there was no evidence that he had been deliberately pursuing a course of conduct calculated to injure her health.

Husband succeeds

But in the same year a wife was held to have treated her husband with cruelty by refusing to have sexual intercourse even though this was due to an invincible fear of conception and childbirth. The wife had been prone to stopping at the last moment. "And it may well be that to excite a husband in that way and then to stop him at the last moment might be a very serious and a very cruel thing to do."

Trying out a vasectomy

In a 1980 case on the modern unreasonable behaviour ground the husband was thirty and the wife thirty-one when they married. They had two children. Then, over a period of about five years, the wife refused intercourse because she was frightened of getting pregnant, the husband failing to buy contraceptives for himself and the wife unable to use any for medical reasons. But, thereafter, the husband underwent a vasectomy operation and it became necessary for him to have intercourse on at least twelve occasions over a three months period (an average of once per week) before he went back for a test as to whether or not the vasectomy had been successful. Intercourse did take place about once per week but not as often as the husband would have liked and there was some lack of co-operation by the wife as she knew the husband was associating with another married woman; a little over four months after the vasectomy the husband left the wife and moved in with the woman. He asked the divorce court to grant him an unreasonable behaviour decree. The wife resisted. The divorce court obliged the husband. She appealed. The Court of Appeal backed her and took the husband's divorce decree away. In view of the length of the marriage and the sexual difficulties there had been, the wife's post-vasectomy behaviour had not been unreasonable and especially when the husband was, at the time, deeply involved with another married woman.

No sex agreement

- Man is impotent but desires marriage with woman who is fully aware of the situation and is agreeable to the arrangement. Can he legally protect himself from nullity, divorce and maintenance should she later become disagreeable?

- Man and woman are capable of sexual intercourse but desire a marriage without intercourse. Can they

> protect themselves from divorce, nullity and maintenance should the other change his mind after the marriage has been celebrated?

We have devised a no sexual intercourse agreement to be entered into before marriage. It can be affirmed after the marriage. It is aimed at protecting an impotent man, our couple in search of a marriage without intercourse and others with different permutations who are after the same end. But we give a warning: in the majority of cases, if tested in court, the agreement will probably be held void as being contrary to public policy and so unenforceable. Say, for example, a healthy, young couple enter into the agreement and marry but the wife changes her mind about sex and the husband refuses to submit though capable of intercourse. The agreement would almost certainly be held to be void if the husband sought to use it as a defence to either nullity or divorce proceedings, but we venture to suggest it might have its use in that situation should the wife go on and claim maintenance: she could hardly deny the existence of the pre-marriage agreement and the court might well quietly take the agreement into account in deciding whether it was reasonable for the husband to maintain the wife following annulment or divorce and, if so, to what extent.

And where, say, the wife who truly remained disinclined towards intercourse but sought to divorce her husband on the ground of unreasonable behaviour on the false premise that she was aggrieved by his refusal, the fact she had entered into the agreement before the marriage would lend colour to the husband's argument that she did not want sex after it so that his behaviour was not unreasonable to *her*.

Companionship will do, thank you

In the case of, say, older persons who seek companionship in marriage without intercourse, we believe that the agreement could be helpful not only in relation to any maintenance dispute which surfaced, but as to whether there was actually a decree of nullity or divorce. Here, we believe, the court might say that the agreement was not contrary to public policy and that, for example, it was not open to a party to go after a nullity decree on the ground of incapacity or wilful refusal or a divorce decree on the ground of unreasonable behaviour when all the other party was doing was complying with the terms of the agreement. And we believe the court might well refuse a nullity decree to a party to an agreement where he sought to rely on his own impotence.

```
THIS AGREEMENT is made on the 14th July 1988
BETWEEN RICHARD NUNN of 13 Peace Cottages
Hasslefree near Rochester Kent of the one part
and SALLY BATE of Chaste Towers Alresford
Hampshire of the other part

BACKGROUND:
(1) The parties are engaged to be married to each
    other
(2) The parties wish intend and have agreed that
    each shall display love and affection to the
    other and that during the subsistence of the
    marriage each shall engage in natural sexual
    activity with the other but shall not engage
    in sexual intercourse with the other (or any
    other person)
(3) The parties are desirous of the said wish
    intention and agreement being recorded in
    manner set out herein

NOW IT IS HEREBY AGREED AS FOLLOWS:
1.  Neither party shall require the other to
    submit to sexual intercourse with such party
    during the subsistence of the said marriage.
```

2. Neither party shall engage in sexual intercourse or any other sexual activity with any third party during the subsistence of the said marriage.
3. In any matrimonial or other proceedings between the parties or their personal representatives in which the conduct of either of the parties during the subsistence of the said marriage shall be relevant -
   (a) no reliance shall be placed by one or by his or her personal representatives on the abstinence from sexual intercourse by the other
   (b) the parties or their personal representatives shall invite the court concerned to refrain from taking such abstinence into account in determining any question or matter in issue or which shall be relevant in the proceedings between the parties or their personal representatives.
4. Neither party nor their personal representatives shall institute or prosecute any matrimonial inheritance or other proceedings against the other or the estate of the other for relief on the ground of the abstinence from or failure or refusal of the other to engage in sexual intercourse with that party during the subsistence of the said marriage or the compliance with any of the terms of this agreement or in which such party or his or her personal representatives shall rely on such abstinence failure refusal or compliance.
5. Both parties shall affirm this agreement following the celebration of the said marriage if required by the other to do so.

IN WITNESS whereof the said Richard Nunn and Sally Bate have hereunto placed their hands the day and year first before written

SIGNED by the said RICHARD) R. Nunn
NUNN in the presence of:)

Millie Combes
747 Abbeywood Drive
Catisfield. Housewife

SIGNED by the said SALLY) Sally Bate
BATE in the presence of:)

Nosie Parker
29 Woodbine Park
Catisfield.
Civil Servant

Second thoughts

More about jobs

Nottingham solicitor Nigel Elliott agreed to employ twenty year old Justine Leverton from Newark as a secretary, and sent off the usual commiserations to the unsuccessful applicants. Miss Leverton signed an acceptance letter which detailed the employment conditions. And, then, one and a half working days before she was due to start, Miss Leverton telephoned her would-be boss to tell him she would not be starting as she had fixed up another job.

Not a particularly uncommon story, but what singles it out from the ordinary is the reaction of Mr. Elliott. Instead of ripping up a few dozen law reports and slitting his throat, he sued Miss Leverton in the county court. He claimed the cost of re-advertising the position and one and a half hour's re-interviewing time at the rate of £50 per hour.

Miss Leverton paid £79 into court which was less than the total claim, but included the legal costs of Mr. Elliott's firm and the appropriate court fee. Mr. Elliott accepted and that was the end of the matter. His stand was (and you wouldn't expect anything else, would you?) legally sound, and it is a stand which other disappointed employers might care to follow: they might even throw in a claim for the difference between hiring a temp until a new full-timer was found and what the reneging applicant would have been paid had she turned up.

The prospective reneger might find it less costly and painful to start the job and give notice on the first day. The length of the notice will be dictated by her contract. Once she has been in the job for one month she is obliged under section 49(2) of the Employment Protection (Consolidation) Act 1978 to give one week's notice although her contract may provide for longer.

Real cool

How to change your mind

The law protects from themselves those who get silly at their doorsteps. Sign up an agreement at home and the customer will probably be able to back out later. Cooling off they call it. Housewives, the impetuous and the gullible have been cooling off in relation to credit agreements for years: since July 1 1988 cooling off in respect of cash agreements as well has been available. Cooling off operates provided the amount advanced under a credit agreement or the price to be paid under a cash agreement exceeds £35. But there's a clutch of cash agreements which do not get the cooling off treatment including those of the land, insurance and investment variety; agreements for the supply by roundsmen of food, drink and other household perishables; and agreements for catalogue goods where the supplier operates its own cooling off machinery.

Don't pop up and see me sometime

So precisely where does the deal have to be made for the customer to qualify for cooling off? Let's start with cash agreements. The trader must have signed the customer up during an unsolicited visit—a visit without the express request of the customer—to his home or place of work, the home of somebody else or an excursion organised by the trader away from his business premises. A solicited visit will be treated as an unsolicited visit if the customer ends up agreeing or offering to buy goods or services which, when he was solicited, he did not know and could not reasonably have known formed part of the trader's business—a set of encyclopaedias when you were after a set of teasing silk lingerie with accoutrements. If the trader has telephoned the customer in the absence of a request by the customer for him to do so, indicated he is willing to visit and does then visit, the law pretends that is an unsolicited visit.

That's cash agreements. With credit agreements, the old Consumer Credit Act 1974 provisions still apply and they are similar. But the credit cooler has five days following the date on which he receives through the post a copy of his agreement to cancel, whereas the cash cooler has seven days from the date on which he makes his contract.

Cooling notice

This is the really good bit (we've been working up to it). If the cash customer is entitled to cool off he must be given a notice to this effect by the trader. And the notice must contain the following information—

- trader's name

- trader's reference number, code or other details to enable the contract or offer to be identified

- a statement that the customer has a right to cancel the contract if he wishes and that the right can be exercised by sending or taking a written notice to the person who must be identified within seven days following the making of the contract

- a statement that, if he wishes, the customer can use a cancellation form which has to be provided with the notice.

Now if the notice—which is to be dated—is not delivered when the contract or offer is made, the contract is unenforceable against the customer. It doesn't matter that the customer has omitted to cancel. Because of the trader's failure to comply with the law, he is punished. No enforcement. And that means that if part of the price is still outstanding, the customer can refuse to pay it and still keep the goods: the trader will not be able to sue him.

If it's in relation to a credit deal that the trader has failed to give the notice of cooling off rights, he may still be in trouble, but not quite so deeply as with a cash deal. He will need permission from the court to enforce the agreement should there be arrears, and permission will probably be granted unless the customer has been prejudiced and the trader deliberately forgot the notice. The court could always give permission but reduce the customer's liability.

Way out, man

It's highly arguable that the trader can technically avoid serving a notice of cooling off rights by providing for the price to be paid in cash except for £35 which would have to be passed over shortly afterwards.

Battering bonanza

And how to stop it

The wife who is battered by her pig of a husband can ask the police to prosecute him, can seek a divorce and a court injunction to restrain him from biffing her again and, in bad cases, may be able to get him expelled from the matrimonial home. Where he's worth a few bob, she might additionally take the rare course of suing the husband in the county court or High Court for damages for assault. She could go after legal aid and the wife has an excellent prospect of persuading the divorce court to ignore the damages when it comes to decide on the maintenance and property provision which the husband is to make for her and any children.

Mrs. C. showed the way in 1983. A High Court judge awarded her £9,605 damages against her husband after an assault in which she had sustained a broken nose and cheek bone and which gave her double vision and ear, nose and throat problems. The assault had taken place whilst divorce proceedings between her and her husband were pending. The same judge then went on to decide on maintenance and property in her divorce and ignored the £9,605 in assessing her reasonable needs and the husband's income and capital.

It's open to the husband to defend the damages case and so the wife should turn her mind to the available evidence before the blood has dried. If the neighbour didn't have her ear to the wall, a call to the police may not only secure the husband's arrest (though there will often be a police reluctance to interfere except in the more serious situations) but a couple of respectable witnesses. And off to her doctor the wife should go as soon as she can: his evidence later on of what he saw, diagnosed and prescribed could prove most helpful.

The law would work the same way against a battering wife. If possible, the rolling pin should be seized for evidential purposes.

The time limit for bringing proceedings for damages? Three years from the date of the assault.

Battering bonanza

Court fees only

IN THE HIGH COURT OF JUSTICE 19 88 . G , No. 674

QUEENS'S BENCH DIVISION

HAPPINESS DISTRICT REGISTRY

Between

MELANIE GARFIELD

Plaintiff

and

IVOR ADENUF McGREGOR GARFIELD

Defendant

* Insert name of Defendant

† Insert address of Defendant

To the Defendant* Ivor Adenuf McGregor Garfield

of† 15a Sin Row Happiness in the County of Great Joy

THIS WRIT OF SUMMONS has been issued against you by the above-named Plaintiff in respect of the claim set out on the back.

Within [14 days] after service of this Writ on you, counting the day of service, you must either satisfy the claim or return to the Court Office mentioned below the accompanying ACKNOWLEDGEMENT OF SERVICE stating therein whether you intend to contest these proceedings.

If you fail to satisfy the claim or to return the Acknowledgement within the time stated, or if you return the Acknowledgement without stating therein an intention to contest the proceedings, the Plaintiff may proceed with the action and judgment may be entered against you forthwith without further notice.

Issued from the Happiness District Registry of the High Court this 14th day of July 19 88

Writ indorsed with statement of claim
(unliquidated demand)
(District Registry)

Form F1206

27 & 28 St Albans Place
London N1 0NX
October 1982

Note: This Writ may not be served later than 12 calendar months beginning with that date unless renewed by order of the Court

IMPORTANT

Directions for Acknowledgement of Service are given with the accompanying form

Statement of claim

~~**The Plaintiff's claim is for**~~

1. At all material times the Plaintiff and the Defendant were intermarried.

2. On or about the 2nd December 1987 at approximately 10.30 a.m. at the former matrimonial home "Chez Garfield" 41 Albert Road, Happiness aforesaid the Defendant assaulted and beat the Plaintiff by initially striking her about the head with a copy of a certain book, namely "Gold's Law" and then with great force repeatedly about the head and body using his clenched fist.

<u>Particulars of Injury</u>

The Plaintiff sustained a displaced fracture of the nose, fractures of the 11th and 12th ribs, a cut upper lip, extensive bruising, pain and shock. She was admitted to Happiness General Hospital and detained for treatment and observation for two days. The Plaintiff was incapacitated from her employment as a waitress for a period of three months after the said assault and battery during which period she was dismissed because of such incapacity and has been unable to find other employment. The Plaintiff's nose is disfigured and she will have to undergo surgery to rectify such disfigurement.

<u>Particulars of Special Damage</u>

(a) Loss of earnings from the 2nd December 1987 (and continuing)- £600.00

(b) Prescriptions - £12.00

(c) Travelling and out-of-pocket expenses - £25.00

3. The Plaintiff claims interest on such damages as are due to her at such rate and for such period as the court thinks fit pursuant to the provisions of section 35A of the Supreme Court Act 1981.

And the Plaintiff claims damages and interest pursuant to section 35A of the said Act.

(Signed) Cut and Thrust

[The cause of action] [~~One of the causes of action~~] in respect of which the Plaintiff claims relief in this action arose wholly or in part in‡ Happiness

‡ Insert name of place

in the district of the District Registry named overleaf.

THIS WRIT was issued by Cut & Thrust

of Equity Chambers, Fish Street, Happiness, Great Joy GJ12 9BC

Reference: SG/MM Telephone: 91837 34782 4235

~~[agent for~~

~~of~~

]

Solicitor for the said plaintiff whose address is "Chez Garfield", 41 Albert Road, Happiness, Great Joy.

~~[THIS WRIT was issued by the said plaintiff who resides at~~

§If the Plaintiff does not reside within the jurisdiction

~~[§and whose address for service is~~

]]

IN THE HIGH COURT OF JUSTICE

QUEEN'S BENCH DIVISION

HAPPINESS DISTRICT REGISTRY

19 88 . G , No 674

Between

MELANIE GARFIELD Plaintiff

and

IVOR ADENUF

McGREGOR GARFIELD Defendant

Writ of Summons indorsed with Statement of Claim

MESSRS CUT AND THRUST
Equity Chambers
Fish Street, Happiness
Great Joy

Plaintiff's Solicitors

Train pains

A chapter to hide from BR

THIS CHAPTER IS SUITABLE FOR READING AT STATIONS AND DURING RAIL JOURNEYS—KEEP HIDDEN FROM GUARD

WAYS AND WAYS

The criminal way

An accountant who protested at BR's lack of service and communications by squatting on the track with his brief case was convicted in January 1987 at Bodmin Crown Court of obstructing the railway—a high speed train was forced to halt only yards away—and conditionally discharged for twelve months and ordered to pay £300 costs. The trial judge Mr. Recorder T. G. Field-Fisher QC promised him: "If I meet you outside one day, I shall tell you how I managed to stop the Liverpool-Euston express and was wholly in the right."

The psychological way

The judge had been returning to London for the weekend during the handless corpse drugs trial at which he was appearing as advocate. He had a number of his legal cronies with him. About three miles outside

Stafford the train stopped. It stayed motionless for half an hour, and then the guard announced that the legal first-class carriage was unsafe. The whole train went back to Stafford at 5 mph where the legal party, the judge presiding, refused to vacate on the ground that there were no vacant seats or, certainly, no vacant first class seats in the rest of the train. The station master was summoned, but threatened to call BR police. Still the party would not budge. The judge then pulled off a psychological coup. He submitted that the station master had a choice: he could put another first class coach on or, bearing in mind his senior position, stop the next through express and allow them on to that. The latter course was followed and an irrevocable undertaking extracted that the party would vacate. Seven minutes later the express was waiting. It got into Euston half an hour before the slower train on which the party had started.

Other ways

It may not always be necessary to take steps as extreme as those of the accountant and his sentencer. BR's conditions of carriage and code of practice and the address of the regional Transport Users Consultative Committee could provide salvation.

BR's tickets are issued subject to its standard conditions of carriage then prevailing and available for inspection at all good ticket offices:

"You want to go to Concarriage, mate? Where's that?"

"Sir, I said I wanted to see a copy of your standard conditions of carriage."

"Is that a single or return?"

The ticket holder is bound by the conditions though he has neither seen them nor has a clue what they contain, but the conditions are subject to a test of reasonableness in so far as they attempt to exclude or restrict the liability of BR for breach of contract, or attempt to entitle BR to render a service substantially different from what the passenger reasonably expects, or to render no service at all. The code of practice does not have any legal effect. That's what BR maintains, but we suggest it is strongly arguable that BR is under a contractual duty to act as it promises it will do in the code. And what the code certainly does is to indicate how, in practice, BR will deal with particular complaints and claims irrespective of what the conditions say. It was due to be rewritten in the autumn of 1988 but no changes of any track-shattering importance were expected. The code contains a rarely used arbitration procedure which is generally available for a non-personal injury claim of £500 or less involving a breach of contract relating to the conditions of carriage. Unless there are exceptional circumstances, the arbitration application must be made within three months of BR's "last reply". BR must consent to the arbitration and the arbitrator's decision will be final, which rules out any subsequent county court litigation. £10 is payable by the passenger which he will probably get back if he wins.

Nightmare on the Nightride

Arbitration did work well for a Londoner in August 1986. He had bought a Euston-Glasgow Nightride return so he could attend a funeral in Scotland. The outward "first-class, luxury, air-conditioned coach" was sleazy and filthy with spotted and torn carpet. Seat headrests were missing and the windows were exceptionally dirty. The "subdued lighting" was bright orange and could not be turned off to facilitate sleep. There was no heating whatsoever. The threatened food and refreshment trolley failed to materialise. The return carriage was fractionally less filthy. The high lighting was brilliantly and blindingly white save when, along with the individual seat lighting, it failed for half an hour, and there was a faint warmth from floor level radiators which was just sufficient to remove the chill. BR refunded him ticket money but would do no more. The arbitrator awarded him £150 compensation.

CALL THE COMMITTEE

The regional Transport Users Consultative Committees will take up and push a passenger's complaint against BR free of charge, but opt out if and when the passenger goes to arbitration. They do a good job and whilst they may not thank us for it, we recommend that a disgruntled passenger ask the Committee for his area to pass his letter of complaint on to BR at the outset. Then BR should respond to it more reasonably. Evidence we have seen strongly suggests that the majority of meritorious complaints followed through by a Committee lead to a BR offer when there was no offer before, or to an improvement in the offer originally made. The Committee's offices are in Birmingham (021–643 2144), Norwich (0603–22586), London (01–839 1851 for south and 1898 for London region), Bristol (0272–25703), York (0904–25615), Manchester (061–834 5245), Cardiff (0222–27247) and Scotland (041–221 17760).

UNUSED AND LOST TICKET REFUND

BR conditions provide that *reasonable* consideration will be given to a refund for an unused ticket which is returned within twenty-eight days of expiry, together with such supportive evidence as may *reasonably* be required. And that the amount, if refunded, will be the price less the cost for any journey made (for example, one way on a return) and an administrative charge. In its code of practice BR says that when the return portion of a journey has not been made it will want supporting written evidence verifying the circumstances of the claim—as a safeguard against fraud. But this will not be required from a passenger producing a half-used return ticket at his outward destination station. BR tries to settle refund claims within fourteen days.

The conditions and code are definitive about lost tickets. They will not be replaced and the price will not be refunded. The reason given in the code is that someone else may find the ticket and use it dishonestly. It follows that a passenger who cannot produce his lost ticket can be required, on the face of it, to pay again and it has to be the standard fare second time round. We suggest that such a severe and blanket treatment in the conditions could be unreasonable and held by a court to be invalid. Is it reasonable, for example, that a nun who has been robbed without carelessness on her part of her expensive Portsmouth & Southsea—Glasgow return and can prove by paid cheque or credit card statement that BR received the loot, should be powerless against a refusal to refund her one penny?

TUCC fought cases:

1988 Lady purchased London—Southport saver return—return portion lost when purse stolen —ticket clerk assured her she would be refunded return portion if she purchased another saver for £19—she did but was refused anything when she claimed. RESULT: £10 in travel vouchers.

1987 Boy returning home from school in Ipswich for the holidays left return portion of ticket in his shirt—when mother washed shirt, ticket disintegrated—BR refused to honour it. RESULT: After ticket pieced together and sent to BR, complimentary single ticket issued.

1987 Lady having left return portion of ticket in another handbag, unable to produce when required and surcharged full £41.50 fare—collapsed in tears and so collector told her she could claim refund—after rude, dismissive and then polite response at Reading declined refund for fear of setting a precedent. RESULT: full refund.

CLASS DISTINCTIONS

No standard class accommodation—first class accommodation used

BR staff, say the conditions, may give permission for standard class (we used to call it second class in the good old days) single or return ticket holder without accommodation to occupy first class accommodation, and if permission is given, the first class ticket holder cannot claim a refund: otherwise, the standard class ticket holder may travel in first class accommodation (corridors and gangways included) if he pays the difference in fare. The code adds nothing. But nor does the code say a word about the permission provision which appears in the conditions. There is a different regime for a standard class season ticket holder who travels in first class accommodation. If he pays up before the commencement of the journey he will only be charged for the difference in fares: in all other cases he will be charged the full first class standard fare for the journey. The conditions do not provide for a surcharge-less journey with BR staff permission.

So standard class single or return ticket holders who cannot find a seat in standard class accommodation should ask permission to sit in a first class carriage free. If permission is refused and a surcharge is paid, is there any hope of getting it back through the county court? We suggest there is an arguable case that a standard class ticket holder—including a season ticket holder—who cannot find standard class accommodation is entitled to go into first without surcharge and so should be able to claim back the surcharge. Whilst the conditions provide that BR will not be under any liability for failing to come up with sufficient accommodation of a particular class, we contend it may well be legally unreasonable (particularly on long journeys) for BR to go on to effectively make a profit out of its own inadequacies by surcharging accommodation-less standard ticket holders who travel in first class accommodation instead of standing in a corridor. Most passengers expect to be able to sit somewhere when they buy their tickets and to travel in a corridor is substantially different from travelling with bum on seat. Ask BR to look at the Unfair Contract Terms Act 1977:

TUCC fought case:

1987 Euston—Manchester passenger given permission by member of platform staff to sit in first class accommodation because train was full—guard duly surcharged him £14 after heated exchange. RESULT: £14 refunded.

No first class accommodation—in with the riff-raff

The conditions provide that if there is insufficient first class accommodation available for a first class single or return ticket holder (not a season ticket holder) he may travel in standard class accommodation and claim the appropriate difference in fares, but he must have on-train staff confirm the circumstances in writing and he must submit the confirmation in support of his refund claim.

TUCC fought cases

1987 Couple bought first class return tickets from travel agents for "The Rhinelander" but it is a standard class train—on both journeys no buffet or lighting. RESULT: £20 travel vouchers.

1987 Regular first class traveller had to stand in standard class coach Euston—Manchester and no full meals service available—£13.50 ticket difference refunded without compensation. RESULT: £10 travel vouchers.

1987 First class Plymouth—Liverpool return passenger changed at Crewe into standard class only train – on return journey no buffet till Birmingham and then no hot food or heat and train broke down and two and a half hours late. RESULT: first class complimentary return ticket.

NO TRAIN—LATE TRAIN

The conditions purport to exclude BR from liability for trains starting or arriving early or late, and entitle BR to:

- alter timetables without notice
- allow trains to leave stations before the arrival of other trains shown in the timetables as connecting trains
- withdraw all passenger services from any station on any day or suspend or discontinue the running of trains or alter the times of starting or arrival of trains.

So there! Sounds pretty draconian, but given the size and complexity of its operation, generally, we could not hold out much hope to a passenger (or intended passenger) who wished to drive a steam engine through that lot (although misinformation by BR staff is another matter). But in their code of practice BR say that every effort is made to ensure persons awaiting the arrival of passengers are advised of service problems and that its aim is to run all timetabled services. And it does seem that a claim which might have run into difficulty in court because of the contract conditions may lead to some *ex gratia* settlement if only in the form of travel tokens when pressed through the passenger's TUCC.

TUCC fought cases:

1987 Bath—Liverpool passenger arrived late at Bristol after all outgoing connections missed—no apologies and nobody to explain how to proceed. RESULT: £10 travel vouchers.

1987 Reading—Gatwick train cancelled and so Tunisian bound passenger went to Clapham and changed, as advised—flight made but missed planned visit to duty free shop—stressed. RESULT: £20 travel vouchers.

1987 Exeter—Paddington passenger 70 minutes late on a Sunday night—no refreshment—no apology—underground finished—£11.50 taxi fare incurred. RESULT: £11.50 cheque plus £10 travel vouchers.

1988 Bootle—Southport train delayed by fatality on line—lecturer asked BR staff to telephone college to say she would be late, but message relayed was that she would not be coming so class cancelled causing £27 pay loss—in meantime passenger took taxi to college at £10 fare—£1 offered. RESULT: £10 taxi fare reimbursed.

LOOK! NO TICKET!

Under the conditions, if a passenger joins a train without a valid ticket he must pay the full standard single fare for the journey and will not be entitled to any reduction or discount he would otherwise have enjoyed. But this does not apply where the ticket office was closed or unstaffed and there was no ticket machine which was in working order. Then the passenger can insist on only paying the fare he would have paid if all had been well.

TUCC fought cases:

1987 Lady travelling into Reading abandoned queue believing she would miss train—charged full single fare and had to purchase another single on return journey. RESULT: single fare refunded which gave her a 10p profit.

1987 Bath doctor delayed by late bus so bought ticket on train costing him an extra £14.60. RESULT: BR could not be blamed for delayed bus; no compensation.

1987 Weston-super-Mare mum outraged that son who worked in City had to abandon ticket queue at Paddington after twenty minutes and surcharged £11 when buying ticket on train. RESULT: £11 travel vouchers to hand to the lad.

1987 Because of lengthy queues at Grange-Over-Sands station reached nine minutes before departure, lady abandoned and bought ticket on train with £1.15 surcharge. RESULT: £3 travel vouchers.

RESERVED SEATS

We submit that the failure by BR to have accommodation available for which a reservation fee has been paid is probably a contract breach for which damages could be claimed. The code of practice says that seats can be reserved in advance on most Inter-City services for a "modest charge" and that the guard should be contacted if the passenger has any problem with the reservation.

TUCC fought cases

1987 Passenger had reserved a smoker, allocated a non-smoker—to reach toilet with door handle, had to walk through three carriages—no towels. RESULT: £5 travel vouchers.

1987 First class reservation made for Wigan—Pitlochry journey—double booked—standard class unreserved accommodation occupied. RESULT: First and standard fare differences plus reservation fee refunded.

1988 Reservation on Oxenholme—Edinburgh train for school party—because of gross overcrowding, party unable to board to get to reserved seats—next 90 minutes spent at Oxenholme until BR conveyed party to Edinburgh by road but visit had to be severely curtailed. RESULT: Free trip to Edinburgh for party on future date.

1987 Australian non-smoking couple found reserved seats occupied on Reading—Gatwick train—"This happens nearly every day" said the guard and found them seats at rear of train in smoking compartment without checking rights of bums in reserved seats. RESULT: £2 compensation.

'ORRIBLE JOURNEYS

The conditions and code are silent about the standard accommodation—the degree of comfort of the seat, how many toilets per thousand passengers, bulbs in light sockets. We suggest it is strongly arguable that if a passenger has not been able to travel in reasonable comfort, he has a right to claim damages but, without a reservation, the absence of a seat would not of itself be any help. You can see how well our Euston—Glasgow Nightrider did with his arbitration claim (see *Nightmare on the Nightride*, page 339).

TUCC fought cases:

1987 83 year old lady and daughter, both severely disabled, travelled Exeter—Manchester—train was 90 minutes late in arriving at Exeter—no seating—buffet full and when refreshment eventually obtained, lady assistant insulting—train arrived at Manchester two hours behind schedule by which time friend due to meet them had had to go on to work. RESULT: £50 travel vouchers (but lady felt she could not face BR again).

1987 Lady travelling with daughter Bristol—Edinburgh first class—standard class passengers in compartment—no air conditioning—wafting smoke—no trolley service, no restaurant, no chance of reaching buffet due to overcrowding

—disgusting toilets with some doors which did not lock—£124 fare. RESULT: £25 travel vouchers.

1987 Senior partner in design company with first class ticket forced to travel standard class Bristol—Paddington—no breakfast as advertised—guard rude, obstructive and incoherent—accommodation cold—refused to show ticket—at Paddington called at manager's office to be met by guard and police—refused to pay standard class single fare but later produced photocopy of first class season ticket. RESULT: Apology that service not as should have been but Bristol area manager felt incident was caused by refusal to show ticket. Warned he was required to provide ticket on demand and failure to do so in future could lead to prosecution.

TUCC Ragbag

1987 Buffet steward refused Northern Ireland bank note as payment for phone card and refreshments—passenger had long wait at destination because unable to make call to be collected—hungry and thirsty (only Bank of England notes are legal tender and so, strictly speaking, Northern Ireland and Scottish bank notes can reasonably be refused in England and Wales). RESULT: £2 travel vouchers.

1987 Passenger queued in rain for thirteen minutes for ticket and then boarded Taplow—Reading train—£2.20 surcharge demanded—asked to see senior official at Reading but confronted by two

BR police constables and embarrassed in front of constant stream of travellers. RESULT: £5 travel vouchers.

1987 Fifteen-year-old denied child ticket at Paddington and paid extra £6.45—mother questioned whether BR's policy is to assume young are lying. RESULT: Copy birth certificate sent in—£6.45 refunded.

BRBB

If another passenger is causing pain the British Railways Board Byelaws may be brought to his attention (it is wise to first ensure there are other, non-spectacled, male and reasonably strong, sympathetic commuters in close proximity) and, should he not desist, the guard notified.

- "No person shall smoke or carry a lighted pipe, cigar or cigarette . . . upon the railway, where smoking is prohibited by the Board by a notice exhibited in a conspicuous position . . ."

- "No person, while upon the railway shall, to the annoyance of any other person, sing, perform on any musical instrument or use any gramophone, record player, tape recorder or portable wireless apparatus."

- "No person shall occupy or use any compartment, sleeping berth or seat on the railway, upon which or in relation to which notice has been fixed or given by the Board that such compartment, sleeping berth or seat is reserved, except the holder of a reservation ticket issued by the Board in respect of the holder's occupation or use of such compartment, sleeping berth or seat."

THIS BOOK IS NOW COMING TO AN END. WE APOLOGISE FOR THE DELAY IN GETTING THERE, ANY OFFENCE GIVEN AND THE POOR GRAMMAR. WE HOPE YOU HAD AN ENJOYABLE READ. PLEASE ENSURE YOU DO NOT LEAVE ANY OF THE PAGES BEHIND. THANK YOU.

Index

page

page

Index

page

page